PREFACE

FINDING EGYPT'S POOR

It is February 1994, and I am working in the principal reading room of the Egyptian National Archives. As I shiver from
the damp of the Cairo winter, I struggle to understand events
that transpired in this city nearly a century and a half earlier:
The director of Mahall al-Khayriyyat issues appeals to the
government storehouse for bread to feed the poor who show
up daily. Beggars are arrested and sent to another building,
Takiyyat Tulun. A young girl, having been expelled from
Takiyyat Tulun, pleads to be let back in. What are these institutions? I ask myself. Why are beggars being arrested?

"What are these institutions? And why are beggars being
arrested?" I ask fellow researchers in the archives. Mahall al-
Khayriyyat is clearly a soup kitchen, but is it a religious endowment? Everyone is certain that Takiyyat Tulun is a Sufi
lodge (or *tekke*) in the neighborhood of Ahmad ibn Tulun
Mosque, but although I know that tekkes traditionally cared
for the indigent and their own members, I am sure that this
cannot be the case. In response to my second question, my
colleagues simply shrug; one of them jokingly gives me a
five-piaster coin. This group of friends are used to my crazy
questions, and they constantly tease me about my research
topic. They cannot understand why I, as an American, am so
fascinated with begging.

But in the weeks and months that follow, my suspicions
about these two institutions are confirmed. I learn that the
Mahall al-Khayriyyat served as a government soup kitchen
in the mid-nineteenth century, providing one thousand meals
daily, and that Takiyyat Tulun was a state-run shelter located
within the walls of the Ahmad ibn Tulun Mosque. Both reflected the state's appropriation of traditional concepts of
care for the poor. Attempts to arrest beggars, I discover, represented novel approaches to poor relief during this era. As I
continue my research, I realize that I am not the only for-
eigner who has ever displayed an interest in Egypt's beggars.

AT THE DABTIYYA, the Central Police Department, of Cairo, interchanges between the Egyptian populace and the state demonstrate the central role this office played in assisting the needy and gave me more clues on the function of Takiyyat Tulun and other institutions: Aysha bint Hasan appeared at the Dabtiyya in January 1854, anxious to find her sister. "Might my sister be among the poor of Takiyyat Tulun?" she asked. A few weeks later, Sheikh Hasan told officials of the Dabtiyya, "I'm looking for my wife, Suhag." If she is among the poor of Takiyyat Tulun, I would like to procure her release. I promise to take care of her." In 1863 Sulayman, seeking his daughter Khadra, who had been committed to the insane asylum, traveled 13.5 miles from his hometown of Nawa in Qalyubiyya Province to Cairo. He too hoped that officials of the Dabtiyya could help him locate his loved one. In each of these three instances, the Dabtiyya sent word to the Civilian Hospital, which was responsible for the administration of Takiyyat Tulun and the insane asylum, to find out whether the people being sought were in these institutions.

Takiyyat Tulun, a poorhouse established within the structure of Ahmad ibn Tulun Mosque, and the insane asylum, located after the mid-nineteenth century in Bulaq, were two places to which Egypt's indigent sought admission or were involuntarily confined.[1] Established at nearly midcentury, these institutions gave shelter and care to individuals whose families could not provide for them. In each instance cited here, the people who made queries at the Dabtiyya came prepared to prove to officials that they were ready and able to care for their relatives.

We do not know the outcomes of the familial dramas that led Aysha, Sheikh Hasan, and Sulayman to the Dabtiyya. Nor do these particular accounts of their quests reveal whether their inquiries were their first or their last. Like Aysha, Sheikh Hasan, and Sulayman, I set out to find missing people, individuals who until recently had fallen through the cracks of Egyptian historiography. The people I sought identified themselves and were described by others, such as state officials and European and Egyptian observers and reformers, as "the poor." Like the three people who hoped to obtain help from the police, I too consulted numerous state agencies — or rather their records — to find information on their circumstances and the options for assistance that they pursued. Takiyyat Tulun and the insane asylum were not the only formal recourses for care available during this period. Before the establishment of Takiyyat Tulun, the poor had been sheltered in a structure known as the

Maristan Qalawun. This institution, which had been founded by the
Mamluk sultan Qalawun in 1284, housed a hospital, an insane asylum,
and an almshouse. A civilian hospital admitted the indigent for medical
services, free of charge, and an orphanage and foundling home took in
children whose parents could not provide for them, as well as abandoned children found in the streets of Cairo. In addition, toward the
end of the nineteenth century, members of the indigenous elite and foreigners residing in Egypt established private charitable associations that
distributed food and clothing and provided other means of assistance to
Egypt's destitute. By the mid-twentieth century, concern about the poor
had taken another turn and resulted in the creation of other avenues of
poor relief: during of the 1940s and the early 1950s, political parties
and Egypt's monarch, King Farouk, vied with one another to prove
their ability to provide for the poor.

Records of these various state and private institutions and discussions
demonstrating the poor's centrality to political struggles gave me insights on the experiences of the poor. But of equal importance, these
materials also illuminated the various uses charity served over the course
of the nineteenth and early twentieth centuries in Egypt.

My queries led me to records pertaining to the most desperately poor,
individuals who claimed that they had "no one" to take care of them
and that they owned "nothing." In many cases, these individuals could
not work due to physical difficulties, such as blindness or lameness, or
due to the responsibilities of taking care of children without the help of
a spouse or an extended family. In some cases, the individuals I encountered could not speak for themselves; these people included abandoned
infants as well as the mute and the insane. Without resources or families
and relatives to provide assistance, these people were entirely dependent
on the charity of their neighbors and, as I illustrate in this book, the
benevolence of the state and emergent philanthropic organizations.

※

This book takes the initiation of new state interventions in poor relief in
the first half of the nineteenth century as its point of departure to put
the itinerant poor, the benevolent actions of the state and private actors,
and transformations in attitudes and policies toward the poor in Egypt
at the center of its historical analysis. Although Alexandria was also the
site of two poor shelters, the Qishla al-Sadaqa (Hospital of Charity) and
the Takiyyat Qabbari (the Tekke of Qabbari), the focus is largely on the
establishment and use of two shelters in Cairo as well as the discourse
(on the part of indigenous Egyptians and foreigners) concerning the

public presence of the poor in this city. Although I provide a survey of various forms of assistance to the poor (including religious endowments and funds from the state treasury — the Bayt al-Mal) in the introductory chapter, my focus is on specific institutions and organizations whose primary concerns were the "public" (that is, publicly visible) poor. Given the paucity of sources on income and the absence of information on caloric intake or quality of housing, I do not endeavor to document poverty and the extent of impoverishment. Nor do I undertake an examination of relative poverty and the conditions of the laboring poor. Rather, I focus almost entirely on those poor whose presence in public spaces made them an object of government concern and, in the late nineteenth century and onward, a target of numerous actors (private associations as well as members of Egypt's government) who sought to demonstrate their commitment to ameliorating the conditions in which the most destitute lived. While recognizing that the laboring poor and the lives and experiences of the lower classes are an important topic of analysis, I have restricted myself to individuals whom others (such as the state, foreigners, and religious organizations) identified as "the poor" and their interactions with the state and private groups at moments when they sought assistance or became the targets of criticism. In looking at those individuals whom others have identified in this fashion, I endeavor to understand the very criteria of need that the state and private individuals and organizations introduced as a means of measuring whether a poor person deserved assistance. As I show, the charitable actions of the government and of associations were kept in check by emergent notions of who constituted the deserving poor and who merited assistance.

Drawing from a range of sources–including police registers, government correspondence pertaining to policies toward the itinerant poor, records of petitions, lists of shelter residents, the notes of foreign and indigenous observers, and records documenting the care provided to abandoned infants and children — located in the Egyptian National Archives, the British Museum, and the Public Records Office, the first three chapters detail transformations in poor relief over the course of the nineteenth century. Through analysis of these materials, I situate these developments within the context of Islamic and Ottoman practices of charity and policies toward the poor to demonstrate that the unique features of Egypt's poor-relief practices must be understood within the economic changes under way during this period. Making use of materials available in the Başbakanlık Archives in Istanbul and other primary sources, I compare historical and contemporaneous practices of poor relief at the center of the Ottoman Empire — in the capital of Istanbul — with those of Cairo so as to enhance our understanding of the extent to which policies toward the poor in Egypt at times emulated and at times diverged from those at the center.

In the following two chapters, my scope narrows from an analysis of state-sponsored practices to the perceptions and actions of private individuals and associations. In these chapters, drawing from materials in Egyptian and British archives and travel literature published in the nineteenth and early twentieth centuries, I document how the public poor were politicized. The *spectacle* of the poor and tropes of Egypt's poverty were key features in foreign accounts of conditions in Egypt during the nineteenth century. Toward the end of the century, concern about the public presence of the poor became an important aspect of the programs of indigenous and multiethnic associations founded in Egypt. During the last decades of the monarchy, the poor became a political pawn in the struggles for political legitimacy that were waged between the palace and political parties.

The experiences of the poor, their interactions with the state, and the institutions in which they sought shelter (or in which they were incarcerated) form one of the core structures of this text. Again and again, I present the figure of the beggar, the foundling, and the anxious family member. I examine the circumstances that led them to seek assistance and the care they received. Woven throughout this text are the sometimes incriminating, sometimes compassionate remarks that observers (government officials, foreigners visiting or working in Egypt, and reformers) made regarding the public presence of beggars. At the same time, we repeatedly encounter the state and private actors who engaged in charitable actions. In this latter regard, I provide an analysis of the motivations behind the establishment of specialized institutions for the poor and the goals of the foundations established by philanthropic associations.

As this book explores the emergence of new institutions and the involvement of new actors in the field of poor relief, it also presents developments in practices and policies toward the poor. The economic and political context of poor relief, the colonial framework, and changing perceptions toward the poor serve as lenses through which to view transformations and understand the politicization of the poor.

In each aspect of our interactions with the public poor, the state, its institutions, and individuals involved in philanthropy, we witness Egypt's encounters with modernity. Within the frame of poor relief, we see the development of bureaucratized apparatuses through which many of Egypt's poor astutely navigated as they sought assistance, we come face to face with secularized and specialized institutions that replaced traditional structures, and we see how by the early twentieth century charity came to serve practical and political purposes. Although charity never ceased to be grounded in religious prerogatives, its very implementation had meanings that extended well beyond religious doctrines.

❧

Until now, the poor and practices of poor relief in nineteenth- and early-twentieth-century Egypt have not been topics of inquiry for historians and social scientists. However, the findings of scholars who have examined the consequences of state building and the economic, social, and political developments initiated by Muhammad Ali, Egypt's governor, in the early nineteenth century and their discussions of the ramifications of his projects and the subsequent transformations initiated by his successors highlight how new state interventions affected the lives of the populace as a whole.

Given his position as the architect of many programs in Egypt, and due to his military exploits, which challenged the sovereignty of the Ottoman sultan Mahmud II and brought the British more prominently into the Middle East (both in terms of trade and as allies of the Ottomans in their wars against Egypt's armies), Muhammad Ali has figured prominently in the historiography of Egypt in the first part of the nineteenth century. On one hand scholars have explored the motivations behind his numerous domestic and foreign projects, arguing that his programs had as one of their goals the creation of an independent nation.[2] On the other hand, recent scholarship has challenged this perspective, instead arguing that Muhammad Ali's intentions, and specifically his establishment of an army and numerous industries geared toward the military, were directed toward his own dynastic ends, not the goal of securing an independent Egyptian nation.[3] As much as the intentions behind Muhammad Ali's actions are a source of contention, the very identity of Egypt in the nineteenth century is a source of fierce debate: some scholars, such as Ehud Toledano, contend that Egypt was, during the period of Muhammad Ali as well as in the reigns of his successors, Ottoman. The language of Egypt's rulers, their cultural orientations, and their political allegiances make clear that throughout the nineteenth century, Egypt remained culturally and politically within the Ottoman fold.[4]

Historians have examined the era of Muhammad Ali and the reigns of his successors from the perspective of the domestic programs they introduced as well as from the angle of the impact these programs had on the Egyptian populace. In their works, some information on the experiences of the poor can be found. Timothy Mitchell documents the advent of the increasingly interventionist state in nineteenth-century Egypt through an exploration of the myriad ways in which Muhammad

Ali's government and the regimes of his successors attempted to control, order, and discipline the Egyptian populace. Mitchell's discussion of this era has highlighted the coercive and discursive means through which governments in the period preceding and during the British occupation (1882–1952) sought to maintain control over and make the best use of Egypt's populace. However, as Khaled Fahmy argues, Mitchell's book does not illustrate the points at which these projects failed or never came to fruition. Although state intervention commencing in the reign of Muhammad Ali was pervasive, it was not absolute. Rural and urban inhabitants resisted the actions of the state, fleeing conscription and other government exactions on their lives.[5]

Many of Mitchell's findings rest on blueprints for programs or plans that were not necessarily enacted completely (or successfully). Economic historians, however, provide us with a more complete understanding of the impact that actual programs and agricultural transformations — under way in eighteenth-, nineteenth-, and early-twentieth-century Egypt — had on the rural peasantry. Roger Owen illustrates how the production of cotton, and specifically the movement to create a mono-culture of cotton, transformed the economy and the peasantry's relationship with their land and the state. By the second half of the nineteenth century, taxation and other privations had turned many rural Egyptians into landless tenants or had forced peasants to find work in the cities.[6] Kenneth Cuno's analysis of land ownership in Lower Egypt illustrates how features of the Egyptian countryside previously posited as nineteenth-century transformations (such as the commodification of land, cash-crop agriculture, and marked differences between the rural rich and poor) were well in place decades before the rise of Muhammad Ali. In addition to eloquently demonstrating how rural transformations were a feature of eighteenth-century Egypt, Cuno's analysis of the changes under way during Muhammad Ali's rule provide insights on the impact of taxation demands and the resulting indebtedness of peasants. Indicative of the scope of economic difficulties the rural poor experienced were transactions such as the reassignment of land to other peasants and officials who paid peasants' tax arrears (even though in some cases peasants continued working the land they had lost) as well as the redistribution of land whose owners were in tax arrears due to peasant flight.[7]

Judith Tucker's groundbreaking work (*Women in Nineteenth-Century Egypt*) on the experiences of urban and rural women from the beginning of the nineteenth century until World War I lays an essential foundation for our understanding of the multiple avenues of women's participation in Egyptian society. Her use of Shari'a (Islamic Law) Court registers sheds light on the experiences of many lower-class urban women as well as peasant women of modest means. Contextualizing her anal-

ysis within the rapid political, economic, and social changes of the period, Tucker documents the ways in which peasant and urban women
partook in agricultural production, disputes over property, and urban
occupations. Throughout the extensive transformations under way in
nineteenth-century Egypt, women struggled with increasing state intervention in their lives and state-imposed practices such as agricultural
monopolies (during the reign of Muhammad Ali), military conscription,
and the demands corvée (a system that lasted into the first decades of
the twentieth century) made on them and their families.[8]

Laverne Kuhnke's book on public health projects in nineteenth-
century Egypt, though state centered in its analysis, gives us further
glimpses of the interaction between the populace of Egypt and the government in terms of the establishment of hospitals, vaccination programs, and quarantines. Showing how the introduction of such programs was set against the backdrop of increased governmental concern
about issues of sanitation and efforts to stop the spread and devastation
caused by plagues and cholera, *Lives at Risk* provides insights into the
conditions in which many Egyptians lived, their initial rejection of gov-
ernment-sponsored vaccination programs (out of fear that these projects
were intended to "mark" children for future military service), and their
attempts to avoid being admitted to government-run hospitals.[9] However, contrary to Kuhnke's findings, records document the number of
Egyptians who sought medical assistance, thus indicating that many of
the poor — perhaps out of desperation — resorted to state forms of medical care.[10]

More than any other scholars of modern Egypt, Tucker and Toledano
have sought to understand the effects that changing economic and political circumstances had on Egypt's population, centering their analyses
on women (Tucker) and individuals described as marginal (Toledano),
who included the poor and the unemployed. Tucker closely examines
the ways in which families took care of their dependents and briefly
notes the existence of "a few embryonic state institutions" that evolved
"in response to dire need for assistance which grew as traditional forms
of mutual aid faltered."[11] However, she does not discuss the nature and
function of these emerging institutions. Toledano's astute analysis of
police records from the middle of the nineteenth century, an era that
has received less attention than the reigns of Muhammad Ali, Ismail
(1863–79), and Tawfiq (1879–92), which immediately preceded the
British occupation, elucidates the range of assistance options available
to the destitute of Cairo as well as recent migrants. Toledano discusses
the role of institutions such as Sufi lodges, which served as temporary
residences for recent migrants, and provides an in-depth analysis of the
precarious position in which migrants and people without networks of

support found themselves upon their arrival to cities such as Cairo. Although Toledano focuses on the criminalization of Egypt's "marginals," he does not explore the ways in which some of these people also sought and received assistance from the state.

My own research on poor relief during this era draws heavily on Toledano's and Tucker's discussions of the dislocations and other difficulties that the rural peasantry and urban dwellers experienced. But my analysis of sources focuses almost exclusively on the lives of men, women, and children who fell outside the scope of their research and the assistance options available to them. The individuals whose history I seek to recover include the invalid, the elderly, orphaned and abandoned children, women who could not depend on their families to take care of them, and people who did not come into contact with the law as a result of criminal wrongdoing.

A further feature of my research that sheds light on Egypt's social history in the nineteenth and twentieth centuries is my analysis of the ways in which the poor actively sought the assistance of state and private agencies. Until now, scholars of Egypt have focused on the disciplining aspects of the creation of modern state apparatuses, interpreting the actions of the increasingly interventionist state (particularly during Muhammad Ali's nearly four decades of governance) as efforts of social control. However, as I illustrate, the ultimate outcomes of poor-relief strategies were not what their founders had intended. To put it succinctly, although shelters for the poor were established with the intent of clearing the streets of the itinerant poor, by the 1850s the poor came to make increasing requests to the state for admission to these shelters. Over time, the number of individuals seeking assistance from the state overtaxed the available resources. The end result was that Cairo authorities were never able to completely control the public presence of the urban poor. Much to the consternation of city officials and foreign and indigenous reformers and observers, beggars and the itinerant poor continued to be a constant feature of Cairo's public spaces.

Works on the economic, political, and social changes under way in nineteenth-century Egypt have for the most part been devoid of discussion of the continued role that religion played in the Egyptian practice of statecraft. While scholars of Ottoman history in the central Ottoman lands are attentive to these issues in, for example, their discussions of how religious symbols are utilized to legitimize rule, assumptions about the modern and hence increasingly secular nature of the Egyptian state held by scholars of Egypt have resulted in their distancing themselves from an analysis of the continued ways in which religion was a part of the state apparatus and ideology. By examining the charitable initiatives of Muhammad Ali's government as well as the governments of his successors, we have the opportunity to witness how a particular religious language of benevolence (albeit at times formulaic) served to maintain and reinforce connections between the populace and the state. Contributing to studies geared toward understanding the Ottoman identity of Egypt during the nineteenth century, my research demonstrates that many of the poor-relief policies that Muhammad Ali and his successors undertook were imitations and modifications of practices applied at the center of the Ottoman Empire: their context was both Islamic and Ottoman.

The religious component of poor relief continued to pervade the discourse and actions of members of philanthropic organizations that became active in the field of poor relief at the end of the nineteenth century. But equally important to our understanding of the rise of associations during this period is analysis of the ways in which care for the poor was politicized. Many organizations were founded in reaction to missionary actions and the activities of British residents of Egypt. These associations sought to prove that they were best able to provide for Egypt's poor. Scholars of the late nineteenth and early twentieth centuries, for instance, Afaf Lutfi al-Sayyid Marsot, Leila Ahmed, Beth Baron, and Margot Badran, have examined the creation of philanthropic organizations to understand how women's participation led to their greater involvement in the public sphere. In my analysis of the actions of a variety of philanthropic groups that emerged during this era, I explore the motivations behind charitable actions, and I analyze the means by which the poor made use of these groups' services and how they were used by both these organizations and other political actors.[12] As I illustrate, the bestowal of charity in nineteenth- and early-twentieth-century Egypt meant more than just benevolence.

To find "the poor" in Egypt has been a formidable task. Unlike Europe, where the poor have been a category of analysis with scores of scholars making use of records of, for example, almshouses, workhouses, insane asylums, hospitals, and foundling homes, the topic of the poor in Egypt, as well as elsewhere in the Middle East, has not received scholarly attention, due in great part to the difficulty of finding sources on their experiences.[13]

Whereas the marginalization of the poor in Europe resulted in the creation of separate institutions charged with maintaining these individuals and keeping them out of the public eye, the poor of the Middle East did not suffer from the same stigmatization; nor do we find, with the exception of Egypt, as detailed in this book, the creation of facilities for segregating the poor from society at large. In the Middle East, the poor remained integrated into society; their families, as well as the community at large, saw it as their duty to take care of them.

Research on religious endowments (*awqaf*; sing *waqf*) provides partial answers to queries about how the urban and rural poor who had no families or other sources of support received assistance. Awqaf, established by statesmen, their families, and private individuals, funded institutions such as mosques, Sufi lodges, soup kitchens, schools, and hospitals. However, the records of institutions that have been examined by scholars to date provide extensive information only on the *ideals* of charity and the goals of each institution. Documents pertaining to the founding of a religious endowment mention that the poor were to receive care from that endowment, but they do not reveal the numbers, identities, or circumstances of individuals who received assistance. However, in the works of Miriam Hoexter and Amy Singer, which include analyses of the day-to-day workings of institutions funded through endowments, we learn more about the identities of those who received aid. Many of them, as these two authors find, were not impoverished.[14]

Assumptions about the religious nature of poor relief have also deflected scholars' attention away from sources other than awqaf for studying poor relief and the experiences of the poor. Recent works by Abraham Marcus, Eyal Ginio, and Ehud Toledano demonstrate the fruitfulness of analyzing state-generated sources such as Shari'a Court registers and police records. Marcus's use of Shari'a Court registers enabled him to document the assistance available to Aleppo's poor in the eighteenth century as well as the vulnerability of women and children. Ginio's work on Shari'a Court materials for eighteenth-century Salonika demonstrated how destitute young girls, taken in as servants in households, were often the targets of abuse.[15] Toledano's use of police records located in the Egyptian archives demonstrated how these materials proved to be an important source for understanding the moments at which the poor came into contact with law enforcement officials. My own work, inspired by the richness of sources in Toledano's *State and Society in Mid-Nineteenth-Century Egypt*, but utilizing a different series of police records from the same era, has confirmed that historians of the Middle East need to look beyond religious institutions to understand the experiences of the poor.

The records of government bodies charged with maintaining public order in other Middle Eastern locales of the nineteenth century and previous eras might well yield results as interesting as Toledano's. However, the Egyptian state's involvement in poor relief during this era was unique. Even if we draw comparisons between authorities' policies toward the poor in Cairo and in Istanbul, we find that practices of actual confinement of the poor in Istanbul did not occur until nearly the turn of the century. Only in 1896, with the establishment of Darülaceze, did Istanbul officials successfully enact prohibitions on begging and endeavor to clear the city's streets of the able-bodied and the deserving poor. The Egyptian government used novel approaches (unseen in other areas of the Middle East at this time) to restrict the publicly visible poor and used shelters to confine them. These approaches were motivated by pragmatic desires to monitor the mobility of the Egyptian peasantry, make use of the populace's labor, and regulate even the "deserving" poor's access to their neighbors' charity. State-generated sources found in the Egyptian National Archives provide us with previously inaccessible information regarding these new practices of benevolence and the development of policies over the course of the nineteenth and twentieth centuries.

However, since documents were not classified under the subject heading "the poor," finding the poor was no easy matter. In my research, I skimmed police records and health reports as well as government correspondence pertaining to Cairo for any mention, whatsoever, of the poor. Although I encountered a number of dead ends, I also found gold mines of materials. Government orders issued by the Khedival Cabinet (Diwan al-Khidiwi and Al-Ma'iyya al-Saniyya) as well as by consultative bodies such as the Privy Council (Majlis al-Khususi) illustrated governmental concerns about peasant flight from the countryside (not all of these peasants, arguably, were "poor") and referred to the public presence of the poor, the conditions of prisons, and crime due to vagabondage. The central police departments of Cairo and Alexandria (respectively, Dabtiyyat Misr and Dabtiyyat Iskandiriyya) contained the richest documents. By examining registers of incoming reports from various departments as well as outgoing orders from police departments, I learned that the most extensive accounts were hidden among one particular set of outgoing police records, Dabtiyyat Misr: Sadir. There I found mention of individuals like Aysha, Sulayman, and Sheikh Hasan, who sought family members in various state institutions, as well as accounts of the arrest of poor persons, their petitions to the state for assistance (whether poor prisoners in the Iblikhane, a women's prison, or male prisoners in other jails), and requests by indigent pilgrims from other areas of the Islamic world who sought free passage to their home countries.

Accounts of the poor found in the Dabtiyya series provide brief details on the poor and their circumstances. Generally one paragraph in length, each entry recounts the name of the person, mentions his or her condition, and describes the course of action to be taken. Despite the sparseness of information, the entries are a rich source of information about the practice of poor relief during this era. They elucidate the frequency of the poor's interaction with the government and the ways in which the poor actively sought assistance.

Although the police records are extensive, they contain gaps. I was unable to find records in the series which had provided the richest accounts of arrests and other documentation pertaining to the poor, Dabtiyyat Misr: Sadir, for the period preceding 1844 (the police department was established in 1835), due perhaps to their having been misclassified in the archives or due to their having been destroyed in an 1889 fire.[16] In addition, since looking through any one register (some reports of one or two months were bound together in a two- or three-hundred-page volume) was a time-consuming task, I relied on a sampling of registers, scrutinizing most closely registers that were five years apart.

Because the responsibilities of various offices shifted over time, the poor fell out of sight. While the outgoing series of Dabtiyyat Misr had contained accounts of individuals requesting assistance through the 1840s and early 1850s, by the late 1850s petitions began to be recorded in registers entitled Dabtiyyat Misr: Sadir al-Ardhallat (Responses to petitions), and other petitions became available in an entirely separate office, Muhafazat Misr (the Governorate of Cairo) Sadir al-Ardhallat. Finally, records of various offices such as Dabtiyyat Misr and Muhafazat Misr end abruptly in 1880. The ongoing classification of materials in the Egyptian archives may shed light on other police and municipal records from the 1880s on which pertain to the poor. The cataloguing of Dabtiyya documents (loose-leaf pages stored in boxes) may also reveal petitions by the poor. During my research in 1993–95 and 1997, only petitions for the late nineteenth century and onward were available. New work by social historians who are studying aspects of crime, gender, and prostitution, such as Khaled Fahmy, Nadi Abdel Ghaffar, Emad Hilal, Liat Kozma, Rudolph Peters, and Mario Ruiz, and their innovative approaches to sources among Dabtiyya registers will reveal further information on the "criminal" poor's interactions with the state.

One series in Muhafazat Misr, records of employees' salaries and rations for the inmates of Takiyyat Tulun, provided valuable data. Even though this series is incomplete — only registers covering two nearly full twelve-month periods are available — it proved to be important for illustrating the record-keeping techniques of the administrators of Takiyyat Tulun as well as providing details about rations, mortality, and the flight of inmates from this shelter. Correlated with records of petitions (which allowed me to cross-reference individuals who came to and left the shelter), this series of twenty registers proved to be an important source. Although this one series was all that was available to me in the course of my research, my hope is that further cataloguing of materials in the Egyptian National Archives will one day reveal the missing registers from this series and further accounts of rations and salaries from preceding and subsequent years.

As scholars of Egypt's social history are well aware, quantifying such issues as population, numbers of births and deaths, and the devastation caused by disease is impossible.[17] The absence of complete information on the number of poor housed in shelters such as Takiyyat Tulun, as well as the fluctuation in their numbers over time and the dispersal of accounts of beggars' arrests throughout a number of different registers, poses great obstacles to any attempt at quantifying the numbers of the public poor who came into contact with the state.

In my research in the Daftarkhane (Archival Office) of the Ministry of Religious Endowments, I did not find information on the numbers or identities of those assisted by or sheltered in Sufi lodges, nor was I able to obtain quantitative evidence of those who sought aid from other institutions funded by religious endowments in the nineteenth century. Without this information, we cannot assess the total numbers of people served by such institutions. We also cannot begin to measure overall fluctuations in the numbers of the poor seeking assistance at any one time; if we were able to do so, we would be able to conclusively document moments at which such institutions, combined with government-run shelters, faced greater or fewer numbers of poor people and could corroborate such data to better understand the full impact of famines, disease, and other destabilizing forces on the lives of Egypt's population.

Materials I consulted for the period of the British occupation in Egypt, such as the series Majlis al-Wuzara', Bulis (Council of Ministers, Police), records from the Wizarat al-Awqaf (the Ministry of Religious Endowments), institutional records, and documents of the Public Records Office, both those pertaining to Egypt and others within the series on the Ottoman Empire as a whole, were another important source of information for forms of assistance available to the poor and concerns about their public presence. In some respects, however, they lacked the richness of the records of petitions and arrest accounts of the period of the nineteenth century preceding the British occupation. Whereas documents from the era prior to the 1880s included the voices of the poor (albeit through the mediation of the state), records from the British occupation almost exclusively provided only official perspectives on the poor.

Because the records I used are state-generated materials, the voices of the poor, readers will notice, do not appear unadulterated. Records of petitions follow a particular formula, as do the actual petitions. Although they may be written within formal conventions, they nonetheless illustrate how the poor portrayed themselves to best obtain particular ends. Actual petitions for admission to poor shelters begin with an honorific directed to the ruler, then shift to the second person, describing the individual's circumstances and providing information on their place of residence, and, finally in closing, shift to the first person as the petitioners make their plea for aid and describe, once again, their circumstances. A single petition or record of petitions cannot tell us the entire story of a poor person's life, but each provides glimpses into the circumstances in which Egypt's most desperate found themselves.

Silences in other sources obscure the motivations behind the actions of the poor. Due to such gaps, we frequently do not know the impetus behind particular events that occurred. For example, we can only guess at why the poor fled from an institution, whether Takiyyat Tulun or orphanages and training schools for adolescents that had been established through the fund-raising efforts of private associations in the early twentieth century. Had they received word that a family member back in the countryside was ill? Did they seek shelter in Takiyyat Tulun only during gaps between seasonal employment in the countryside? Were they escaping from the monotony and conditions of the shelter or training facility? Were the poor, given their vulnerability and dependence on the state or private associations, ever subject to abuse?

Finally, the poor's experiences, as well as the actions of the state, are mediated through yet another voice, that of indigenous and foreign reformers who commented extensively on the conditions of the poor and made proposals for their treatment. For events taking place in the early part of the nineteenth century, I have relied on accounts provided by advisers to the viceroy of Egypt, Muhammad Ali. Key among them were Antoine Barthélemy Clot (Clot Bey), Muhammad Ali's French medical adviser, and Joseph Hekekyan, a British-trained Armenian engineer in his service. These individuals had numerous interactions with the poor who received assistance in state-run shelters. Their portrayals of the poor, as is made clear in chapters 2, "Discerning between the Deserving and the Undeserving Poor," and 3, "Among the Poor of Takiyyat Tulun," and how they represented the treatment of the poor to foreign audiences were motivated by particular agendas—neither adviser provides complete or unbiased stories. The same holds true for foreigners residing in Egypt during the nineteenth and twentieth centuries who commented on the conditions of Egypt's poor and poverty. Despite their biases, as chapter 4 "The Spectacle of the Poor," illustrates, the use of foreigners' representations of Egypt's poor combined with indigenously generated materials allows us to come closer to a clearer understanding of the circumstances of the poor and the state's and private associations' involvement in their lives.

Alongside the representations provided by foreign and indigenous observers of Egypt in the nineteenth century, I draw heavily on the accounts provided by reformers active in the early twentieth century who
established a series of charitable associations. One shortcoming is that
these associations provided information only on the successes of their
endeavors. I have not found more detailed accounts of the day-to-day
running of particular institutions established by these groups or obtained information, for example, on the rate of employment of boys
who entered reformers' industrial training schools. A further difficulty
with this material is that the perspectives of association members and
reformers active during this period were very much shaped by interna-
tionalized discourses on the poor; simultaneously, since some of their
writings and presentations were directed toward international audiences, they might have portrayed themselves and their programs in particular ways to win favor and praise.

In documenting new forms of managing the public presence of the
poor and the poor's interactions with the state and philanthropic associations, this book constitutes one of the first attempts to understand
policies of poor relief in the Middle East. Although the story it tells
reveals, for the first time, the bureaucratization of assistance to the needy,
the role and functioning of state-run shelters, the activities of a number
of philanthropic organizations, and the politicization of the poor, it is
not the final chapter in the study of poor relief in Egypt; nor does it
provide a complete picture of the poor and the full range of their experiences, interactions with charitable organizations, and attitudes toward
authority or providers of assistance. Having identified the richness of
particular series of documents, I hope that other researchers will take
on similar projects to fill in subsequent layers, more fully document the
experiences of the poor, and ascribe further meaning to the actions of
the state and private actors during this era.

※

For this book, I used Arabic, Ottoman Turkish, and modern Turkish
sources. When transliterating Ottoman Turkish, I used modern Turkish
spelling. For Arabic materials, I followed the conventions of the *International Journal of Middle East Studies* but used diacritics only for the
letters *ayn* (ʿ) and *hamza* (ʾ) when they appeared in the middle or the
end of a word or name. For Egyptian names of people, places, and
institutions that contained the letter *j*, rather than using the sound of
the letter *j*, I used the Egyptian colloquial *g*. Hence the reader will find
discussion of the Malga' al-Hurriyya (Shelter of Freedom), which should
properly be Malja' al-Hurriyya, and mention of a foundling rescued

from the steps of a mosque in the Cairo neighborhood of al-Gamaliyya. More familiar names, such as those of the khedive Said or Ismail, are spelled without diacritics. Arabic words that are found in the English language, such as *ulema* or *sheikh*, are also written according to their English spellings.

ACKNOWLEDGMENTS

*I*HSAN, a word that I translate as "benevolence," "beneficence," and "charity" throughout this book, is also understood as generosity. Since I first became involved in the lives of Egypt's nineteenth- and early-twentieth-century beggars and other needy people, I have been the recipient of countless acts of generosity.

Numerous institutions provided financial support for my dissertation research and work on subsequent revisions, including the comparative component with Ottoman Istanbul. Grants from the Social Science Research Council and American Council for Learned Societies, Fulbright-Hays, and the American Association of University Women allowed me to conduct research and write my dissertation. During my graduate study, the University of Michigan Horace H. Rackham School of Graduate Studies, Center for Middle East and North African Studies, and History Department provided the support and intellectual environment that nurtured my graduate work. As I began to revise and expand my study, a comparative research grant from the Council for American Overseas Research Centers allowed me to travel to Cairo and Istanbul. Summer research support and the creation of a database were made possible through a Villanova University Faculty Research Grant and Research Support Grant. I am also grateful to Villanova University for providing me with a generous publication subvention grant that partly covered the cost of reproducing the images used in this book.

Generosity is at the very core of Egyptian society. Given that Egypt was my primary research site, it is clear that I have incurred a great many debts there and that I have been profoundly shaped by my experiences in Egypt's archives and the city of Cairo. The welcome I received in the numerous sites of my research, personnel's patience with my queries, and the warmth, acceptance, assistance, and encouragement I felt in every interaction — in intellectual environments as well as in the homes of the numerous families who took me in — made my research in Egypt a truly wonderful experience.

For facilitating my research and encouraging my work at the Egyptian National Archives, I wish to thank Dr. Ibrahim Fathullah, Madame Sawsun Abd al-Ghani, the employees of the main reading room, and the personnel attending to document delivery. I am also grateful to the staff of the periodical reading room at the Egyptian National Library. At the Ministry of Religious Endowments, Dr. Husam al-Din King Uthman and the able staff of the Daftarkhane shared their knowledge of *waq-*

fiyya documents and allowed me to work with their holdings. Dr. Abd al-Fattah Hasan of the Muslim Benevolent Society of Cairo took time out from his busy schedule to discuss the society's projects and also arranged tours for me of some of the institutions they currently fund. Joyce Arnold, Nihal Tamraz, Lesley Wilkins, and other members of the staff of the American University in Cairo's Rare Book Collection gave me valuable access to their library's collections.

My access to these research venues could not have been possible without the help of the Binational Fulbright Commission of Egypt; I am particularly grateful to Dr. Ann Radwan and Nevine Gad al-Mawla for their assistance. In addition to facilitating every aspect of my research in Cairo, they paired me up with two experts of Egypt's modern history, Dr. Ra'uf Abbas Hamid and Dr. Abd al-Wahhab Bakr. These scholars shared with me their extensive knowledge of Egypt's history and the Egyptian National Archive's holdings, patiently listened to my queries about the materials I found, gave me ideas for other sources, and went out of their way to make me feel welcome in Egypt. My gratitude to these scholars is immeasurable, and I hope that they are satisfied with the results of my findings.

In other locales, various institutions made my research possible and fruitful. I wish to thank the staffs of the Public Record Office in London and the library and archival staff of the Wellcome Center for Medical Science and the British Library. In Istanbul, the staff and archivists of the Başbakanlık Archives reminded me that although I might love Egypt more than any other place in the world, I had truly come home when I began work in their collections. I am grateful to them for the welcome that they provided and their efficient and expedient handling of my requests.

In a project that has been a long time in the making, I have had the good fortune of meeting and working with many scholars. Daniel Crecelius, Kenneth Cuno, Khaled Fahmy, Jan Goldberg, Magdi Guirguis, Nelly Hanna, Abd al-Mu'nim al-Jami'i, Khalaf Abd al-Azim Sayyid al-Miri, Rudolph Peters, and Amira Sonbol shared their extensive knowledge of the Egyptian National Archives and witnessed both my triumphs and my defeats as I struggled to make sense of my findings. In the archives and in the Egyptian National Library, Vickie Langohr, Mona Russell, and Lisa Pollard kept me focused and brought tears of laughter to my eyes when, as our hours of work seemed to drag on and exhausted from hand copying materials, I was ready to give up. In the archives, Mona Attollah always saved a space for me at the table where she worked with other Egyptian researchers. They, like Ms. Attollah, did not mind being frequently interrupted by my questions. Sharing their time and welcoming me into their midst, this group of Masters and Ph.D. students made my experiences in Egypt unforgettable. I will forever be enamored by their good-natured approach to research, their willingness to help, and their sense of humor.

The richness of Egypt's history, its wealth of archival materials, and the strengths of its various research institutions meant that I could benefit from the insights of other scholars who also made Cairo their temporary home. The American University in Cairo, the American Research Center in Egypt, and the Dutch Institute of Cairo were three venues where I discussed my work and gained from the knowledge of others. In these and other exchanges, I am particularly grateful to Walter Armbrust, Nathan Brown, Imco Brouwer, Peter Gran, Michael Reimer, Ted Swedenburg, and Katherine Zirbel for feedback during conversations and in early drafts of this project.

As I (and my research notebooks) crossed both the Atlantic and the Mediterranean, I had the opportunity to discuss my work in many forums. Audiences of panels in which I participated at the annual conferences of the Middle East Studies Association and the Social Science History Association, working groups organized by graduate students at the University of Michigan, and attendees at workshops (at the American Research Center in Cairo, the American Research Institute in Turkey, Ben-Gurion University, Bosphorus University, City University of New York, the University of Michigan, New York University, Oxford University, the University of Pennsylvania, and Princeton University) and commentators on my papers helped me to further develop my ideas. Of all the audience members, I am perhaps most grateful to Engin Akarlı, who first suggested that I orient my point of comparison of poor relief to Istanbul rather than Europe. For reminding me, however, that understanding Egypt's poor-relief projects in comparison with both the Ottoman Empire and the West would have an import for scholarship on poor relief in the Middle East, North America, and Europe, I thank Sandra Cavallo, Mark Cohen, Natalie Zemon Davis, Lori Ginzburg, Seth Koven, Adele Lindenmeyr, and Leslie Peirce.

Many scholars have taken me under their wing as they read drafts of my work and generously gave of their time. Above everyone else, I wish to thank Juan Cole, who saw this project through from the beginning and who served as a foundational source of inspiration and support during my graduate work through the present. Beth Baron, Joel Beinin, Mark Cohen, John Fine, Sally Humphreys, Adele Lindenmeyr, Zachary Lockman, Brinkley Messick, Karen Pfeifer, Robert Vitalis, Mary Wilson, and Dror Ze'evi have been key critics and mentors; without them, I know that I would not love history and Middle East studies as much as I do. Kenneth Cuno and Amira Sonbol read an earlier draft of this manuscript from start to finish and provided insights and criticism that helped me better formulate my ideas. Michael Bonner and Amy Singer, in addition to teaching me the value of collaboration, shared the excitement of making new inroads into the study of charity and philanthropy in the Middle East. I also wish to acknowledge my appreciation of Seth Koven, who understood better than anyone else my concerns about the voyeurism of charitable work and the historians' craft. Although many scholars have had an impact on the questions I ask and my approach to sources, I bear sole responsibility for any errors and recognize that my work might not measure up to all of their expectations.

At Princeton University Press, I wish to thank Brigitta van Rheinberg for her interest and support for my project and also extend my gratitude to the able staff of the press, especially Jonathan Hall, Hugh Lippincott, Carmina Alvarez, and Gail Schmitt. I also extend my sincerest thanks and appreciation to my copy editor, Dalia Geffen, for her meticulous attention to my manuscript and her patience.

Friends and colleagues in the United States and across the world have been supportive at every stage of my work. I am particularly grateful to Sevim Çakmak, Rochelle Davis, Lessie Jo Frazier, Paisley Harris, Meghan Hays, Vickie Langohr, Nadir Özbek, Figen Satar, Stephanie Singer, and Rebecca Winer for their many years of friendship and to my colleagues at Villanova University for their collegiality and intellectual support. Linda Thomas, in addition to being a great friend, also helped design and create a database for two sets of sources.

Last, I extend my deepest gratitude to my family for generously serving as a constant source of support and refuge but also for understanding when I could not go home due to travel or the necessity of working, and to my husband, Ron Donagi, for standing by me through thick and thin and for sharing the adventure of life with me.

MANAGING EGYPT'S POOR AND

THE POLITICS OF BENEVOLENCE,

1800–1952

I

BENEVOLENCE, CHARITY, AND PHILANTHROPY

REMARKING ON his travels in the Ottoman Empire in the first decades of the nineteenth century, the Englishman Thomas Thornton described how Islam was imbued with a genuine spirit of piety and noted that as a religion it was best characterized by its acts of public utility.[1] Thornton was impressed by the benevolent works he saw all around him: the fountains that provided clean water to townspeople and villagers, the stately mosques in the capital, Istanbul, and the care and respect that he saw neighbors and strangers express for one another. The sum of all that Thornton noticed was Islamic society's ideal imperative to take care of its members.

This introductory chapter explores the structures that existed to provide for the poor in Islamic societies, beginning with an overview of the avenues of care that the poor could pursue. It then turns to a discussion of some of the silences in contemporary scholarship on Middle East poor relief and illustrates how transformations in early-nineteenth-century Egypt and the resulting documentation on this era and subsequent decades provide us with important new insights on state involvement in poor relief. The chapter concludes with a methodological and theoretical discussion to highlight the ways in which this book—exploring the new attitudes, new policies, and new actors in the field of poor relief—gains from and complements our understanding of poor relief in the context of the Middle East, North America, and Europe.

Ihsan (beneficence, generosity) and *sadaqa* (almsgiving) are core features of Islamic societies. In addition to the requirement that Muslims pay an alms tax (*zakat*), the Quran and the Hadith (sayings and actions attributed to the prophet Muhammad) frequently call on the believers to care for the needy among their members. Although *charity* has connotations specific to the Christian world, throughout this book I utilize this term and describe forms of assistance and care for the needy as "charitable acts." To better capture the meaning of *ihsan*—meaning generosity or benevolence—for an English-speaking audience, I interchange the translation of this term as "charity and benevolence." However they might be translated, the meaning of these words, as will become clear, is grounded in Islamic prerogatives of caring for the needy. The opening pages of this chapter explores how a range of ideological, cultural, and physical aspects of Islamic society were intended to ensure that all of its members received care.

From birth to young adulthood, the family was the first bulwark of safety and security and the primary site of socialization. As a child matured, he or she contributed to the family's income; depending on the circumstances, marriage could mean the loss of that child's participation in the original family unit; as the parents advanced in age, children were expected to care for them.[2]

But changes throughout a person's life cycle could endanger the security and well-being of even those who had once had adequate means of support. For instance, parents relied on their children to support them in their old age, but when migration, disease, death, or natural disasters took such forms of assistance away from them, the elderly became dependent on relatives or members of their community. Women and children were particularly vulnerable to fluctuations in income and the weakening of support networks.[3] Divorce or the death of a spouse could mean that women frequently returned for assistance to their families.[4] Hence, for women, more than for men, it was imperative to stay close to networks of support.

Outside of one's immediate family, those in need of assistance could also look to their broader kin network. Relatives provided monetary assistance and training to nephews and nieces and, when necessary, took in their orphaned kin.[5] Intermarriage (cousin to cousin) enabled land and inheritances to stay in the family and ensured a solid network of support when needed.

If a person in need was without relatives or family, or if the support they provided was insufficient, she or he could next turn to the neighborhood and community. Neighbors watched out for their fellow neighbors, with richer members of the community distributing food and clothing on religious occasions. The more well off set up tables during the month of Ramadan to serve dinners marking the breaking of the fast (*iftar*) and distributed an allotment of meat and clothing to poorer families on the occasion of the Id al-Fitr (Feast of Breaking the Ramadan Fast) and Id al-Adha (Feast of Immolation). Some wealthier families even went so far as to adopt poorer families who expected, given a sense of moral economy, forms of assistance.[6] In rural areas of Turkey, through to the present, neighbors still assist nonrelatives; in previous centuries, urban areas' support provisions included guilds, which provided mutual aid to their members.[7]

Another means of receiving aid — and also a means of a livelihood — was begging. In cities such as Cairo or Istanbul, beggars were sure to acquire at least a minimum subsistence, given the charity of these cities' inhabitants. Ogier Ghiselin de Busbecq, a Flemish diplomat residing in Istanbul in the sixteenth century, noted how beggars forced on passersby "a tallow candle, a lemon, or a pomegranate, for which they expect double or treble its value, that so by pretense of selling they may avoid the disgrace of asking."[8] Other beggars seemed less inhibited. At Istanbul mosques in the 1830s, Reverend Walsh saw "crowds of needy persons," to whom members of the congregation gave "liberal alms" as they entered and left.[9] Baroness Minutoli, visiting Egypt in the early 1820s, remarked that the numerous beggars of Cairo were sure to receive food from owners of shops, and in this manner they could easily survive.[10]

Since almsgiving was never intended to be ostentatious and was not a means to call attention to one's benevolence in public, documenting its practice is difficult. "Charity," noted Thornton, citing the Persian poet Jami, "was comparable to musk." Its substance, "though concealed from the sight, is discovered by the grateful odour which it diffuses."[11]

"Islamic society" in the Middle East comprised a multiethnic and multireligious civilization. Within this society, from the era of the Umayyad Dynasty through the Ottoman Empire, in a geographic sweep of territory extending from Islamic Spain to India and beyond, each religious community had the responsibility of caring for its needy.[12] To have fallen into poverty, as Mark Cohen shows in his analysis of requests for assistance by the poor found in the Cairo Geniza, brings shame to the poor person.[13] Most assuredly, to have one's religious community members visible among the "public poor," I would argue, could bring shame upon the entire community, for that meant that they proved themselves unable to protect their own members. In addition to hiding the shamefaced poor, as Abraham Marcus shows, ensuring care for the poor members of their communities was intended as protection against conversion: minority religious groups' impoverished members might be tempted to convert to escape the financial burden of their poll taxes.[14]

Family members felt a moral obligation to their needy kin, but the necessity of providing for their dependents was also due to a need to hide the impoverishment afflicting the family from people outside of the family. Since caring for one's family's destitute members was such a private matter, it is difficult to find sources delineating its practice.

A more visible means of assisting the needy, a practice utilized by private persons as well as rulers and statesmen, was the creation of religious endowments. A person creating a religious endowment designated the profits from land or other real estate (such as shops), to go toward a charitable project.[15] Since the creation of a religious endowment was both religious and contractual, written records known as *waqfiyya* remain. These documents provide important information on the founder's goals in creating a religious endowment, the property that would go toward its establishment and upkeep, and detailed notes on the administration of funds. Given that many of the targets of religious endowments went toward buildings, such as mosques, schools, and even hospitals, physical evidence of this form of charity remains with us to the present day.

The most physically imposing institutions funded by religious endowments — and the most thoroughly researched structures — are those established by rulers, statesmen, and other prominent people in Islamic history. But private persons also created religious endowments. All endowments, whether established by the state or by private individuals, fulfilled a pious obligation: the founder of a religious endowment brought him- or herself closer to God by providing for the poor.

The revenues from religious endowments could be directed toward the endower's family (*waqf ahli*) as well as the community as a whole (*waqf khayri*), but all religious endowments were ultimately intended to serve the community. In this manner, they were directed toward a variety of services and institutions. The institutions funded by awqaf could be buildings such as schools, mosques, and hospitals; or they could consist of services, such as prayers on religious occasions and the distribution of food and water.[16] Given the possibility of the extinction of family lineages due to disease, infant mortality, and overall low life expectancies, even *ahli* religious endowments (endowments designating family beneficiaries first and then, ultimately, the community's poor) were likely to benefit the larger community within a few generations.[17] Private individuals frequently designated a prominent institution (such as an imperial waqf) as their ultimate beneficiary. As Miriam Hoexter has shown, a populace's trust in the sound management of a religious endowment could be measured by the number of private persons who named a larger institution (such as the Waqf al-Haramayn in Algiers) as the ultimate beneficiary of their endowments.[18]

Religious endowments served numerous personal economic ends. Theoretically, waqf property was not subject to taxation and could not be seized by the state. Designating one's heirs as beneficiaries or managers of religious endowments prevented property from being reappropriated by the state or divided up following death and enabled specific family members to profit from the endowments. Women established religious endowments so as to "safeguard their own property and its income from encroachment by their husbands and their husbands' families."[19] As Carl Petry argues, during times of economic or political instability, the designation of properties as religious endowments was intended to protect the properties from state confiscation and hence enabled individuals such as Mamluk emirs, the military elite (the Mamluks ruled Egypt between 1250 and 1517), to not only amass large amounts of property, but also maintain this wealth after their fall from power, thus allowing them to pass on these riches to their own progeny.[20]

Institutions funded through religious endowments also benefited their founders in other ways. As Adam Sabra argues, Mamluk sultans included tombs for themselves in the institutions they funded. Those who attended the mosque — or hospital, Sufi lodge, or school — offered prayers for the founder and his descendants.[21]

The ruling elite's creation of religious endowments also served political purposes. In creating institutions for the poor, as we will see later, they drew attention to themselves as benefactors. Their cognizance of the political import of their actions is evident in the strategic placement of the institutions they established and in royal ceremonies displaying their beneficence. However, as I argue, while acknowledging the political purposes of endowments, we must not lose sight of how the creation of endowments, grounded in religion and piety, also served the needs of a society.

Imperial Forms of Assistance to the Poor

Until recently, scholars have primarily focused on how the creation of religious endowments fulfilled economic ends. However, Paula Sanders's work on the Fatimids, Adam Sabra's book on poverty and charity in Mamluk Egypt, and works on the Ottoman period by Kenneth Cuno, Halil Inalcık, Leslie Peirce, Amy Singer, and Bahaeddin Yediyıldız have revealed the extensive public services that awqaf provided and the ways in which imperial ceremonies and other practices assisted the poor.

Our most detailed records of religious endowments are not available until the Mamluk period. However, for the era of the Fatimids, a Shiʿite dynasty that ruled Egypt from 969 to 1171, accounts of their ceremonial practices show how imperial largesse was extended to the populace at royal ceremonies, religious celebrations, and seasonal festivities.[22]

As Sabra shows, although the Mamluks' role in poor relief constituted primarily a safety net (rather than being a means to ameliorate poverty), the services they provided were extensive. In the capital of Cairo, Mamluk sultans established mosques, Sufi institutions, schools, and hospitals; they arranged the burial of the dead (during times of plague); and they attempted to implement price controls and distribute grain during times of scarcity. Endowments by the military elite included funds for the distribution of bread and water to the poor throughout the year.[23]

Building on the models and ideals of beneficence of prior Islamic rulers, Ottoman imperial religious endowments established by rulers, statesmen (administrators, governors, and important personages in various regions), and their families enabled the construction of buildings and the provisioning of services that benefited the general public as well as people who were identified as being particularly needy of assistance.[24] They funded the vast infrastructure necessary for commerce and trade as well as the very sanitation apparatuses of cities and towns. *Sabils* (fountains), set along public thoroughfares, granted all who passed clean water and refreshment. Bridges were founded and maintained through religious endowments, as were waterworks. A key characteristic of these institutions was how in the words of Busbecq, they "helped not only everyone, but everyone equally."[25]

Caravansaries and Sufi lodges provided temporary shelter, a meal, and drinking water. Mosques were another example of a public institution that Ottoman rulers and statesmen founded and supported through religious endowments. These buildings served as more than places of worship; they also were places in which the weary could rest and wash. Attached to the more prominent and richly endowed mosques were vast complexes that housed charitable establishments such as soup kitchens, shelters, schools, and, in some cases, hospitals.

Mosque complexes, founded and maintained through religious endowments, were at the center of society, both physically and in terms of being a central point for the distribution for services. The Fatih mosque complex of Istanbul, established by Mehmed II (ruled 1444–46, 1451–81), illustrates the centrality of such an institution. In addition to serving as a place of worship, this complex initially housed the treasury (Bayt al-Mal) that allocated pensions to disabled soldiers and the widows and children of soldiers killed in combat. It also served as a distribution point for food and services to the needy and orphans in its most immediate neighborhood.[26]

Ottoman rulers, women of the royal family, and prominent officials not only endowed religious institutions such as mosques and Quran schools but also erected and supported Sufi lodges as a demonstration of their piety and religious commitments.[27] Given their asceticism and renouncement of material possessions, Sufis were referred to as "poor" (*faqir*; pl. *fuqara*) and were closely associated with poverty and mendicancy. They also helped care for the needy.[28] Sufi orders gave assistance to the poor in thirteenth-century Seljuq Anatolia, and in Ottoman Anatolia their lodges provided care for the mentally ill. In late-seventeenth-century Ottoman Egypt, Sufi orders managed hospitals that cared for the insane, the government—according to the Ottoman traveler Evliya Çelebi—having previously confiscated the funds that allowed these institutions to function.[29] Sufi lodges in Tunis gave assistance to the poor, serving as a distribution point for food and, in some instances, sheltering those who had no other means of support.[30] Those of nineteenth-century Egypt also functioned as shelters for impoverished nonmembers.[31] Although Sufi lodges continued to serve members and nonmembers during this period, the Egyptian government's use of the term *takiyya* to refer to state-run poorhouses reflects its appropriation of these lodges' traditional function.

With the exception of Sufi lodges, which were dispersed throughout the empire, the Ottomans' involvement in establishing religious endowments and extending care to the poor was largely confined to major urban cities or religious sites such as Istanbul, Mecca, Medina, and Jerusalem. Istanbul, as the Ottoman capital, had extensive provisions that drew students as well as the poor to the city. In the seventeenth century Çelebi noted that having traveled in nineteen different dominions over the course of fifty-one years, he found that the *imaret* (soup kitchens) of this city were the best and most extensive he had seen anywhere. The poor were offered food three times a day at the Fatih imaret, and twice a day at imarets such as those of Sultan Bayezid, Khaseki Sultan, and Eyüp. In addition, "hundreds of kitchens" in various dervish lodges provided at least a loaf of bread and a bowl of soup to the poor.[32] Through the imaret system, as Halil Inalcık argues, the immense wealth concentrated in the hands of the ruling elite was redistributed among the poor.[33] But the strategic placement of institutions funded through religious endowments often meant that inhabitants in cities of lesser administrative or religious importance were denied access to imperially funded forms of relief. In provincial cities — for example, Aleppo in the eighteenth century — the poor could turn to their families and, to communal forms of charity and use other survival tactics such as begging or stealing, but the state's charity was conspicuous by its absence.[34]

The very act of feeding the poor was rife with symbolism associated with the Ottoman state. Following customs stemming from a Turkic and Persian heritage as well as Islamic traditions, during the month of Ramadan Ottoman rulers fed their subordinates at nightly *iftar* (dinners marking the end of the daily fast during Ramadan) and distributed (sometimes personally) food to the poor during the Id al-Adha. The soup kitchens that Ottoman rulers and their families established were a further extension of the patrimonial symbolism that suffused the very act of feeding the poor. Representing the means by which the sultan bestowed his benevolence on the poor, soup kitchens and ceremonies of food distribution served to strengthen the bonds between the ruler and his subjects.[35]

Principal urban areas, such as Cairo under Mamluk rule and Istanbul or other important administrative centers in the Ottoman provinces, were also sites of other forms of benevolence. In Cairo the Mamluk sultans distributed food to the poor on religious holidays and at banquets celebrating the opening of institutions funded by religious endowments.[36] Ottoman sultans and administrators extended their benevolence to the populace during specific religious holidays and the celebrations that they staged to mark an ascension to the throne, victories in battle, or the birth or circumcision of a son. During Ottoman royal celebrations, the poor were not designated as the sole beneficiaries; rather food and money were distributed to all those in attendance, and the whole society had the opportunity to benefit from these displays of generosity.

In addition to imperial endowments, members of the Ottoman royal family, as Leslie Peirce has documented in her study of the imperial harem in the sixteenth and seventeenth centuries, might choose to allocate funds toward specific persons or purposes. Hence, alongside the foundation of soup kitchens or other endowments, for example, women of the royal family designated funds that would pay for the dowries of poor women.[37] Like other forms of royal largesse, each display of charity served multiple purposes: it represented the piety and beneficence of the person making the bequest, served the persons receiving the assistance, advertised the munificence of those in power, and functioned as a model for members of the elite.

As scholars have shown, in the case of the Mamluks and the Ottomans, the central state also administered specific funds for orphans, families of soldiers, and other people designated as deserving (*mustahiqqin*). The Mamluks created an orphans' depository (*mawdiʿ al-hukm*) to safeguard the inheritances of rich and poor orphans until they reached the age of discretion.[38] In the Ottoman context the treasury (Bayt al-Mal) provided funds to orphans and widows of soldiers.[39] The state was responsible for the distribution of assistance to the needy through the office of the treasury in later periods as well. As Kenneth Cuno has documented, in Ottoman Syria and Egypt one source of funds for the treasury was state land set aside as an endowment by a ruler or his deputies (*irsad*). This form of endowment differed from waqf in that it was not the sole property of the sovereign, nor could he or his family be the beneficiaries of the endowment. Rather, "the beneficiaries of an irsad must be chosen from among those activities, institutions and persons that are legitimately deserving of support (*al-mustahiqqun fi bayt al-mal*)."[40] Legal treatises specified institutions and people who were deemed legitimate beneficiaries. They included religious clerics, the poor, orphans, women, and widows. Mosque and tekke construction, their upkeep, and the salaries of those who performed religious duties were also included as legitimate targets of funding through irsad.[41] The state treasury's stipends to those deemed deserving of charity and its compliance with definitions of *deservedness* grounded in religious doctrine, like the state's role in the establishment of other imperial awqaf, placed the state (as personified by the ruler) at the center of charitable giving.

Together with imperial forms of assistance, the multiple assistance options available to the needy in Islamic society constituted what has been described in Europe as a "mixed economy" of relief.[42] Such a range of options represented a perfect world of close connections between the ruler and his subjects, a wealth of endowments that provided for the destitute, social networks in which family, kin, and neighbors took care of their own, and ample alms for beggars who congregated in a town's or city's public areas. Yet in many cases this symbiosis of care remained only an ideal. Istanbul, for example, was richly endowed with imarets and other provisions of relief, but nevertheless not all of the poor received as warm a welcome as Thomas Thornton, the early-nineteenth-century visitor to the Ottoman Empire, described in his portrayal of Islamic charity in the Ottoman realms.[43] Systems of inclusion and exclusion meant that many were denied access to the very city space of Istanbul. The undesirable poor — specifically able-bodied men and men without networks or persons to vouch for their good behavior — were frequently expelled from the city.[44] Such practices of distinguishing between the sturdy poor and those deemed deserving of assistance were traditions that went back centuries, to the early Islamic period.[45] The presence of the undesirable poor in urban spaces was controlled through systems such as the *tezkere* (*tadhkira* in Arabic), a passport or document allowing a person to travel from one place to another.[46] Employment came only with sureties or within the structure of guilds; the unemployed who sought casual work were frequently denied access to the city. The very spaces of neighborhoods were also circumscribed to keep strangers out.

At the level of the family and kin networks, we also find silences and instances when practices did not measure up to ideals. Although we can surmise the means by which a family and neighbors cared for their indigent, documenting these actions of providing assistance is more difficult. Even more challenging is ascertaining the survival strategies of the most desperately needy, cut off from kin or family support. Poor women frequently resorted to the courts to be sure to obtain maintenance allowances that were their due.[47] Court records and other run-ins the poor had with the law (for theft, for example) are one means of finding information on poor people's efforts to get by.[48] Yet what of the invalids, the elderly, single women, and women with small children who had no networks of support and whose actions had not brought them to the courts? To whom or what did desperate individuals who had no other means of assistance turn?

Finally, a further shortcoming in our understanding of poor relief in the Middle East stems from the nature of source materials on religious endowments. Religious endowments instructing how a soup kitchen was to feed the poor or listing the provisions made for a particular neighborhood's needy did not, unfortunately, include information beyond the *ideal* of poor relief. The information such records provide is limited to the services to be provided and the actions and goals of donors. Records of individual endowments—for example, Ottoman imaret—entail discussions of the day-to-day upkeep of the institution and the salaries of employees; but the poor who received sustenance from them remain anonymous. The circumstances of those who sought assistance, the ways in which the poor presented their requests for assistance, the means by which waqf administrators and other personnel prioritized among the needy and perhaps distinguished between the deserving and the undeserving poor, and the extent of care the poor received are all issues that are absent from historical scholarship on poor relief in the Middle East.

The Benevolence of the State

Thanks to the centralization efforts of Muhammad Ali's government and the governments of his successors (policies that included direct interventions in poor relief and efforts that built on the centralization processes of rulers before them),[49] we *do* have extensive information on one Ottoman province's practices of poor relief and the poor's use of state assistance. An analysis of the registers and documents of various state departments and institutions and an examination of the records and publications of associations active at the end of the nineteenth century and the early twentieth century allow us to gain an understanding of features of poor relief and the experiences of the poor. These materials provide information on the circumstances of the poor, the delineation of the two categories of the deserving and the undeserving poor, the use of poorhouses to shelter the desperately poor, the means by which the indigent sought the state's (and, later, assocations') assistance, and the motivations of individuals (Egypt's rulers as well as private persons and groups) in providing poor relief.

It was within an environment of a religious tradition of charity that Egypt's government (a government based on a household elite comprising blood relatives, in-laws, freed slaves, and other close retainers)[50] established a series of institutions intended to provide for the poor and needy of Cairo and other areas of the Ottoman Empire in the first half of the nineteenth century. As governor of Egypt, the attention Muhammad Ali gave to the indigent in this province could be seen to fall in line with the beneficence of other Ottoman rulers. And the construction of shelters and other means of caring for the poor had a long indigenous history in Egypt as well.[51] Many institutions funded by religious endowments were established and maintained in Cairo, a city that had served as the central locus of power since the Fatimid era.

The institutions established during the rule of Muhammad Ali, those that were introduced and maintained during the reigns of his successors, and the ongoing provisioning of assistance to Egypt's poor during the nineteenth and early twentieth centuries reflected numerous features that highlighted their religious nature. Individuals who were received into any one of these institutions — the poor shelters of Cairo and Alexandria, state-run hospitals, an orphanage and foundling home, and insane asylums — as records documenting their admission note, were admitted "out of the charity" or "out of the benevolence" (*ihsanan* or *min ihsanat*) of Egypt's ruler. The government's recognition of its obligations to the poor and needy, through the establishment and maintenance of a variety of facilities — facilities that supplemented or at times took the place of traditional structures such as religious endowments and the government's provisions for the needy through the Bayt al-Mal — illustrates that these institutions were founded within an Islamic rubric of attention to society's vulnerable members.

However, the Egyptian government's initiatives, although reflecting religious prerogatives, also featured aspects of a modern state apparatus.[52] Familial and community practices of assistance continued to exist, but alongside these forms of care, the state introduced and managed specialized institutions that sheltered the deserving poor (and helped enforce newly initiated restrictions on the public presence of the idle poor) and established specialized facilities such as hospitals and a foundling home and orphanage. The introduction of state-initiated poor-relief policies demonstrated new levels of bureaucratization (and hence depersonalization) via new and more interventionist means. In the urban centers of Cairo and Alexandria and throughout Egypt's provinces, the office of the Dabtiyya best represented this bureaucratization and the introduction of new levels of intervention. This office served as one of the points of intersection between the Egyptian populace and the state in terms of providing various kinds of poor relief. Its responsibilities in Cairo and Alexandria included applying government directives for the treatment of beggars and the insane who had been rounded up by the municipal authorities. Simultaneously, it served as a medium through which needy individuals sought the state's assistance. The individuals requesting assistance presented their petitions to numerous offices of the state (including the Dabtiyya), hence giving the ruler—in reality—little or no contact with those on whom he bestowed his charity. At this juncture, the precise strategies and tactics of poor relief were centralized and secularized; a range of government-appointed personnel applied the government's new policies toward the poor.

Although these new interventions resulted in the appropriation of traditional forms of charity (as evidenced in, for example, terminology such as government-run shelters being labeled as *takiyya*) and the bureaucratization of care, they did not mean the entire displacement of other forms of assistance. Religious endowments such as al-Azhar continued to function as a site of food distribution to designated recipients. Families, neighborhoods, and—at least in the early part of the century—guilds continued to provide for their members. New government interventions, however, reflected, a growing concern about the public presence of the poor, new, and increasingly centralized ways of clearing the streets of the idle poor, and, by the beginning of the twentieth century, a new role for the elite in caring for those deemed Egypt's most vulnerable members.[53]

The Poor in the Public Eye

"In our cities, and especially in Cairo and Alexandria," remarked Kamel Greiss to an audience attending his presentation before the Sultanic Society of Political Economy, Statistics, and Legislation in 1916, "the streets and public spaces are cluttered with the infirm, the crippled, children in rags, and the unemployed, all with outstretched hands." The blind people one encountered, like mothers with small children who beseeched passersby to give them alms and the entire range of beggars who pleaded for assistance, were, in Greiss's view, impostors. Mendicancy in Egypt, as he explained to his audience, had become a true profession.[54]

Greiss's perspectives on begging were not unique. European travelers to Egypt commented on beggars who had amassed fortunes thanks to the charity of sympathetic inhabitants. Visitors to Istanbul also remarked that, for the most part, beggars were primarily "religious impostors" who could easily subsist thanks to the kindness of the urban populace. Even as far back as the first centuries of Islam, city authorities attempted to distinguish the deserving poor from those who feigned illness or destitution so as to solicit alms. In other eras and Middle Eastern locales, the presence of beggars had been termed a public nuisance as well as a potential threat to public order and security.

Nearly a century before Greiss's calls for denial of assistance to "impostors," the public presence of Egypt's poor had been a source of consternation for Egypt's government. In the first half of the nineteenth century, Muhammad Ali and city officials had expressed frustration over the large number of peasants fleeing from the countryside to, among other places, Cairo and Alexandria. In this period, the government initiated intensive efforts to expel nonresident beggars from the city and introduced ways to distinguish between the able-bodied and the deserving poor. Labor demands — stemming from efforts to maintain agricultural monopolies and to establish industry and due to the engagement of Muhammad Ali's armies in Greater Syria — and the need to direct government expenditures and manpower toward this occupation and hostilities with Mahmud II — resulted in a new official intolerance for religious mendicants as well as other beggars.

Concern about appearances and issues of public health, order, and security was a further reason for the government's comments on the presence of beggars in Cairo's streets and public spaces. By the time of Ismail's reign, when increasing numbers of Europeans were arriving in Egypt, the government had issued numerous calls for the removal of the poor from the streets and markets of cities such as Cairo and Alexandria. In each instance, institutions in existence, such as Takiyyat Tulun and Takiyyat Qabbari (in Alexandria) were mentioned as possible places in which the poor could be cared for and hence kept out of the public eye. Simultaneous to this era, as well as in decades preceding Ismail's rule, references to the itinerant poor included discussions of issues of public health and, in some instances, public security. Regarding order (*dabt wa rabt*) and security, the authorities of Cairo and Alexandria, like Istanbul authorities, were most concerned about loitering and the public presence of unemployed but able-bodied men. Government decrees set forth regulations as to what to do with these individuals. Forced employment and military training were just two options that the government initiated in an attempt to clear the streets of those who were deemed potentially troublesome or dangerous.

Beggars' seemingly unfettered existence in Cairo's public spaces was also a topic object for comment and concern for foreigners residing in or traveling through Egypt during this era. In many ways, parts of my analysis of the poor and the state's actions are mediated through the sometimes sympathetic but often condemnatory comments of Westerners residing in Egypt. In many cases, the official stance of their home governments vis-à-vis Muhammad Ali (the British were belligerent, and the French more conciliatory) colored their perceptions as well as their portrayal of conditions in Egypt. As Afaf Lutfi al-Sayyid Marsot has warned us in her analysis of portrayals of Muhammad Ali, we must be mindful of how particular biases led to misrepresentations of his rule and policies.[55]

Given these portrayals' political nature (these descriptions were intended to represent Egypt in a way that served imperial ends), we need to be attentive to Western travelers' potential for exaggeration and misrepresentation. However, as long as we recognize their intended political import, we can make use of the descriptions of Egypt that they provide. Leaving aside the "fantastic" and utilizing descriptions that corroborate other sources allows us to present a more vivid picture of Egypt's social history. At the same time, by analyzing these sources' intended impact on European audiences we can see how certain representations of Egypt's poor fulfilled imperial objectives.

Egypt's importance to the Ottoman Empire and new trade initiatives in the first decades· of the nineteenth century, its integration into the world economy, and specifically its increasing strategic importance in the second half of the century brought growing numbers of foreigners to Egypt. Tourists (thanks to steamships and the opening of the Suez Canal) joined diplomats, military officials, merchants, and entrepreneurs resident in Egypt during this era. They commented on the conditions of Egypt's poor as well as on the public presence of beggars. These various groups of outsiders frequently remarked on the large number of beggars they saw, as well as the ease with which beggars were able to subsist on the charity of Cairo's inhabitants. But of equal importance in their discussion of the public presence of beggars were remarks on how the conditions of Egypt's poor were indicative of the despotic government of Muhammad Ali (as well as his successors) and the Egyptian government's inability (and disinterest) in providing for the poor. Such tropes of Egypt's poverty and the topos of the government's lack of regard for the poor (as well as, later in the nineteenth century, accusations that indigenous private persons neglected their obligations toward them) were key features of foreigners' perceptions of Egypt. During the first decades of the British occupation (1882–1922), British medical authorities as well as journalists argued that Egyptians' disregard of their own poor and their inability to care for their impoverished citizens indicated that British expertise was crucial in public health and social welfare and that Egyptians were not ready for independence from British rule.

The practice of poor relief in the nineteenth and early twentieth centuries reflected a hybridity. Government efforts represented a melding of different religious traditions and simultaneously spoke to Egypt's unique placement at the crossroads of a series of empires.[56] Egypt's traditions of poor relief were grounded in Islamic practices and an Islamic ethos of caring for the poor, but state involvement in this realm also reflected Ottoman influences. Finally, European actors (advisers, outside observers, and colonial officials), through their proposals, their critiques, and, by the end of the nineteenth century, their programs, influenced the very shape of poor relief.

Managing the Poor

The initiation of direct state intervention in poor relief during this period in Egypt differed markedly from policies in other times and locales of the Middle East. From secondary research addressing policies toward the poor in the contexts of Mamluk Egypt (1250–1517), eighteenth- and nineteenth-century Tunis, and eighteenth-century Aleppo and secondary sources and available archival materials for seventeenth-through nineteenth-century Istanbul, we learn that city officials did not implement broad-scale practices of arresting and interning the poor. In each region, begging was an accepted feature of society. City officials in Istanbul did not make extensive efforts to clear the streets of the poor until the 1890s. Direct state involvement in poor relief, centralized institutions and apparatuses of record keeping which kept track of the poor's involvement with the state, and the broad-scale implementation of restrictions on the public presence of the poor set Egypt apart from other areas. In some respects, practices in Egypt came closer to those of Western Europe and Russia. At the same time, the continued religious ethos that pervaded state involvement in poor relief distinguished Egypt's initiatives from those of countries such as France and England.

In the process of documenting the initiation of direct state involvement in poor relief and charting transformations in state and private initiatives of charity over the course of the nineteenth century, this book posits that poor-relief practices in Egypt did not fit neatly into a distinct rubric of social control.[57] Despite the introduction of restrictions on poor people's public presence and increasing interventions in their lives, the word *policing* is not an apt description of policies implemented in the nineteenth and early twentieth centuries, for the state and private organizations were incapable of entirely controlling the poor. The conjuring of an apparatus of control that *policing* implies, furthermore, fails to capture how benevolence was in great part religiously inspired. Nor was the state's and private organizations' *provisioning* of assistance to the poor inexhaustible and unrestricted. The establishment of priorities in provisioning resulted in the forging of distinctions between the sturdy poor and those deemed "deserving" of assistance. The idleness of the able-bodied poor (predominantly men) served as a justification for punishments ranging from forced employment to transportation. Finally, poor relief was neither unilaterally determined nor unilaterally imposed. The *intent* of the state and private philanthropists differed from the *outcome* and *effect* of their actions.[58] Furthermore, the requests the poor made for assistance influenced the shape and scope of assistance. In sum, the state (through its agents in the Dabtiyya) and well-intentioned philanthropic groups active in Egypt from the end of the nineteenth century onward *managed* the poor. They implemented policies, introduced plans (frequently positing these programs within a religious discourse of care for the poor), and succeeded in providing a range of assistance. But inadequate resources and a certain measure of inefficacy meant that they could not completely regulate or control the public poor.

That Egypt's rulers and philanthropists had a difficult time fully implementing poor-relief projects is understandable given the failings of their northern neighbors in this same realm. Studies of poor relief in Europe have illustrated the difficulties that numerous governmental agencies and private bodies encountered as they sought to impose restrictions on the itinerant poor. This scholarship also demonstrates that social-control models are insufficient explanatory modes of analysis, for they represent only the intent of poor-relief officials, for example, and not the outcomes of their endeavors. In England application of the poor law varied depending on local circumstances, and workhouses never resembled Benthamite panopticons. Due to new policies, some people might have been categorized as marginal or deviant, but the assumption that these practices were geared solely toward social control does not account for the relief that families felt when, unable to care for a dangerously insane relative, they committed him or her to a state-funded institution. Nor does the assumption that such policies were all-pervasive explain how the "quiet" insane continued to evade confinement due to a lack of space. Sunday schools, rather than being the preserve of outsiders and a means of imposing middle-class values and ideas of deference to authority on the British working classes, were run by members of working-class communities and promoted self-help and advancement through merit.[59]

To truly understand poor-relief practices in the contexts of North America, Western Europe, and Russia, we need only look at the more nuanced and detailed studies that have emerged. These works explore the economic and social goals of the administrators and statesmen who shaped poor-relief policies and examine the successes and failures of their objectives. For example, in her exploration of the application of the poor law in nineteenth-century England, Lynn Lees documents the operation of poorhouses and how the poor utilized these institutions and viewed the actions of officials charged with administering the poor law. She also shows how local decisions and administrators' actions affected the functioning of workhouses. Administrators frequently did not enforce the purported discipline and punishment the workhouse was intended to introduce. Although workhouses were intended as a means to stigmatize the poor, at times the most destitute, lacking other means of assistance, considered the workhouse as a viable (and often temporary) solution and not an institution to be avoided at all costs.[60]

Cultural norms and predominant attitudes toward the poor could also impede the implementation of restrictive policies. As Adele Lindenmeyr illustrates, imperial Russia's experiments in poor relief were distinct from those of Western Europe due to cultural differences. Giving aid to the needy was ingrained in Russian culture, and the recognition that "poverty was not a vice" was pervasive. Despite reformers' efforts to secularize poor relief, cultural attitudes toward poverty and charity and tolerance toward begging prevented government authorities from enforcing restrictions on the public presence of beggars.

Works that closely examine how the poor took advantage of assistance options serve as a further critique of social-control models. Contributors to *The Uses of Charity*, Peter Mandler's edited volume, discuss how the poor actively sought the assistance of the state, navigating through a variety of resources and presenting their cases in ways in which they could best benefit from the sympathies of poor-relief officials. Just as contributors to this edited volume document the agency of the poor, Rachel Fuchs's analysis of impoverished unmarried pregnant women in nineteenth-century Paris recovers the voices and actions of women whose experiences have remained outside the historical record. Utilizing court documents about women accused of abortion and infanticide, she analyzes the absence of options available to single, poor, and pregnant women, the motivations behind the choices they made, and the ways in which they procured assistance.

Other scholarship on poor relief in Western countries has attempted to contextualize the rise of the welfare state, documenting the extent to which demands from those in need of assistance and the activities of philanthropists helped shape emerging institutions. In this line, the work of Theda Skocpol sets discussions of Civil War pensions and aid for women and children within Progressive Era politics and contingencies.[61] A "maternalist welfare state," with female-dominated public agencies implementing regulations and extending assistance to women and children, came into being. Contributors to Seth Koven and Sonya Michel's *Mothers of a New World* also show how maternalist discourses were used to fashion welfare policies. Women activists, couching their demands within a maternalist rhetoric, made demands on the state that influenced political policy and ensured a space for themselves (as social workers and in health care fields) within emergent institutions. As authors in this edited volume show, the formation of welfare policies was predicated upon the actions of numerous actors.[62]

Nor did "welfare institutions" in the West ever develop along a linear trajectory. Two recently edited volumes, *The Locus of Care* and *Medicine and Charity before the Welfare State*, call into question the delineation between familial forms of charity and the "rise" of the welfare state. They argue that there never was a "golden age" of the family, nor was there a time when state-funded relief was paramount. Contributors to *The Locus of Care* document how multiple forms of assistance have always existed side by side. Even separating "state" charity from "private" forms of assistance, as the essays in *Medicine and Charity before the Welfare State* illustrate, is impossible. In Western Europe, the church and the state frequently subsidized "private" charities. The central government and political parties also often chose to promote some charities at the expense of others for their own political ends.[63]

The questions that these scholars of poor relief in the West have posed of their research materials and the means by which they have contributed to our understanding of poor relief and state-society relations have, in turn, enriched my analysis of the initiation of more interventionist forms of poor relief, the development of state-run charitable institutions in Egypt, and the rise of philanthropic organizations. Like Fahmy's book on the Egyptian army in which he illustrates the failure of many "disciplining" projects, I acknowledge the allure of social-control models.[64] But I also recognize that calls for the prohibition of begging and the confinement of beggars, and private philanthropists' efforts to promote vocational training and enforce respectability among Egypt's street children, remained but blueprints in terms of their successful enactment. Beggars continued to be a constant presence in public spaces, poorhouses in Egypt (like those in Europe and North America) had insufficient space and resources, and philanthropists' vocational training centers were more frequently used by families who enrolled their children in these institutions than by the street children such institutions sought to reform. Despite their intended goal of removing potentially criminal boys and girls from the streets of Cairo and Alexandria, juvenile "vagrants" remained a public presence.[65]

Our understanding of Egypt's social history must take into account the actions of the poor themselves, and not only the means by which they were acted upon. Although on one hand we can explore state-initiated plans for clearing the streets of beggars and how such projects involved the establishment of poor shelters and other attempts to restrict the public presence of the poor, on the other hand we must look at poor people's *use* of these facilities and how they learned to negotiate through the various bureaucratic offices established at this time. We must also examine how the poor portrayed their poverty and need to state officials as well as to private philanthropists. As contributors to Mandler's collection *The Uses of Charity* seek to understand, how did the poor present themselves so as to best take advantage of services and the sympathy of those who provided assistance? How, as scholars contributing to *Medicine and Charity before the Welfare State* ask, did the poor use charity for purposes for which it might not have been intended?

In books on poor relief in the contexts of Western Europe, Russia, and North America, we find many points of similarity in the practices and the development of services. Like institutions in Europe, the state's involvement in charity in Egypt did not proceed along a linear track. Familial, community, and traditional forms of assistance operated along-side new, state-run institutions. The centrality of the poor to the state changed depending on the economic and political conditions of Egypt, and the demands of the poor overwhelmed the state's capacity to provide for them. As in Europe, multiple options for care existed. Poor people's first line of defense was their families, but even their receipt of some forms of state assistance (that is, admission to government-run shelters) did not cut them off entirely from their loved ones. Although at the outset state-run shelters in Egypt were designed to punish beggars (by restricting their access to private charity, casual labor, and their freedom of movement), the poor of Egypt *sought* admission to shelters, considering it just one among many options for care. Like the poor of nineteenth-century England and eighteenth- and nineteenth-century Antwerp, many of the poor who requested admission to shelters in Egypt made use of government facilities for only short periods of time.[66]

The cultural aspect of Egypt's experiences with poor relief was similar to that of imperial Russia. In both locales, a religious ethos of care for the poor permeated charitable practices.[67] As in Russia, the inability of Egypt's state officials to enforce prohibitions on begging might very well have been due to private persons' continued tolerance of the poor. In both Egypt and Russia, religious obligations also underlay the motivations of philanthropic associations established at the end of the nineteenth century.

Developments in poor relief and attitudes toward the poor in Egypt, as in Western Europe, Russia, and North America, were contingent upon transformations in the economy and the changing ability of the state to respond to the needs of the poor. Simultaneously, the actions of well-intentioned philanthropists also set the perimeters of forms of assistance. As in North America and Western Europe, associations, many of which included prominent women, called for the implementation of programs to ameliorate the conditions of the poor. The targets of such organizations, as in the other regions, were society's most vulnerable people: women and children. What differed from the development of welfare provisions in the Western world, however, was the colonial component of Egypt's experiences with poor relief. Many associations came into being in response to interventions by missionaries and foreign groups, and they frequently equated care for the poor with nationalist ideals.

Transformations in Poor Relief

State-sponsored shelters functioned in only two urban areas of Egypt, Cairo and Alexandria. In addition to the lack of any mention of such facilities in rural or other urban areas of Egypt, the presence of indigent people from outside of Cairo and Alexandria who gained admission to these shelters confirms that these four institutions (the Maristan — also referred to as Mahall al-Fuqara', Takiyyat Tulun, Qishla al-Sadaqa, and Takiyyat Qabbari) were all that existed. Like Istanbul, whose imaret were a draw for the empire's poor, many needy people from outside these cities came to Cairo and Alexandria and petitioned for admission, noting that they had no other means of support. Their requests for admission might well have followed other attempts to obtain a livelihood by begging in the cities. Unlike poor-relief programs in Europe, which stipulated that poor persons could receive aid only in their home districts, the poor shelters in Cairo and Alexandria did not make such distinctions. As long as individuals could prove their deserving status (for example, by demonstrating their inability to work and provide for themselves and by proving that they had no other means of support), they would be considered eligible for state charity.

The state's ability to assist the poor, however, was limited. As early as the 1830s, the government imposed its own criteria of deservedness on the poor whom the police had arrested on Cairo's streets and markets. As described in chapter 2, those who were able to work were put to work, and those deemed "unfit" were admitted to the state-run shelter located in the Maristan Qalawun. Confining the poor was never absolute. Once confined to these shelters, beggars could gain release if they met a number of conditions. As discussed extensively in chapter 3, family members and the relatives of beggars petitioned for the release of their kin, vouching for the beggars' good behavior and providing guarantees that the beggars would not engage in this activity again.

By the 1850s, shelter officials also had to deny admission to other individuals who requested shelter. Those deemed healthy were considered ineligible. And those who wished to become permanent residents of Takiyyat Tulun, Cairo's second poor shelter, could not stay unconditionally. Shelter administrators frequently screened residents and determined who would be allowed to continue residing in the shelter and who would be expelled. In many instances, individuals who had been expelled subsequently requested readmission, attempting to prove yet again that they deserved state assistance.

Poor shelters established in Egypt differed from similar facilities in Europe. Unlike the workhouses of England, for example, they were not intended to enforce strictures of less-eligibility, nor were they designed to inculcate an appreciation for work. On only one occasion did I find evidence that the poor within the walls of Takiyyat Tulun were to be put to work (during the reign of Khedive Ismail).[68] However, this project to create a *workhaus* was never implemented. The four Egyptian poorhouses were distinctly charitable in that they were intended to provide food and shelter to individuals who had no other recourse for care. The poor housed in these institutions could leave, and many did leave: they fled, were released through the intercession of family and kin, or proved to shelter administrators that they were capable of caring for themselves and promised that they would not return to begging. In many ways, Egypt's poor shelters were a temporary home for the indigent. In some instances, the poor made these institutions their permanent residence.

The poor were never absent from the public eye. Throughout accounts of this era, we see that they were a source of frustration for city authorities who sought to remove them from public spaces, and they were an object of charity and sometimes of criticism, for private persons and charitable organizations alike. Chapter 4, "The Spectacle of the Poor," focuses on the fact that the very spectacle of the poor was politically charged. For Westerners, the poor's ubiquitous public presence and the supposed inadequacy of poor-relief institutions and insane asylums at the beginning of the nineteenth century demonstrated the despotism of Egypt's rulers. In the second half of the nineteenth century and later, their public presence indicated not only the negligence of Egypt's rulers but also the Egyptian elite's lack of concern for the indigent and the "need" for Western nations to teach Egyptians how to care for their own poor.

The state's overall abilities to provide for the poor diminished by the end of the century. Upon the closing of Takiyyat Tulun (to protect and preserve this important monument of Islamic art and architecture), the shelters that replaced it were smaller, with a combined capacity of just over three hundred persons, unlike the nearly five hundred who could be housed in Takiyyat Tulun (figures 1.1 and 1.2 depict Ahmad ibn Tulun Mosque when it was used as a shelter in the 1860s and as it

Figure 1.1. This photograph shows the Mosque of Ahmad ibn Tulun when it served as a shelter for the poor, circa 1860s. (Courtesy of the Iverson Collection)

appeared in the 1980s).[69] In addition, the priorities of the Egyptian government during the British occupation also affected the state's involvement in poor relief. Whereas public health concerns and the medical aspects of charity continued to be a priority, assistance to the truly destitute received less governmental attention. At the same time, more restrictive prohibitions were imposed on able-bodied beggars. These restrictions, which targeted chiefly vagrant men (considered sturdy men who were capable of working), included punishments as harsh as imprisonment or transportation.

During this era, as I illustrate in chapter 5, "The Future of the Nation," associations entered the field of poor relief. Their activities point to how a particular cause, namely ameliorating the conditions of Egypt's poor children, became a rallying point that brought different individuals together with a common goal. A second feature of these associations was that instead of giving assistance for the sake of charity alone, they began to focus on assisting the poor in obtaining viable means of employment. Programs initiated by these organizations — projects that the government replicated in later years — centered primarily on industrial and vocational training for boys, but they also included

Figure 1.2. By 1880 the Mosque of Ahmad ibn Tulun ceased to be used as a shelter for the poor. During the last decades of the nineteenth century and the first decades of the twentieth, extensive restoration work was completed. The repairs and restoration have erased any traces of its use as a shelter. (Courtesy of the Iverson Collection, 1985)

opportunities for girls to gain skills for employment. A third aspect of the advent of associations was the politicization of poverty and the ways in which associations and individuals, although directing their efforts toward charitable ends, made use of the poor for political purposes.

The rise of charitable associations in late-nineteenth-century Egypt stemmed from the convergence of the inadequacy of state-sponsored services, a collective threat felt in communities, the emergence of an educated elite, and the availability of forums and means of communication (such as the press) through which an organization could advertise its actions and efforts and solicit funds. The conjuncture of these various factors was similar to the one that gave rise to associations at the center of the Ottoman Empire. There, a period of political turmoil and revolution concurred with the development of civil society and the subsequent creation of political organizations and associations.[70] In Istanbul the bestowal of charity was itself politicized as Sultan Abdul Hamid

II pitted himself against associations in an effort to prove his ability to care for the poor.[71] In the case of Egypt, despite charitable goals, philanthropic organizations (as well as other associations founded during this period) also represented a threat to Egypt's monarchy. Egypt's government attempted to temper the emergence of civil society (as represented by the associational movement active since the last decades of the nineteenth century) through a variety of means.[72]

Even though the charitable projects of numerous associations were ostensibly geared toward the amelioration of the conditions of the poor, the Egyptian government, as early as the 1920s, sought to make sure that the aims of these groups were solely charitable. Each organization was required to demonstrate that it was not in any way involved in politics. Such concern became increasingly acute from the 1930s on as the government sought to curtail the activities of communist groups who were likely to agitate among the poor. A second source of anxiety was the activities of the Muslim Brotherhood, whose projects were geared toward improving the lives of the poor.

From the 1920s on, Egypt's monarch and politicians recognized the political import of the poor and became involved in poor relief at various levels so as to counter the activities of associations and organizations engaging in charitable activities. At one level, they instituted surveillance over the activities of philanthropic organizations. At the same time, they endeavored to advertise their own concern for the poor. The Ministry of Social Affairs, established in 1939, assumed surveillance of the activities of all associations active during this period. Simultaneously, this ministry also sought to detract attention from the activities of private associations by placing King Farouk, Egypt's ruler, at the center of numerous benevolence projects. As Nancy Gallagher has argued, competition between the king and various political parties drew the poor into a public discourse during the Second World War. In this era, politicians vied with one another in the press and advertised their philanthropic activities among the rural poor, to prove their benevolence and ability to best address the needs of Egypt's poor.[73]

In the first decades of the twentieth century, the politics of benevolence had come to mean the forms and scope of competition between Europeans and Egyptians as to who was best suited to care for Egypt's poor. But the politics of benevolence also entailed competition among Egypt's own elites and politicians, with each drawing attention to the poor and to ameliorating poverty. The various actors on the field of poor relief put the poor in full public view so as to advertise their own abilities to care for them and in this manner lay claim to their own political legitimacy.

The extent to which charitable associations could assist the poor, coupled with the increased difficulties the poor faced during the Depression and the Second World War, as I emphasize in chapter 6, "Conclusion: From 'the Poor' to 'Poverty,'" made poverty and discussions of the means to ameliorate it topics of political debate. During the 1940s and on, political parties and the king competed with one another to prove their abilities to care for the poor.

II

DISCERNING BETWEEN THE DESERVING

AND THE UNDESERVING POOR

WHEN THE SPANIARD Ali Bey toured the al-Azhar Mosque in 1806, he was perplexed to find that its floors were devoid of the beautiful Persian carpets another traveler had described. Instead, he found that the floors were covered with mats. In response to his inquiry as to why the carpets were no longer there, the sheikhs of the mosque informed him that such coverings had never existed. Mats, they noted, were preferable because the vermin of beggars and the poor who slept there could be easily washed off of them.[1]

The Mosque of al-Azhar was not the only place in Cairo where beggars and the poor congregated. Other mosques (as in the Islamic world as a whole) also served as areas where those in desperate circumstances could wash, rest, and perhaps even be offered food and water.[2] In the words of a late-nineteenth-century traveler to Egypt, mosques were "as much a place of rest and refuge as of prayer . . . a houseless Arab may take shelter there by night or day."[3] Mosques throughout the Middle East, funded by religious endowments, could be small—serving solely as a place of worship and including running water for ablutions—or large—including such facilities as a school, a hospital, an orphanage, a shelter, and a soup kitchen. Whatever their size, mosques were spaces where at the very least the weary could find a temporary refuge.

Al-Azhar, built in 971–973, was one of the larger mosque complexes of Cairo, its facilities including a university as well as a soup kitchen. As a center of learning, al-Azhar provided housing to students from various regions of the Islamic world. As a distribution point, it supplied food to its religious clerics, their families, and other people deemed deserving of these rations.[4] Qalawun, another large complex, included a mosque, a hospital, and at one time a school for orphans.[5] Like Ottoman mosque complexes in other areas of the Middle East, the motivations behind the establishment of the complexes of al-Azhar and Qalawun were manifold. They all fulfilled pious goals, served the needy, and proved to be a lasting legacy to their founders and to the individuals who bequeathed subsequent funds to ensure their proper functioning.[6]

In addition to the provisions and shelter they might obtain at mosques, the poor of nineteenth-century Cairo had various means of assistance available to them. Throughout Egypt, they could seek help from kin and other networks of support. As in eighteenth-century Aleppo, those in need turned to their families, who were obligated to provide for them.[7] For newcomers, networks of support (family members, relatives, and village friends and acquaintances) in Cairo were essential for obtaining jobs and enabling individuals in dire circumstances to borrow money.[8]

When help from kin was absent or inadequate, the indigent received charity from their better-off neighbors. Travelers to Egypt noted that beggars could easily gain sustenance. Baroness Minutoli, visiting Egypt in the early 1820s, remarked, "[A]s for beggars in the city, who are very numerous, they rarely pass a shop containing provisions, without receiving from the owner some food, which, at least, supports life."[9] Celebrations of religious holidays included the distribution of food and clothes to the needy in one's neighborhood; and shrines, like mosques, were also places where the poor obtained food.[10] During religiously significant days, such as Ashura — the tenth of the month of Muharrem and the nine days that precede it — pious people distributed alms to the needy; even women of "respectable circumstances," with young children in their arms, solicited money in the streets of the city.[11]

Charity benefited both the giver and the recipient. Michael Dols argued that charity "did the almsgiver a necessary service. Charity was a means for a Muslim to atone for sin and express his or her gratitude for God's bounty."[12] Edward Lane, residing in Egypt in the early nineteenth century, noted how benevolence and charity to the poor "are virtues which the Egyptians possess in an eminent degree," remarking that public fountains (essential sources of clean water) were prominent examples of the charity found in Cairo and the countryside.[13] He concluded that charity (whether it was endowing a fountain or giving alms) was practiced as much out of pity as out of an expectation of eternal rewards in the hereafter. Aside from any benefit to the giver, or any sense of compassion, the poor regarded assistance as their right. In Morocco, for example, every family of means had its regular clientele of needy persons who appeared on specific dates to receive charitable gifts, which they considered their due (haqq).[14] The needy in Cairo might also have felt this same sense of moral economy, relying on specific families to provide aid.

Within a family or among members of a small community, it is possible to identify those individuals genuinely requiring assistance. They were frequently the invalid and the elderly, women with no other means of support, and orphaned children. Within a family or community, all of these were individuals whose history and personal circumstances other members of the family or community knew. But in larger communities — or cities — discerning between the "deserving" (*mustahiqq*) and those who feigned illness or destitution was more difficult. Legists such as the Ottoman Şeyhülislam Ebu's-su'ud Effendi grappled with this problem in the sixteenth century. As he touched upon issues of begging and the virtues of charity, Ebu's-su'ud noted that *cerrarlar* (troublesome beggars) should be reprimanded and forbidden from gathering at mosques, though the actions of those who gave them alms were virtuous. In earlier centuries in Arab regions, one of the duties of the *muhtasib* (the market inspector) had been to confiscate the belongings of sturdy beggars and have them hired out to work. He also had the authority to expel sturdy beggars from the mosques where they congregated. Hadith (the sayings and actions attributed to the prophet Muhammad) warned that importunate begging would be punished by hellfire.[15]

European travelers to nineteenth-century Egypt frequently commented on the existence of "imposters" among beggars, aiming their criticism primarily at religious mendicants.[16] However, since we do not have a way of documenting the daily charitable acts of private persons, we have no information on how inhabitants of Cairo might have discerned between the truly needy and the undeserving beggars. Given the strength of religious convictions and the extent to which charity was valued, it is likely that in many cases almsgivers did not distinguish between the deserving and the undeserving. However, in times of economic crises, or when migration brought increasing numbers of people (among them the poor) to urban areas, the charitable impulses of people were certainly strained. Economic necessity, as Mark Cohen documents in his analysis of the Cairo Geniza, forced members of the Jewish community to limit their charitable activities. First one's household received assistance, then, if funds remained, members of the broader community received aid. "Strangers" were less important, because, among other reasons, they had no one to vouch that they were indeed worthy of assistance.[17] In the broader society, during times of economic difficulty or when the poor became a public nuisance, charity could not be extended to everyone.

Although we lack detailed information on individual responses to supplications in nineteenth-century Cairo (other than Europeans' statements that the poor of the city had little difficulty procuring food and sustenance, given the charity of their neighbors), records of *state* actions toward the poor do offer a glimpse of how government authorities discerned between the deserving and the undeserving poor. Before the nineteenth century, a person's place of residence offered one distinction between meriting and being unworthy of assistance. City authorities in Istanbul returned Egyptian peasants caught begging in the markets in the sixteenth century to their home villages; officials in Cairo severely punished peasants who had come to Cairo during times of famine in the countryside and forcibly returned them to their land.[18] The drawing of such distinctions between country and city dwellers served to maintain order and security. Such distinctions, like efforts under way in Europe, also implied that the poor of a particular area should be provided for in their place of residence instead of taxing the charitable resources of other areas.[19]

Efforts to distinguish between beggars who "belonged" in the cities and those who should remain in the countryside were also a feature of the policies initiated in nineteenth-century Egypt during the rule of Muhammad Ali. However, whereas Muhammad Ali's concern focused partly on issues of public security, his government and those of his successors took these distinctions one step further. Egyptian governments attempted to impose more refined criteria of deservedness by implementing broad prohibitions on begging and creating new, specialized institutions for beggars, abandoned children, and individuals in need of medical care. In preindustrial Western Europe, the centralization of poor relief and the use of almshouses and other means to intern the poor occurred where commercial capital dominated production and necessitated the regulation of labor.[20] In nineteenth-century Egypt, the arrest and admission of beggars deemed deserving of assistance (due to their inability to provide for themselves) to state-run shelters and the forced employment of the able-bodied were initiated during a period of high labor demands due to the nascent industrial works and the introduction of agricultural and military projects.[21] Other factors, including a new concern for the appearance of public spaces and the emergence of new discourses about responsibility toward the poor, also influenced attitudes toward the poor and charitable practices.

The government's attentiveness to events in Cairo's streets and markets built upon previous centuries of Ottoman rule, but the initiation of new policies must be understood within the context of numerous government objectives distinctive to the early nineteenth century and the geography of this entire province. New policies signaled a transformation in state involvement in charity and changes in official attitudes toward the itinerant poor. The introduction of new taxonomies of locale (determining who had the right to reside in the city and who belonged in the countryside) and space and productivity (clearing the streets of beggars and distinguishing between the deserving poor and those capable of supporting themselves through work) were at the core of state initiatives in charity.

The ways in which the Egyptian government sought to introduce these taxonomies were unique to the Middle East at this time: they were implemented in conjunction with the introduction of new economic policies and new state involvement in public health and poor-relief projects. The police played an essential role in applying these new practices. However, although the imposition of such taxonomies demonstrated new levels of centralization and new forms of bureaucratization, both the rhetoric and the practice of benevolence continued to reflect the religious features of charity.

In the decades that followed the implementation of new practices, the poor took advantage of the state's new inroads. As the government imposed restrictions on the poor and introduced specialized institutions, the poor, in many cases out of desperation, actively made use of these services.

Dabt (to record or arrest)

On a September day in 1846, the Cairo police arrested Muhammad ibn al-Shahhata and his young son Ahir for begging in the streets. Upon questioning him, the police learned that the two beggars had fled from their village in Minufiyya. As was the policy with absconders from the countryside, Muhammad and his son were sent to the *Ma'mur al-mutasahibin*, the official in charge of those who absconded, for their transport back to the countryside. After staying in a large area (described as a "keep" or "close") until a sufficient number of absconders had been gathered, the two of them were sent to their villages either by boat or on foot, as part of a chained group.[22]

The arrest and conveyance of Muhammad and his son resemble other efforts made by Ottoman officials to control access to major cities in the empire. Istanbul authorities in the nineteenth century and earlier frequently tried to stop migrants from coming to the city and attempted to enforce orders specifying that permission to live and work there was to be granted only to individuals who had obtained a *tadhkira* (Ottoman *tezkere*), a sort of passport or permission document that contained a physical description of the person as well as his or her place of origin and destination.[23] Istanbul authorities also expelled unemployed nonresidents (as well as vagrant residents) and sometimes punished them with hard labor.[24] Even single men who had found employment in Istanbul—in casual day labor or other trades—were eyed with suspicion.[25]

Istanbul authorities' interest in denying nonresidents access to the city grew out of a concern about preserving public order.[26] Although the Egyptian government made use of similar mechanisms (namely, the tadhkira and various types of patrols) to control the mobility of the Egyptian peasantry, these measures were in part motivated by fears for public security. But the arrest of Muhammad and his son and prohibitions

on begging during this time must also be understood within more specific concerns about labor control, attempts to monitor the Egyptian
population's mobility, and new attitudes toward the use of public spaces.
These concerns resulted in the use of agencies, such as the police,
charged with regulating access to Cairo and its streets and markets. The
surveillance of Cairo's public spaces affected the lives of both the itinerant able-bodied poor and beggars deemed incapable of working. From
the 1830s on, invalid and elderly men, women, and children seeking
charity from better-off inhabitants in the streets and markets of Cairo
found themselves facing officials attempting to maintain order and clearing the streets of the itinerant poor.

The 1846 arrest of Muhammad and his son and their expulsion from
Cairo were among a series of attempts made in the previous three decades to keep the Egyptian peasantry tied to their land; they also reflected Muhammad Ali's extensive efforts to preserve order and public
security and to use the peasantry for his own economic and military
goals. Determining who had the "right" to reside in Cairo (*haqq al-
Mahrusa*) and who was obliged to work the land in the countryside
required modern state apparatuses. Thus, the expulsion of peasants became possible through the imposition of laws and the creation of agencies devoted to their capture and conveyance back to their land.

✄

After consolidating power in Egypt in the first decades of the nineteenth
century, Muhammad Ali endeavored to reap the greatest profit from the
labor of Egypt's populace. His efforts were geared toward fulfilling
three goals: cultivating long-staple cotton on a large scale, building a
modern army, and ultimately establishing hereditary rule for his family
in Egypt.[27] In cotton production and other agricultural endeavors, he
sought to create and maintain government monopolies on produce for
export, a goal that relied on peasant labor for cultivation and required
their corvée labor for maintaining irrigation works and building an infrastructure capable of transporting these products. In industry, geared
primarily toward the army, the state employed men in numerous textile,
armaments, and shipbuilding projects, and it employed women and
children in textile manufacture and cotton ginning. To develop a military, Muhammad Ali introduced conscription for male peasants (sometimes for a lifetime of service) and excessively taxed the populace to
fund his aims.[28] Overseas, he engaged in diplomatic efforts as well as
wars to achieve autonomous rule over Egypt.[29]

Whereas these endeavors built on prior centuries of administrative
centralization, tax-collection procedures, and efforts to extract Egypt's

wealth from its soil, the projects initiated during Muhammad Ali's reign resulted in increased government intervention in the lives of the Egyptian populace and ever more pervasive demands on the full labor potential of rural and urban inhabitants. In the countryside, entire families provided labor for corvée, and families lost their primary breadwinners to conscription levies, initiated in 1822. The imposition of monopolies on agricultural production and the introduction of new crops transformed peasants' relations with both the land and the state.[30]

In many realms, both peasants and urban dwellers resisted government incursions into their lives. They fled from conscription and deserted the army, they burned their crops and fled from their villages to protest taxes and the monopoly system, they committed acts of sabotage in the factories where they were forced to work, and they even resorted to suicide.[31] In response to individual acts of rebellion, as well as broad-scale insurrections, the Egyptian government imposed harsh punishments on those who obstructed government projects. To control the mobility of the peasantry, whose presence in the countryside was essential for producing crops, paying taxes, and the success of recruitment drives, the government introduced laws and regulations intended to keep peasants tied to their particular locale. These laws and regulations had at their core systems of hierarchy, which made a range of individuals (from village sheikhs to provincial administrators) responsible for the conduct of "their" peasants.

Collective punishments and holding village and provincial officials directly responsible for the conduct of the peasants in their regions were intended as ways of ensuring compliance with governmental directives.[32] Laws in the Qanun al-Filaha (Law of Peasantry, 1829–1830) promulgated the punishment (most often a certain number of lashes with the *kurbaj*, or whip) to be meted out to peasants who fled conscription or agricultural work. Punishment was also inflicted on anyone who attacked or threatened the sheikh or other superiors, the *mashayikh al-hissa* (sheikhs of the districts), the *mashayikh al-kibar* (the highest-ranking sheikhs), or the administrative district head, the *qa'imaqqam* (article 26). Village sheikhs were punished together with the peasantry for participating in rebellions, either by imprisonment or with lashes of the kurbaj (articles 27 and 24). Rebellions were not the only crime punishable by beatings: sheikhs and inhabitants of the villages who failed to cultivate their land were also punished (article 43). Officials and guards who sometimes aided peasants in their attempts to flee the countryside were also punished harshly.[33]

The demand for labor throughout Egypt's rural areas and attempts to prevent desertion necessitated the maintenance of tight control over peasants' whereabouts. In addition to punitive laws such as the Qanun al-Filaha, the Egyptian government employed the tadhkira system to regulate travel. In Istanbul it was used extensively to control access to this city, and in Egypt peasants intending to travel outside their home villages were required to obtain tadhkiras, giving them permission to leave their place of residence.[34]

Like Istanbul officials, authorities in major cities such as Cairo and Alexandria also attempted to limit access to these cities. Some peasants who had fled military conscription and agricultural obligations sought temporary refuge in areas around their homes, and others tried to find more permanent solutions by moving to urban areas where they might find work.[35] On countless occasions the police of Cairo were charged with apprehending peasants who had fled to the city. In many cases these individuals had already found work. In other instances, with no skills or kin and family networks to ensure an easy transition to the urban landscape, they had resorted to begging. Some of those who migrated to Cairo, "swelling the pauper class" during the era of Muhammad Ali, were the wives of military conscripts.[36] In Cairo, from the 1850s on, residents' exemption from conscription served as another attraction drawing peasants to the city. During this era as well, many conscripted peasants who had been stationed in Cairo decided to stay.[37]

Key to controlling access to Cairo and its policing were the Dabtiyyat Misr (the central police department of Cairo) and the various police outposts (karakol) of the city. Neighborhood sheikhs, spies (bassas), and informants (dallala) kept the Dabtiyya abreast of events in various areas of the city.[38] The extensive records of the Dabtiyya, which detail daily instances in which police officers, neighborhood agents, or other state personnel came into contact with Cairo's populace provide a glimpse of the Dabtiyya's omnipresence in the city and its regulatory responsibilities. Each interaction was recorded (dubita) in the police registers housed at the Dabtiyya located in Muski. Among these registers are entries of day-to-day occurrences in the neighborhoods of Cairo: a warning to neighborhood sheikhs to ensure the vaccination of children, the arrest of a dervish caught sleeping in a coffeehouse, the discovery of a child found abandoned on the steps of a mosque, an accusation made by one neighbor toward another, the arrest of a man found wandering through the streets at night without the required lantern, accounts of the pursuit of peasants who had fled from the countryside, and the arrest (dabt) of beggars found in Cairo's public spaces.

Since the early 1810s, Muhammad Ali's government had endeavored to control peasant flight from the countryside.[39] Archival records and official decrees published in Al-Waqaʾiʿ al-Misriyya (the government news gazette) in the late 1820s recount how Muhammad Ali instructed the police and other authorities in the city to apprehend peasants who had fled from the countryside and to arrest individuals who had avoided conscription to the army or navy. In 1829 one such government decree called for the arrest of indolent peasants who had fled to Cairo. The decree stated that these peasants, who had become beggars, were to be returned to their villages. To guarantee that peasants stay working on the land, provincial authorities were not to allow peasants to travel without a tadhkira.[40]

The itinerant poor were the target of police efforts for other reasons as well. Fear of petty crime was one rationale for the creation of a criminal code that called for the arrest and forced employment of Gypsies, peasant women, orphans, and invalid men found begging (and simultaneously engaging in infractions such as stealing small items worth five piasters) on the outskirts of Cairo.[41]

During the 1830s when Muhammad Ali's armies were involved in the occupation of Syria and wars with Sultan Mahmud II, labor shortages led to attempts to monitor the potential labor supply. The police were charged with finding individuals who had fled from factories where they had been employed and with recruiting labor for industry. John Bowring reported how the means of gathering up workers for factories were similar to conscription policies, yet these efforts also included the recruitment of women and children. He noted how "[t]hey are taken up, men, women, and children, and sent pêle mêle to the manufactories, where they remain until they find a means of escaping."[42]

Government documents and other European accounts confirm Bowring's observations concerning the high demand for workers and efforts to maintain surveillance over labor. During this period of high labor demand, neighborhood sheikhs and other state agents recruited Cairo residents to work in nascent industrial projects. Children were trained in manual trades, and laborers, including vagrants, religious mendicants, and other inhabitants of various quarters, were enlisted in industry. Bonds or sureties (*daman*) from family members were required to guarantee their good conduct and prevent their flight.[43]

The various efforts of the Cairo police to capture agricultural and military absconders and recruit labor for industry brought them into direct contact with the idle poor and beggars seeking charity from the more fortunate inhabitants of the city. Prohibitions on all types of begging, for which we find the first evidence in the 1830s, were intended to deny this activity as a means of subsistence and applied to the invalid, the elderly, and, most importantly sturdy (or able-bodied) beggars. The same rationale behind government calls to deport peasants (issued in the interest of maintaining public order but also meant to deny this means of livelihood to the sturdy poor who turned to begging) also applied to religious mendicants. In the words of an unnamed government official interviewed by James August St. John: "[D]emands for labor [had] made begging a crime."[44]

Growing concerns about sanitation, public health, and appearances also led to increased attention to urban spaces. In the 1830s and 1840s, efforts were under way to remove rubbish, fill stagnant ponds, and improve the overall appearance of cities such as Cairo and Alexandria. Municipal officials were responsible for making general improvements, but private individuals, shop and home owners, were also required to partake in cleanup efforts, keeping the entryways to their shops and homes swept and their buildings whitewashed.[45] Public health measures, including vaccination programs and the imposition of quarantines, resulted in the creation of new offices and the appointment of officials who would ensure compliance with governmental directives. As a result of new knowledge about the spread of disease, individuals identified as carriers were singled out. In 1834, fearing the spread of sexually transmitted diseases, government authorities expelled prostitutes from urban centers.[46] Prohibitions on begging (and the expulsion of nonresident beggars as well as the forced admission of others deemed deserving of assistance to state-run shelters) were yet another aspect of city authorities' increased attentiveness to public spaces. Beggars, like the prostitutes who were singled out and expelled from the city, found themselves the targets of state actions.

Records of intensified efforts to capture absconders in (from 1844 on) clearly illustrate the Dabtiyya's role in controlling peasants' flight and access to Cairo. Although such efforts were part of a series of attempts the government had made in the previous decades, the actions toward fleeing peasants in the 1840s were mostly motivated by Muhammad Ali's desperate need to acquire revenues for his government and ensure agricultural production on land that had been granted to members of his family and retinue, to officers in the army, and to other government officials.[47] In 1844 and later, the Dabtiyya was instructed to gather up all nonresidents of Cairo and deport them to their land.[48] Within the context of such efforts, individuals who had found sanctuary in al-Azhar Mosque could not evade capture.[49] Aiding the police where village sheikhs who came into the city seeking peasants who had fled from their villages.[50] Only individuals who had a tadhkira, proving that they had permission to be out of their home villages, were allowed to stay in Cairo.[51]

Muhammad Ali's government and his successors' governments recognized that difficult circumstances in the countryside were, in part, a catalyst for migration. For this reason, these governments sent commissions of inquiry into the rural areas and, at mid-century, attempted to ameliorate conditions there through the redistribution of land.[52]

Cairo authorities' continued attention to public spaces and the implementation of orders prohibiting begging in the 1840s indicated ongoing intolerance for individuals whose actions in public spaces had once been permitted. Sheikh Issawi ibn Ahmad was a beggar who found himself face to face with government authorities responsible for clearing the streets of beggars and the idle poor. As the Cairo police made their rounds through the city's neighborhoods in February 1846, they came upon him reciting the Quran (with "the intention of demanding charity") and immediately arrested him. At the police station officers recorded the particulars of his case, intending to admit him, like other beggars, to Mahall al-Fuqara', a poor shelter located in the Maristan Qalawun. However, upon identifying Sheikh Issawi ibn Ahmad as someone who "knew the Quran," the police sent him to the Mosque of al-Azhar. There, a religious leader of al-Azhar delivered a stern warning to Sheikh Issawi ibn Ahmad to never beg again. Although Sheikh Issawi ibn Ahmad escaped punishment, other religious mendicants caught begging or idle in Cairo's public spaces were punished by forced labor or confinement.[53]

In the 1850s and 1860s, continued efforts to capture absconding peasants represented the government's concern about agricultural production, but these efforts also indicated anxiety over the number of unemployed (and potentially criminal) men found wandering (*da'ir*) in both the urban and the rural areas. Wandering around without work (*da'ir 'ala hawa infasu bidun/bi ghayr sina'a*) or being homeless (*da'ir 'ala hawa infasu bidun ma'wan*) was cause for arrest. Such policing of idleness included calls for the prohibition of casual labor such as magic performances and prohibitions on games of chance and gambling in public areas. Efforts to put a stop to wandering about without work sometimes included the mass arrests of loiterers. In 1862, when a total of 725 individuals were arrested in various districts of Egypt for loitering (wandering around without work and having no place of residence), they were sent to the *orta al-madhnubin* (punishment battalion). Fear of brigandage and of the theft of agricultural produce prompted the Egyptian government to enforce laws calling for the arrest, punishment, and training of vagabonds in 1863 and again in 1866.[54]

The imperative of *dabt wa rabt* (order) was central to Cairo authorities' application of restrictions on the mobility of the populace. As Cairo authorities enforced laws designed to control migration to Cairo and restrict beggars' abilities to solicit, Muhammad ibn al-Shahhata, his son, and hundreds of other peasants (beggars as well as individuals who had acquired employment in the city) found themselves being escorted, under guard, back to the villages from which they had fled or to the agricultural estates of Muhammad Ali and his family.[55] In Europe authorities in various locales expelled nonresident beggars to ensure that people outside the beggars' original place of residence would not be burdened with their care.[56] At first glance, when we look at the case of Muhammad ibn al-Shahhata, the question arises as to whether he was able-bodied (and hence a peasant whose labor would be needed back in the village) or if, as his name implies ("son of a beggar"), he was an invalid for whom Cairo authorities did not want to assume responsibility. However, the fact that other nonresidents caught begging during this time who were deemed invalid or otherwise deserving of assistance were *not* expelled indicates that he was considered fit for work. As discussed in the next section, arrested peasants who were deemed deserving of state assistance, together with residents of Cairo, were admitted to the state-run shelter of Mahall al-Fuqara'. Proof that this shelter housed a substantial number of nonresidents is found in an order of 1848. In July of that year, after the indigent of Mahall al-Fuqara' had been transferred to Takiyyat Tulun (which had been renovated to serve as a poor shelter), 144 of the 574 men, women, and children of this facility were recognized as nonresidents of Cairo. These individuals included people identified as coming from Egypt's provinces and from al-Sham (Greater Syria) as well as people described as evlad-i Turk (Turks). Those from Egypt's rural areas (numbering approximately 90) were to be transported — if they wished — back to their home villages. The government promised to cover their expenses and assured those returning to their villages that they would be treated with kindness (*zarar ve müzayaka çekdirilmemesi*) during their journey.[57]

Mahall al-Fuqara'

In late 1843 or January 1844, the Commission of Ornato (a joint commission of Europeans and Ottoman subjects charged with overseeing city planning and public health efforts in Alexandria)[58] toured the Maristan Qalawun, the hospital founded as a religious endowment in thirteenth-century Cairo, to assess its conditions and determine how many poor people could be sheltered there. The Ornato's visit to the Maristan came shortly after the transfer of this institution's other residents (the sick together with the insane) to another facility, the Civilian Hospital of Azbakkiya, and coincided with its transformation into a shelter intended solely for the poor — Mahall al-Fuqara' (Place of the Poor).[59]

The Mamluk sultan Qalawun had founded a mosque complex that included the Bimaristan (or, as it was referred to in Egyptian government documents, the Maristan, or hospital) in 1284. With revenues coming from Egyptian lands, public baths, caravansaries, and other investments, the complex that Qalawun commissioned also included a tomb and a school for orphans. The hospital itself was immense: there were separate sections for the blind, those needing surgery, and patients suffering from stomach ailments, as well as separate halls for women and men.[60] By the early nineteenth century the quality of care and the number of patients had diminished, and the hospital had fallen into disrepair.[61] Jomard, one of the participants in the French expedition (1798–1801), noted that ten insane persons and between fifty and sixty sick people were cared for there.[62]

After the French expedition, the Maristan continued to serve as a hospital and, with the government's initiation of prohibitions on begging in 1835, it began admitting beggars. The Maristan was one of the shelters to which John Bowring referred when he noted that the Egyptian government, "desiring to put an end to mendicity, [had] established asylums for those who are unfit to work."[63] One prohibition on begging, which called for beggars' confinement to the Maristan, had been made at the height of the plague; but 1837 documents alluding to the need to employ the able-bodied beggars from among its residents in various forms of industry testify to its continued use as a shelter in the years that followed.[64] Visits by foreigners such as William Yates in the early 1840s, who noted that this institution housed the insane as well as the infirm ("cripples, the aged, and paralytic"), illustrate how the Maristan functioned as a shelter alongside its original role as a hospital and insane asylum in this period.[65] Even before 1835, it is likely that the Maristan served as a shelter for the poor. Hospitals in the Ottoman Empire, unlike *imaret* (soup kitchens) and *tabhane* (shelters), did not impose limits on a person's stay, hence they functioned as places where the indigent could reside for long periods. Nancy Gallagher discusses how the Maristan of Tunis, founded in 1662, not only included medical facilities but was also intended for "the poor who had no shelter or persons to care for them in the city."[66]

The transformation of the Maristan Qalawun into an institution intended solely as a shelter did not occur overnight. Although individuals in need of medical assistance and the insane were to be transferred to the Civilian Hospital in Azbakiyya in 1837, soon after its founding, many continued to be housed in the Maristan.[67] By 1844, however, the transfer of patients was finally complete. And for the next four years, the Maristan, renamed Mahall al-Fuqara', served to shelter the indigent. Its use as a shelter and the establishment of a number of other forms of assistance indicate how during this decade the Egyptian government sought to manage the public presence of the poor.

The Mahall al-Fuqara' was just one of the avenues of relief available to the poor of Cairo, but it proved essential to government objectives of enforcing prohibitions on begging. It only admitted the "deserving" poor—inhabitants of Cairo and nonresidents deemed in need of assistance. Individuals like Muhammad ibn al-Shahhata did not fit into the government-imposed category of "the worthy poor" because of their purported ability to work. The fact that Muhammad constituted a member of the able-bodied and nonresident poor meant that he and his son were categorized as *mutasahibun* (absconders). As we have seen, their status as absconders justified their transport back to the countryside.

Joseph Hekekyan, a British-trained engineer in Muhammad Ali's service, made note of the Ornato Commission's visit to the Maristan in January 1844 and provided his own commentary on the men, women, and children who had already made this "asylum for the poor" their home. He remarked on how the poor of this shelter were lodged, fed, and clothed "by the munificence of the Pasha" (Muhammad Ali) and how many of the shelter's residents had married and had children during their stay. Hekekyan sharply criticized the Egyptian government for providing unlimited charity to the poor, noting that it did not distinguish between residents of Cairo and those of the countryside. In his view (perspectives colored by his own residence in Britain in the 1820s),[68] the "parishes" should be responsible for their own poor.[69] The Cairo police and the shelter's administrators did not entirely heed Hekekyan's advice. Records of that summer indicate their intensified efforts to clear the streets of the itinerant poor; and, contrary to Hekekyan's counsel— although absconders like Muhammad and his son were sent back to the countryside—the invalid and otherwise dependent among them, Cairo residents and nonresidents, were admitted to Mahall al-Fuqara'.

Among the hundreds of beggars who had made Mahall al-Fuqara' their home (in December 1846 inmates numbered 766 men, women, and children)[70] were Mona bint Salim and her brother Muhammad. On a July day in 1844, officers of the Dabtiyya arrested them for begging. In the record of their arrest found in the registers of the Dabtiyya, the scribe noted that Mona was an invalid and that both she and her brother were from Giza. After processing the necessary paperwork for their case, these two beggars were brought to the shelter.

Many other beggars deemed "deserving" of admission joined Mona and Muhammad. During that summer, the police reported additional arrests of beggars found in Cairo's streets and markets and their admission to this shelter (if they were identified as invalids or as residents of Cairo) or their deportation from the city (if considered able-bodied residents of the countryside).[71] Concurrent with the arrests of these people, the Dabtiyya emphasized the necessity of clearing the streets of itinerant peddlers and food sellers in the interest of observing quarantine orders; hence their arrest draws our attention to concerns about public health and similar events in 1835 when, during a plague Cairo authorities had prohibited begging in the streets and markets of Cairo and beggars had been interned in the Maristan.[72]

The practice of confining beggars to the Mahall al-Fuqara' and, later, Takiyyat Tulun (as well as the internment of beggars in Alexandria in two shelters, Qishla al-Sadaqa and Takiyyat Qabbari) became government policy.[73] Records in the Egyptian National Archives indicate that the arrest (*dabt*), deportation, and internment of beggars were policies applied with great rigor over the 1850s, thus showing how the era following Muhammad Ali's death also included increased attention to the itinerant poor.

Within these shelters, the residents received basic necessities such as food and clothing, again highlighting the government's benevolence. But in prohibiting begging and using shelters as a place of internment, the Egyptian government also restricted the autonomy of beggars. If people were mistakenly identified as beggars during the government's roundups, they were released.[74] If those released after being falsely accused of begging were later caught begging, they were sentenced to hard labor.[75] The shelter's personnel was also warned not to allow beggars to leave the shelter "unless a full investigation proves that [the person] is not a beggar."[76] Beggars were to be set free only through the intercession of a relative who promised to take care of the (former) beggar, guaranteeing that this person would never return to begging. The "confinement" of Cairo's beggars, as I discuss in greater detail in the next chapter, was never absolute. Records for later decades show that in addition to gaining their release through the intercession of persons outside the shelter, beggars were given permission to see their families, many beggars fled, and some were released after residing there for only a short period.

In previous centuries, municipal officials (such as the *muhtasib*) had enforced prohibitions on begging by the sturdy poor. Mamluk officials had even gone so far as to transport lepers and beggars to the Fayyum, a region outside Cairo.[77] Hence, the Egyptian government's decision to carry out similar procedures fits prior practices. Yet policies toward the itinerant poor in Egypt were also influenced by ideas about their treatment from outside the Middle East.

French experiences with poor relief in France played a role in shaping Egyptian policies toward beggars and practices of confinement in state-run shelters, although the practices, models, and advice given were applied selectively. Antoine Barthélémy Clot (Clot Bey), the French medical adviser to Muhammad Ali, made frequent visits to the Maristan. On two occasions, in 1846 and 1847, he called for the employment of the able-bodied from among its residents. He was also influential in the decision to transfer the poor from the Maristan to the Mosque of

Ahmad ibn Tulun, which had been renovated for this purpose. During his visits to the Maristan, Clot Bey made numerous remarks about how the poor, once transferred to shelter in the mosque, should be treated. On one occasion, he noted that in the new shelter, men were to be separated from women and the poor were to be engaged in industry, "as is done in Europe."[78]

In addition to Clot Bey's actions and comments affecting how the poor of Cairo were to be treated, French law also served as a model for policies toward beggars and vagrants. In creating criminal legislation, Muhammad Ali looked to the French Code pénal, commissioning a translation of this law code into Arabic. The result, the Qanun al-Muntakhabat, included articles that stipulated beggars and vagrants would be punished with confinement in state-run shelters.[79] Cairo authorities had already begun admitting the poor to shelters before the promulgation of the Qanun al-Muntakhabat in August 1844, so it is clear that this law had only a partial impact on prohibitions on begging and the use of shelters. The economic pragmatism of the Egyptian government, coupled with indigenous concepts of care for the poor, were equally, if not more, influential in shaping the use of shelters and the practice of forcing the sturdy poor to work.

Like numerous other forms of assistance initiated during this period, admission to shelters and the application of other means of care were couched in a discourse of charity. From the 1840s onward, the documentation about government interventions in various forms of poor relief presents the aid given to the poor as stemming from "the charity of the khedive," hence showing that *in intent* the government's provisioning of care replaced the charity of the community. Just as the Ottoman sultan solidified his patrimonial bond with his subjects through the distribution of money, the feeding of the poor in soup kitchens, and other royal bequests, the rulers of Egypt demonstrated their beneficence by bestowing care on their subjects.[80] The act of begging signified a family's inability to care for their own kin. If the family neglected their destitute members, the government stepped in to give them food and shelter.

Intensified efforts to clear the streets of the itinerant poor in the 1840s were concurrent with Muhammad Ali's desperate attempts to return fleeing peasants to the land from which they had fled. These actions necessitated the establishment of offices to expedite nonresidents' expulsion from the city, but the implementation of these policies also required the development of specialized facilities for the internment of the "deserving poor." The creation of Mahall al-Fuqara', intended solely for those deemed deserving, reflected new government interventions in poor relief and the centralization of welfare endeavors. This shelter, while serving ends complementary to those of expelling able-bodied nonresident beggars, did so in a fashion that set its actions within a religious framework.

The Charity of the Khedive

In the middle of November 1846, an unnamed peasant woman appeared at the Dabtiyya carrying an infant boy in her arms. There, she told officers of the Dabtiyya that she had discovered the infant at a mosque in al-Gamaliyya (a neighborhood of Cairo). Following the Dabtiyya's protocol, the officers recorded the particulars of the incident, making sure to note where the child had been found, and then sent the infant to the Madrasat al-Wilada (a midwifery training school and orphanage) located in the Civilian Hospital of Azbakiyya.[81]

Parents abandoned their children, noted Edward Lane, because of financial difficulties, frequently leaving them on the steps of mosques in the hope that a wealthier coreligionist would raise the child as his or her own. Many children thus abandoned would be taken care of by a neighbor.[82] Yet like this peasant woman, many people stumbling upon a child abandoned in this manner did not have the means to care for him or her. Finding infants on the steps of mosques or in the streets of Cairo — or being left with one after the departure of the child's parents — and having no other recourse, these individuals turned to the state for assistance. Individuals seeking assistance by way of the Dabtiyya included the poor who sought medical help for themselves or family members and the relatives of insane persons who requested that the insane be admitted to government-run asylums.[83] The peasant woman's interaction with the Dabtiyya, as well as a multitude of other similar episodes captured in the records of this office, illustrate how inhabitants of Cairo and areas outside the city availed themselves of these state-initiated forms of assistance.

The ways in which the Egyptian government provided medical and other similar services for the populace of Egypt were not entirely unique to the Middle East. Rulers' commissioning of the construction of hospitals in earlier eras were similar to new state initiatives in this realm.[84] Such pious endowments best exemplify the ways in which the state expressed its consciousness of the need to develop medical knowledge and the important role medicine played in Islamic society. However, in nineteenth-century Egypt, we find different avenues of state involvement in medicine and public health. Muhammad Ali's projects were distinguishable from those of earlier rulers in that many were preventive in nature, including vaccination efforts and the application of quarantine strictures. They also involved state expenditures to recruit foreign medical experts, send students to Europe for training, and construct new hospitals. The various institutions and forms of relief established during his reign and during the rule of his nineteenth-century successors included, but were not limited to, an orphanage and foundling home (located in the Civilian Hospital of Azbakiyya, and later in the Qasr al-Ayni Hospital), free medical treatment for indigent civilians, rations and new concern for the health of poor prisoners, an insane asylum (located in the Civilian Hospital, then in a renovated workshop in Bulaq, and finally in an abandoned palace building in Abbasiyya), free transportation for poor pilgrims returning from the Hajj, daily meals at a soup kitchen of Mahall al-Khayriyyat, and state-run shelters.

Government investments in these forms of assistance can be understood from the perspective of charity and the ruler's obligations toward his subjects, but they also represent a new understanding of the importance of medicine and concern for the health of the population at large.[85] These imperatives prompted Muhammad Ali to seek assistance and advisers from France. He recruited doctors to initiate smallpox vaccination efforts as early as 1819 and hired Clot Bey to take charge of Egypt's medical services beginning in 1825.[86] This increased concern for the Egyptian population and its health was most noticeable in the military. But, as Laverne Kuhnke has argued, Muhammad Ali's interest in the health of military personnel also applied to the broader population. With Clot Bey's and other advisers' assistance, the government established medical training facilities, hospitals, and public health programs.[87]

Clot Bey was instrumental in many of the medical advancements in Egypt. His training in France led to interventions in many aspects of health care, and the proposals he brought to Egypt helped transform the government's relations with its populace and helped fulfill particular state ends.[88] The government's interest in the health and well-being of children was evident in child-directed programs such as smallpox vaccination efforts as well as in its practice of raising abandoned infants found in the streets of Cairo.[89] Free medical treatment for the poor represented the government's larger concerns about maintaining sufficient manpower for its army and stopping the spread of disease. The confinement of the insane (both individuals found by the police in urban and rural areas and those committed by their families) indicated governmental attempts to clear public spaces of individuals who might be dangerous to society at large. Providing transport for poor pilgrims returning from the Hajj gave the government direct control over their passage through Egypt, a concern that was particularly acute during cholera outbreaks. Making sure that the indigent among them left Egypt also meant that they could not make Egypt their permanent home. Giving rations to the poor in government shelters or to individuals who congregated at the government-run soup kitchen of Mahall al-Khayriyyat, as well as providing food to needy families at al-Azhar Mosque, guaranteed that individuals in dire straits had at least the bare minimum of food.

These various programs had at their core government concern for the needy, but at the same time they made use of new mechanisms (that is, the creation of new administrative apparatuses and the involvement of the Dabtiyya and medical officers) to ensure the implementation of these policies. The Dabtiyya served to link the state with the populace. It received and acted on requests to care for abandoned infants and applied government directives toward the care of others in need.

Accounts of the care of infants provide details of how family members' attempts to care for their dependents led them to seek the state's aid. In some cases, such as those of two women, Sayyida and Zubayda, they illustrate how children, first left with neighbors or the extended family, were ultimately cared for by the state. In other instances, we see that parents requested care for their infants (and young children) directly.

At some point in 1848 or 1849, Sayyida's daughter-in-law Khadra left her small daughter in Sayyida's care and disappeared. Unable to find Khadra or her son, Abd Allah Sha'ban, and because she was unable to care for her granddaughter on her own, Sayyida brought the child to the Dabtiyya, requesting that she be cared for in the Madrasat al-Wilada.[90] Sayyida's story, as well as other discussions of infants left in the care of extended families, illustrates how the family and extended family were usually the first option. Unable to care for the child on her own, Sayyida saw the state as her last resort.

In the winter of 1853, Zubayda found herself caring for a neighbors' child after the neighbors' departure. When, after two months the child's parents failed to reappear, Zubayda brought him to the Dabtiyya.[91] Contrary to how Sayyida's case illustrates that the family was the first recourse for help, that of Zubayda demonstrates that for some, the neighborhood and the community were primary options for care. At the same time, such accounts illustrate how the poor turned to the state when they were unable to fulfill their own obligations toward their kin or neighbors.

Other records of the Dabtiyya demonstrate how families, having no other means of providing for their infants or small children, requested the state's assistance. When a mother's breast milk was insufficient for her infant (owing perhaps to malnutrition), or when the mother died or abandoned her family, the father might seek to have his infant wet-nursed in the Madrasat al-Wilada. Dabtiyya records contain numerous examples of this practice. When Farg al-Abd's wife died and he had no one who could wet-nurse his daughter, he went to the Dabtiyya with her and requested that she be admitted to the Madrasat al-Wilada.[92] Muhammad Agha, the deputy of the former *kathuda* (governor of Cairo), had bought a pregnant slave, but when the slave died in childbirth, he requested that Hadiyya, the infant girl, be wet-nursed in the Madrasat al-Wilada.[93] When his wife's breast milk was insufficient for his twin daughters, Muhammad Qabili brought one of the girls to the Dabtiyya in the hope of having her admitted to the Madrasat al-Wilada.[94] Ali ibn Ali, a student at al-Azhar, not knowing how to raise his daughter Zaynab when his ex-wife left the child in his care, brought the little girl to the Dabtiyya, requesting that she be raised in the Madrasat al-Wilada.[95] When al-Hagg Muhammad's wife left for the countryside, like Ali ibn Ali, Muhammad did not know how to take care of his daughter Zahra, so he requested that she be admitted to the Madrasat al-Wilada.[96]

Mothers also brought their own children to the Dabtiyya to request that they be admitted to the Madrasat al-Wilada. This institution served not only as a foundling home but also as an orphanage. Fatuma bint Hasan, a resident of Khoronfish Street in Cairo, requested that her son Afifi ibn Hasan be admitted to the Madrasat al-Wilada, for she was "incapable of raising him herself."[97] Takiyyat Tulun also served as an orphanage.[98]

As Miri Shefer has shown in her analysis of hospitals in the Ottoman Empire, those without any kin or other resources frequently sought medical assistance in institutions such as hospitals. Medical attention in one's home was the wealthy's preference, and even less well-off families often did not resort to medical care in hospitals. This aversion to hospitals was also true in Europe. In the era preceding medical advances, only the sick who had no other help made use of hospitals.[99] In Egypt, it was frequently only the poor who made use of gratuitous medical aid. However, as this sampling of cases of infant care illustrates, we find families from a variety of backgrounds seeking state assistance.

Although these new public health programs met secular needs, the khedive's name (in government correspondences and in petitions by the populace) and a discourse of religious obligations pervaded requests for medical assistance and infant care. On the surface, the practice of administering poor relief had become bureaucratized (with the ruler never having direct contact with the people who received his benevolence). However, a language of charity, of Islamic prerogatives of providing for those in need, and of a patrimonial connection between the beneficent ruler and his subjects was maintained in the petitions and their records: individuals' petitions were addressed to the khedive, and responses to these and other requests for assistance were sure to note that the aid provided resulted from the ruler's benevolence, "*ihsanan min al-Khidiwi.*"

In addition to reaffirming the patrimonial bond between ruler and subject, such documents reinforced the ideas of right inherent in Islamic practices of care for the poor. In the eyes of the government—as expressed by the actions of the Dabtiyya—these individuals—infants, the insane, and those in need of medical care—were considered "deserving" of assistance by virtue of their poverty or through other means of proving their dependence. These individuals had a right (*haqq*) to assistance. Hence, for example, infants had *rights* to charity, an insane person would be deemed *deserving* of admission to government hospitals or the state-run insane asylum, for she or he had the *right* of someone who is insane, and an indigent woman found dead in the streets of Cairo would *deserve* a free burial.[100]

Government interventions in poor relief in early-nineteenth-century Egypt were concurrent with endeavors in public health and medicine. The very act of separating the various functions of the Maristan represents the modernization of services. By the 1840s, the Egyptian government, through its health officials, had begun to distinguish between different categories of people needing assistance and to create distinct institutions for their care. In this manner, state-sponsored facilities replaced the multifunctional role Islamic hospitals had once played with more specific, category-centered institutions.[101] While these actions were described as the bestowal of the ruler's benevolence on his subjects, they also reflected the state's knowledge of the importance of public health and the increasing interventions of medical authorities and the police in the lives of Egypt's inhabitants.

A Government Prerogative

Restrictive policies toward the itinerant poor in nineteenth-century Egypt emerged as a byproduct of new government interventions in the lives of the Egyptian populace. The government of Muhammad Ali imposed strictures on the movement of the populace in an effort to procure labor for his various projects (as well as manpower for his military) and at the same time, with the interest of the military in mind, introduced public health measures affecting the populace at large. Efforts to remove the poor from the streets and the application of new public health measures converged in the office of the Dabtiyya. The poor deemed deserving of care received the state's assistance, but those who were considered sturdy or able to work were not worthy of care or sympathy. In enacting new policies toward the poor, the Egyptian government—through the office of the Dabtiyya—imbued the idea of charity and benevolence, and the very structure of the Maristan, with new meanings and uses. The ways in which the Egyptian government applied restrictions on the poor and used shelters to enforce them were unprecedented in other areas of the Middle East at this time. Through the initiation of these policies, the government attempted to regulate even the "deserving" poor's access to their neighbors' charity.

However, concurrent with restrictions on the mobility of the poor, the Egyptian government introduced specialized services and forms of assistance for individuals deemed deserving of assistance. It provided wet nurses and care for abandoned infants and children and medical attention for individuals in need of aid in response to requests for help. A request might come from a person who had found an abandoned child (or one of the child's parents), from the relative of an insane family member, or from a person in need of medical attention. In these many ways, the destitute and needy received the benevolence of the state, a benevolence portrayed as emanating from the khedive himself.

The shelters and hospitals established during the era of Muhammad Ali and the policies toward the poor first implemented during his reign left a mark on Egypt for decades after his death. Despite arguments that the rule of Abbas and of Said brought the demise of numerous projects, including medical assistance, individuals identified as "deserving" of care continued to receive assistance from the government.[102] Dabtiyya and Cairo Governorate records available through the early 1880s recount how the people who benefited from state aid included infants, indigent women, the invalid and elderly, and the sick and insane.

As in the case of beggars rounded up in the periodic sweeps of Cairo's public spaces, officials of the Dabtiyya and other government officials with whom the poor interacted in their quest for aid had the prerogative of determining that person's status of need — it was the government's right to distinguish between the deserving and the undeserving poor. Although we do not have information on the quality of care provided, we know from the 1860s and 1880s (in the accounts of observers who, admittedly, had their own agendas) that Egyptians distrusted the medical facilities then available. Lucie Duff Gordon recounted how peasants in Upper Egypt avoided government doctors at all costs, and Naguib Mahfouz, an Egyptian medical doctor, noted that the only patients in the Qasr al-Ayni hospital in the 1880s were prostitutes, beggars, and orphaned children. Given the purportedly low quality of care and the population's distrust of hospitals, it is likely that the poor sought the government's assistance as their very last — and most desperate — recourse.[103]

Policies toward beggars rounded up by Cairo's police changed after mid-century. Due to overcrowding and insalubrious conditions in the Maristan, the poor sheltered there were transferred to Takiyyat Tulun (also known as Isbataliyyat al-Tulun, Isbataliyyat al-Fuqara' bi-Tulun, and Takiyyat al-Fuqara'—the Hospital of Tulun, the Hospital of the Poor in Tulun, and the Tekke of the Poor). To avoid overcrowding as the years passed, officials introduced increasingly refined criteria for eligibility. Whereas residents of Cairo—at times without regard to their physical abilities—had been deemed deserving of admission to the Mahall al-Fuqara', from the 1850s on, after the foundation of Takiyyat Tulun, beggars residing in the city who were identified as fit for work were arrested in government sweeps of the city's streets and markets and put to work in government projects. Records for the period following the establishment of Takiyyat Tulun also illustrate how residents of Cairo and areas outside the city (as far away as Mecca) presented petitions to the khedive (again, through the office of the Dabtiyya as well as subsequent offices), asking to be admitted. In this era as well, we find more detailed records of how individuals were admitted to this institution and how they gained their release. These records indicate the government's continued efforts to restrict the public presence of the itinerant poor and demonstrate how, while family and community forms of assistance to the needy prevailed, the poor of Cairo in the second half of the nineteenth century sought help from the state. Their requests for assistance indicated that they were familiar with state services. Their efforts to procure help showed their agency and forthrightness and their ability to navigate through the offices and services of the increasingly bureaucratized and modern state apparatus. To explore these continued interactions between the state and the poor of Cairo and beyond, we must next venture into Takiyyat Tulun to see how this shelter managed the poor.

III

AMONG THE POOR OF TAKIYYAT TULUN

LADY (LUCIE) DUFF GORDON, a Briton residing in Egypt in the 1860s, had the opportunity to visit the Mosque of Ahmad ibn Tulun in November 1862. Her guide during this visit was none other than Joseph Hekekyan, to whom she had been introduced by the British political economist Nassau Senior. As the two approached the mosque, Hekekyan may have given her details of the mosque's long history — how it had been founded during the ninth century by a Turkish slave soldier in the service of the Abbasids who had been sent to Egypt as this region's governor, but who had established himself as an autonomous ruler soon after his arrival. He may have told her that in subsequent centuries the mosque had fallen into disrepair, but that at the end of the eighteenth century it had come to be used as a workshop for producing wool waistbands.[1] And perhaps Hekekyan had told her, just as he was taking his leave to allow Duff Gordon to enter an area of the mosque reserved for women and children, how just fourteen years earlier this mosque had been converted into a poor shelter, replacing the function that the Maristan had served in the first half of the nineteenth century.

Given Hekekyan's harsh remarks on the role of the Maristan in his 1844 notes, it would have been interesting to know his opinion of the use of Ahmad ibn Tulun Mosque as a shelter. Would he, perusing the lists of inmates and surveying the number of children born within the shelter's walls, criticize the length of time that the poor stayed in the shelter, as he had in the case of the Maristan? Might he have bitterly complained — like European and Egyptian members of the commission charged with the preservation of Arab architecture — that the poor sheltered in the mosque were causing damage to this important example of Egypt's Arab heritage?

Certainly other visitors to the Mosque of Ahmad ibn Tulun, in their analysis of this structure, paused to remark that the poor assembled there had ruined the harmonious appearance of its architecture. European visitors were particularly likely to comment on the spectacle of the poor and on the mosque's structural decay.[2] They noted that some features of the building were crumbling and that the presence of the poor had ruined the mosque's original architecture. The renovations that transformed the mosque into a poor shelter in 1847–48 had changed its physical layout considerably: brick walls filled the once-expansive arch-ways, and the arcade areas had been transformed into areas in which the poor were sheltered. The poor, described by Stanley Lane Poole as beggars and casuals, "infest and disfigure the noble building."[3] Smoke from the cooking fires of "a couple hundred of the most ignorant and filthy of the whole population" had blackened the inside of the arcades, "while their carelessness or wantonness has dirtied or destroyed most that was within the reach of their hands."[4]

Art historian K.A.C. Creswell has described the decision to convert the Mosque of Ahmad ibn Tulun into a poorhouse and the concomitant renovations as a "most shameful act of vandalism," attributable to Muhammad Ali's French medical adviser, Clot Bey.[5] Yet, rather than view the decision to convert the mosque into a poor shelter as an af-front to its architectural and artistic integrity, the mosque's mid-century renovations can be understood in the context of the Cairo authorities' simultaneously pious and pragmatic approaches to dealing with the itin-erant poor. From one perspective, we can view the mosque's conversion into a shelter as a manifestation of the Islamic community's obligation to take care of the poor; the Tulun shelter is one example of charitable efforts made in the later decades of Muhammad Ali's rule and the eras of his successors. From another perspective, the use of this mosque as a shelter reflects the Egyptian government's attempts to centralize poor-relief services. Using the mosque as a shelter in part fulfilled the ruler's obligations of charity. But it also—like providing care for abandoned children, free hospital treatment, and free passage for pilgrims traveling home from the Hajj—was one example of the increasingly central role the Egyptian state played in providing assistance to the needy. From yet another angle, the conversion of the mosque and its use as a shelter reflected a continuation of the interventionist and restrictive posture the government adopted toward the itinerant poor, and most specifically the means by which the government could utilize this shelter to enforce prohibitions on begging.

Finally, while the mosque's use as a shelter can provide a lens for clarifying our understanding of the government's involvement in poor relief, we must also look at its use from the perspective of the poor and show how the poor of Cairo and beyond sought admission and other forms of assistance from the state. Thus we will see the extent to which those in need availed themselves of the charity of the state. We will also explore how the charity that the state provided was sometimes a conse-quence of the state's actions in other areas. Thus we see how military conscription and the inability of families to provide for their own kin resulted in the poor having to seek state assistance. To study the shelter at Ahmad ibn Tulun Mosque and to understand the multiple purposes it served, we need to next accompany Duff Gordon into the mosque and examine in more detail the people who made it their temporary or permanent home and the processes by which they entered and left.

"A Vast Poor-House"

In Duff Gordon's discussion of her visit to Takiyyat Tulun, she mentioned that "the Tooloon is now, a vast poor-house." In her letter, dated November 11, 1862, she described in great detail two of the three lodgings she had visited. In one, several Turkish families had partitioned off a larger room with mats hung from ropes. Each family's section, although lacking in furniture, contained "as many bits of carpet, mat, and patchwork as the poor owner could collect." A young boy explained to Duff Gordon in elaborate pantomime how he slept, ate, and cooked in this space. She recounted how she had given a sixpence coin to the families as she departed from the first lodging; they divided it up among themselves — "ten or twelve people at least, mostly blind or lame."

Duff Gordon described the next lodging she entered as "an Arab hut, stuck against the lovely arches." She remarked that she had had to stoop to enter the doorway and that this lodging was poorer than the last. Without mats or carpets to serve as mattresses, the inhabitants of this home were forced to sleep on the floor or on piles of rocks. As she had done on her departure from the homes of the Turkish families, Duff Gordon gave the young woman who had led her into this lodging a sixpence coin; but in this instance, a loud melée ensued as the women in the hut scrambled to claim the coin.[6]

During her tour of parts of Takiyyat Tulun, Duff Gordon was moved by the poverty she witnessed and the lack of physical comfort afforded to the poor. Aside from the absence of bedding, the rations were sparse: each person received a "mere sixpence" (3 piasters) each month, a suit of clothes once a year, and, on festive occasions, lentil soup.[7] The rations were more meager than those they had received in previous years. In 1859 the expenditure for each adult man and woman had been 4 piasters a month, and for each child 2.25 piasters. In earlier decades, the government had distributed clothes, shoes, and mats among the poor, and cooks would have prepared meat, bread, rice, and lentils.[8] The reduction in food provisions may have been due to insufficient funds. In 1863 Khedive Ismail, noting that the shelter's finances were dwindling, called for the use of funds from other sources, such as the religious endowments his grandfather Muhammad Ali had founded to support a school in Kavala.[9] The need for more funds might have been the result of the Egyptian government's budgetary crises, but it was also a consequence of fluctuations in the number of residents and in other demands the poor made on the state for assistance. Takiyyat Tulun could not accommodate sudden influxes of large numbers of poor people. In June 1873, rather than send the 232 beggars apprehended in Cairo's streets to Takiyyat Tulun, the Cairo police brought them to the Qasr al-Ayni Hospital. Owing to insufficient space and the unhealthy conditions there, the 184 men among them were to be sheltered in a rope factory that would be converted to this use. The remaining 48 women were to be admitted to Takiyyat Tulun.[10]

At various times, the number of poor living in Takiyyat Tulun ranged from 400 to 600 men, women, and children. The poor who made this shelter their home constituted only a small percentage of Cairo's estimated population of 267,160 at mid-century or of Egypt's population of 4,752,088.[11] Nonetheless, their presence is indicative of new government interventions in poor relief as well as the manner in which the poor of Egypt and beyond sought the state's assistance. While private charity—the assistance provided by families and one's religious community—continued to prevail in Cairo as well as in Egypt as a whole, the government's involvement in poor relief in the nineteenth century represents a break from prior, noninterventionist practices and the culmination of a new relationship forged between the state and Egypt's populace. This relationship bore features of reciprocity: the state took license to arrest and intern beggars in Takiyyat Tulun (as it had in the Mahall al-Fuqara' of the Maristan Qalawun before it), and the poor actively sought the assistance of the state. An analysis of government correspondence, accounts of arrest, records of petitions, and registers providing information on the residents of Takiyyat Tulun reveals how these two modalities, practices of regulating the public presence of the itinerant poor and the state's beneficence, worked side by side.

The *Kashf* (examination)

Archival documents are an important source complementing the descriptions of Tulun given by visitors such as Duff Gordon. Like other visitors, she provided information on the architecture and presence of the poor in the shelter but did not give any details as to why the families she encountered in Takiyyat Tulun had made this mosque their home; nor does she provide information on the length of their stay. In her descriptions of the people she encountered during her visit, Duff Gordon implied that the scraps of mat and carpet and the few cooking utensils were all that they owned. Reading her account gives the impression that these families had taken up permanent residence in the shelter.

In line with her descriptions, records of residents spanning two nearly twelve-month periods from 1858 to 1860 confirm that a large portion of Takiyyat Tulun's inhabitants had been there for at least twelve months. Yet the same records indicate that many of them stayed only a short time. Given their spartan surroundings and meager food, what would have caused the poor to temporarily or indefinitely reside in this shelter?

Duff Gordon emphasized that many members of the first families she met were "blind and lame." From the records of petitions made by individuals seeking admission to Takiyyat Tulun, as well as accounts of the arrest and admission of beggars, we can infer that many of Takiyyat Tulun's residents were invalids. One family that made Takiyyat Tulun their permanent home consisted of a blind man and his mother. In 1859, a blind man, Giritli Muhammad Agha, together with his half-blind mother, Aysha bint Hasan, and sister Fatma requested admission. As doctors of the Dabtiyya considered the health status and degree of need of these three people, they noted that "there would be no objection" to the admission of both Muhammad Agha and his mother. Yet, as they considered the case of Fatma, they determined that because she was healthy (*salima*), she did not deserve (*ghayr mustahiqq*) to be admitted to the Takiyya.[12]

Between the 1840s and the 1870s, doctors of the Dabtiyya, and then doctors of the Civilian Hospital, and the governorate of Cairo were charged with assessing the health status and needs of applicants to Takiyyat Tulun. As with Muhammad, his mother Aysha, and his sister Fatma, the task before them was to determine the eligibility of each petitioner and each arrested person. With each case, these health officials used a *kashf*, or examination, to assess whether a person was deserving (*mustahiqq*) of care. Whereas in the 1830s and 1840s residents of Cairo had been admitted to the Maristan regardless of their physical abilities (Cairo authorities were most concerned with expelling nonresident able-bodied beggars), from the 1850s on the key criteria for determining people's deservedness became their ability or inability to provide for themselves and the existence or nonexistence of family or kin who could support them. When an individual was deemed incapable of earning a living and could demonstrate the lack of other means of support (family, for example), she or he was considered deserving of state assistance.

The hallmark of the poor, or *fuqara'*, notes Abraham Marcus, is a "state of dependency." Individuals whom Cairo authorities deemed as fuqara', and hence deserving of assistance, included the invalid, elderly men, single men with children, and women. Physical health—and *whether* a person was able to earn a living—was an essential factor in determining a person's status and eligibility for admission to Takiyyat

Tulun. Through the loss of their physical abilities, and their subsequent inability to work and provide for themselves and their families, even men, in the eyes of the state, were considered dependent.

One example of a man who sought the states' charity is Su'uri ibn Ahmad. Su'uri, a resident of Alexandria who said he had previously found shelter in a poorhouse there (Qishla al-Sadaqa), sought admission to Takiyyat Tulun, claiming that he had no one to care for him and that he was an invalid and poor. The Dabtiyya of Cairo, refusing to take Su'uri's claims at facevalue—particularly since he did not have a tadhkira, the required paperwork for travel—contacted the police in Alexandria to corroborate his claim and specifically, to find out if in Alexandria he had been considered "poor and among the invalid."[13]

However, most invalid or elderly men requesting shelter in Takiyyat Tulun had an easier time gaining admission. When Anbar, appeared at the Dabtiyya stating that he was an invalid and poor, he was immediately admitted.[14] Mustafa Hasan, a resident of Khatt Bab al-Fatuh in Cairo, requested admission to Takiyyat Tulun because he was poor and an invalid. He was admitted to the shelter, as were Muhammad Abdul Radiq from Aswan (who had poor eyesight), Jalabi Ahmad from al-Gamaliyya in Cairo (who claimed to be sick), al-Hagg Hamsa (identified as being seventy-five years old, weak, and incapable of earning a living), and al-Hagg Umran Khamsin of the Syrian Community (*ahali al-Sham*), whose advanced age was confirmed by doctors of the Dabtiyya.[15] Al-Hagg Muhammad ibn Ali, doctors determined, though old, had good eyesight. But Al-Hagg Muhammad proved his deserving status in another way: he noted that since he was *gharib* (a stranger), he had no one to take care of him. Officials of the Dabtiyya agreed and admitted him to the poor shelter.[16]

Fathers and their children also requested admission to the shelter and were granted it. The Dabtiyya decided that Ahmad Muhammad and his son Ibrahim deserved admission to the Takiyya, although there was no indication in the record of their petition what circumstances had caused them to make this request.[17] Again, without mentioning physical abilities or other clues as to why Al-Hagg Muhammad al-Iskandirani and his son sought admission to the shelter, the doctor in charge of screening petitions granted the request of this father and son.[18] Hasan Sulayman is another example of a single father who requested to be admitted to Takiyyat Tulun. He arrived at the Dabtiyya with his two daughters and asked if they all could be admitted.[19] In some cases records of petitions note the circumstances of a father and his offspring(s). Yusuf Ismail was admitted along with his crippled daughter. Mustafa ibn Muhammad and his young son were granted admission to Takiyyat Tulun because the father had lost his eyesight.[20]

Entire families requested admission to Takiyyat Tulun as well. Muhammad Ahmad, his wife, Khadija, and their two children were admitted because Muhammad was poor.[21] Gamila, from the neighborhood of Tulun, arrived at the Dabtiyya with her two daughters and requested to be admitted because she was poor. The Dabtiyya granted her request, allowing Gamila and her daughters to join Gamila's husband, who was already in the Takiyya.[22] In 1870 Ibrahim Ali requested admission for himself, his three children, and his parents.[23]

Single women who were elderly or who indicated that they were incapable of taking care of themselves also requested and were granted admission to Takiyyat Tulun. The Dabtiyya confirmed that Nafisa deserved to be admitted because she was ill.[24] Ulama' bint Ali requested admission to the Takiyya on the grounds that she was not only poor but also old.[25] Fatma bint al-Hagg Farah petitioned for admission to the Takiyya, indicating that due to lameness in her right arm she was incapable of working.[26] Maryam bint Ali came to the Dabtiyya claiming that she was poor and without any resources or belongings. A doctor of the Dabtiyya confirmed that Maryam's eyesight was weak and for this reason she was incapable of working (and providing for herself) and approved her application for admission.[27] In the records of Amina bint Nasar Khalifa's request for care, doctors of the Dabtiyya noted that Amina was elderly and blind and incapable of taking care of herself.[28]

But a person's ability to earn a living could be hampered by factors other than physical health. Single women, arriving at the Dabtiyya by themselves—even those who did not describe themselves as elderly or invalid—were considered deserving of assistance solely because of their gender (being female implied a state of dependence) and, consequently, deserving status and frequently, records of their petitions for admission emphasize this feature. Indeed it might have been the bad luck of Fatma—Giritli Muhammad Agha's sister—to have requested admission together with her brother and mother. Had she appeared at the Dabtiyya separately, like other women who stated that they had no one to take care of them, she might have gained admission. This is what happened to Saliha bint Hasan from Al-Sayyida Zaynab, who came to the Dabtiyya claiming that she was poor and requested admission to the Takiyya.[29] Aysha, also from al-Sayyida Zaynab, requested and was granted admission to Takiyyat Tulun because she did not have anyone to take care of her.[30] Fatuma al-Galisa indicated that she had no one to take care of her (literally, that she had "no one to protect her") and was granted admission.[31] After receiving medical care in the hospital, Khadija bint Qirli Ali Agha, who identified herself as someone who was poor and had no family to take care of her, was admitted to the poor shelter.[32]

The women mentioned here were adults; yet their gender, in the eyes of officials determining their eligibility, designated them as dependents. In this manner the state played the role of surrogate father, ensuring the care and protection of individuals deemed unable to take care of themselves. Orphans, on their own or with a guardian, also sought the assistance of the state. For example, when Khadra's father died, she requested admission to Takiyyat Tulun, noting that she no longer had anyone to take care of her.[33] Even children with one parent still alive could be considered orphans and admitted to Takiyyat Tulun. Muhammad Abdu requested that his daughter stay in the Takiyya when her mother died, and "she was accepted to the Takiyya among the poor."[34] Hasan Ahmad was admitted on September, 29, 1868, after claiming to be an orphan with no one to take care of him. But less than two weeks later, his brother Muhammad Nasr Agha appeared, and Hasan was released into his care.[35]

Women with small children, burdened by the responsibility of caring for them, a duty that might have prevented them from finding employment, frequently requested admission to Takiyyat Tulun.[36] Bigaf from Bab al-Nasr arrived at the Dabtiyya in November 1853 and asked whether she and her infant son could be admitted to the shelter. Noting that her son was still nursing, the Civilian Hospital granted her request.[37] Husayna appeared at the Dabtiyya just two days after Bigaf. Together with her four children, she requested admission to the shelter and was granted it.[38] Karima came to the Dabtiyya with her two children, Muhammad and Maryam and, upon requesting admission to the shelter, was accepted.[39]

In most instances, records of women who appeared at the Dabtiyya with children but no husband did not recount what happened to the fathers. Divorce, separation, or death could have explained the absence of a husband. The latter was the case for the unnamed widow of Hasan Agha, who presented a request to the Dabtiyya to be admitted, together with her three orphaned children, to Takiyyat Tulun.[40] In a number of records from the early 1850s, when the Egyptian army was engaged in the Crimean War, we have evidence that the absence of a husband in the military led a woman to seek assistance from the state. With her husband in the army and having "no one to support her," Na'ma and her young son arrived at the Dabtiyya in Cairo, requesting admission to Takiyyat Tulun. Another woman, Aysha, unable to support herself during her husband's service in the military and charged with the care of not only her three children ("little" Nasr, Nasra, and Salima) but also her mother, Misriyya, requested that they all be granted admission to Takiyyat Tulun.[41] Fatma bint Muhammad, the widow of a soldier, came to the Dabtiyya seeking admission for herself and her two children. The

Dabtiyya determined that because her children were young (four-year-old Abdul Rahman and four-month-old Sayd), she would be unable to earn a living and therefore deserved to be admitted to the shelter with her children.[42]

Military conscription had been a source of numerous disruptions in the lives of Egyptians since its inception in 1822. Conscription and corvée levies deprived villages of many able-bodied breadwinners, leaving some women, children, and the elderly to fend for themselves.[43] During the Syrian campaigns of the 1830s, in an attempt to keep their families intact, women whose husbands had been conscripted followed the recruits to the sites of military campaigns, establishing tent cities in the vicinity of the battle.

Outside observers, such as James August St. John, claimed that women who stayed behind frequently turned to begging, and prostitution, to survive.[44] Extreme solutions such as prostitution were certainly not a recourse for all women, as the cases of Na'ma, Aysha, and Fatma illustrate. Women with no families to support them during their husbands' absence or upon a husband's death knew that they could seek state assistance. Takiyyat Tulun was one such resource. Another form of aid for widows was pensions for soldiers and other government employees. Widows who remarried, however, forfeited state assistance.[45]

In some instances, elderly men suffered disruptions because of their sons' military conscription and were forced to seek assistance from the state. While the elderly had traditionally depended upon their sons for financial support, the recruitment of sons could be the cause of destitution. This was the case with Al-Hagg Mustafa, who requested to be admitted to Takiyyat Tulun with his invalid daughter, given that his two sons were in the army.[46] To prevent the destitution of a parent whose son had left for military service, the government of Ismail declared that in families with only one son, the son would be exempt from service (as would the only brother of a man serving in the army).[47] Men who had served in the military were also among the poor requesting and receiving admission to Takiyyat Tulun.[48]

As in other areas of the Ottoman Empire, where the sick went to the hospital only if they had no one to provide for them, women may have used Takiyyat Tulun for the sole purpose of having a safe place to give birth. Over the course of one year, forty-nine children were born in the shelter. Many of these mothers, along with their newborns, stayed for at least eight months, but lists of the residents of Takiyyat Tulun reveal that this shelter also served as a temporary refuge for women about to give birth. Of those forty-nine children, three were dismissed, together with their mothers less than five months after birth. Just as infant mortality was widespread in the general Egyptian population, death struck down numerous shelter children in the first year of life. During that one-year period, four infants died. However, this number does not take into account unrecorded deaths that may have occurred at childbirth. Many of the women in the shelter gave birth in the Civilian Hospital. If their newborns died at the hospital, they were not counted among the poorhouse residents.

Just as hospitals may have been a last resort for those with no one to care for them, Takiyyat Tulun served as a final resting place for some. Malnutrition, infections and diseases, and old age may have been the cause of death for many shelter residents. In some cases, residents died shortly after their arrival. Some died after having resided in the shelter for an extended period, sometimes while receiving attention in the Civilian Hospital. In the course of one year, 93 short- and long-term residents died. They included 25 adult women, 34 adult men, 21 male children, and 13 female children. Given the fact that for many people the shelter represented a place to die, among its employees were a *ghasal* and a *ghasala* (a male and female washer of corpses).

The poor of Cairo and beyond made use of Takiyyat Tulun for their own purposes. Lacking other means of support, some people stayed for months or even years. Others, seeking shelter during the cold and rainy month of February, stayed long enough to remain dry, perhaps receive a free change of clothes, and rest before they ventured out again. Women, awaiting the return of a husband from the military or using the shelter as a safe refuge after the birth of a child or until child could be weaned, also considered the state's charity as a viable — albeit at times temporary — form of assistance. Common to all was the fact that government officials made the final determination as to who deserved to be admitted.

In each instance, the poor took advantage of the shelter and adapted the state's charity to their own needs. In their requests for assistance, they put forth claims that they were worthy of assistance — attempting to use to their best advantage the criteria of deservedness set forth by the state.

Taking Advantage of the State

Although various forms of assistance continued to exist in nineteenth-century Cairo and in other urban centers, and in the rural areas of Egypt, the records of applicants to Takiyyat Tulun reveal that many claimed they had no one to take care of them and, as lists of residents illustrate, entire families received assistance from the state. Many of these individuals could be described by historians of Europe as having experienced *structural* poverty, "the long-term poverty of individuals due to their personal or social circumstances." Arguably, however, *conjunctural* poverty, "temporary poverty into which ordinarily self-sufficient people may be thrown in a crisis," might have damaged or destroyed family networks that in better circumstances, would have allowed families and relatives to care for their needy.[49]

Two sets of sources — requests made by the poor for admission to the shelter and lists of shelter residents — provide information about the identity of the needy. There were entire families, invalid, elderly men (either accompanied by families or alone), and single women (with or without children). A sampling of records of petitions taken at approximately five-year intervals yields clues about the circumstances bringing the poor to Takiyyat Tulun, but the records do not tell the entire story. Available documentation about this shelter's residents — nearly two full years of records detailing the arrival of new residents, their deaths, flight, and release — provide additional information about their identity and how they took advantage of the state's assistance.

Women and children made up a majority of Takiyyat Tulun's residents. During one month in 1859, 318 of the 605 residents were women, and only 188 were men. During the same month, 64 girls and 35 boys resided there. However, in a sampling of petitions for admission for two- and three-month periods in 1853, 1859, 1863, and 1870, men outnumber women.[50] Men also outnumber women in admission. For example, during a month when the number of persons entering Tulun was at its height (70 men, women, and children), 41 were men, and only 22 were women. Yet men stayed for shorter periods than women. Again, during the month in which the shelter admitted 70 new people, a large majority of the women made this shelter their home for at least three and a half months. Conversely, the men admitted during this period stayed for as little as two days and as long as three and a half months, but many left within weeks. One explanation for the larger number of men among monthly admissions is that women could more readily depend on their families for support: only in extreme cases would they rely on the state. The length of their stays further illustrates how assistance from the state was their last viable option. Men, however, were not solely dependent on their families for support: they could travel more easily (and beg) on their own, they could make use of the state's care for more limited periods of time.

Records of petitions, from the Dabtiyya as well as the Muhafazat (Governorate) of Cairo, comprise only a small portion of the overall number of petitions and admissions to the shelter. Again, looking at 1859, a year for which we can corroborate petition records and lists of incoming inmates, petition records among the surveyed Dabtiyya and Muhafazat registers make note of only three people admitted in February, two admitted in March, and three admitted during the three months of summer. Lists of incoming inmates, however, enumerate 70 new arrivals in the Coptic month of Tut (spanning January–February, the coldest month of the year in Egypt), 11 new arrivals in Amshir (February–March), and a total of 78 new arrivals during the three summer months. In part, as will be discussed in the next section, these high numbers reflect the admission of people arrested for begging. Yet the numerical discrepancies also imply that the offices of the police and the governorate were not the sole avenues for gaining admission to the shelter.

Although we cannot rely solely on records of petitions among the Dabtiyya and Muhafaza records to ascertain the numbers of persons admitted to Takiyyat Tulun for any given month, these records are representative (if not exhaustive) of the range of people requesting admission. They indicate that each person claimed to be unable to earn a living (*ghayr qadir 'ala iktisab*) or to be otherwise poor. For the year 1853, for which the most extensive accounts of petitions addressed to the Dabtiyya for admission to the shelter are available, the records show that in October three single men, describing themselves as old, blind, or both, and a family of four sought shelter in Takiyyat Tulun. In November a total of 56 people were admitted to the shelter. They included 8 single mothers with children (with three being the maximum number of children listed with each mothers), 11 elderly or invalid men, an invalid father and son, an elderly woman, two sets of husbands and wives (without children), and two families.

From this sampling, it appears that the majority of Takiyyat Tulun's residents were from Cairo. Areas outside of Cairo were identified as the origins of the petitioners in only two cases: from among the group of 56 people, one man had come from the Sudan and another from Aswan. Records of petitions do not always provide information about the origins of the person being admitted to the shelter, but for cases in which the person's origin is mentioned, most of the time petitioners were identified as coming from various neighborhoods of Cairo. The petitions that the poor presented for aid indicate that among urban families, extended family networks sometimes could not provide for their kin. But before seeking care in Takiyyat Tulun it is likely that they had already relied on their families and their neighbors. Census records analyzed by Kenneth Cuno indicate that households frequently included invalid members, widowed mothers, and the elderly.[51] Such findings confirm that the family unit in both urban and rural areas was an important source of support for all of its members. Families, including one's in-laws, and neighbors also played an essential role in caring for children during their parents' absences or in case of abandonment.

The fact that Takiyyat Tulun (and the Maristan Qalawun before it) also functioned as a shelter for people from outside Cairo illustrates how the city and its forms of assistance attracted nonresidents who were otherwise unable to provide for themselves. Like Istanbul, Cairo was the location of numerous institutions that served benevolent ends. Shrines and Sufi tekkes distributed food to those in need. Sufi lodges also served as a temporary refuge for the destitute.[52] Religious occasions, such as *mulid*s and other holidays, were opportunities for wealthy residents of the city to distribute food and money among the poor. Begging in the city might have been more viable than begging in one's village, in part because of the growing concentrations of foreigners and tourists. A number of beggars arrested and interned in Takiyyat Tulun were released only after promising that they would not return to the city; evidently they had come to the city with the intention of begging.

Takiyyat Tulun also figured in popular knowledge as a place where the poor could receive care and seek refuge. The number of individuals who contacted the Dabtiyya — requesting admission to the shelter or searching for friends or relatives to have them released — indicate the mobility of Egypt's populace (including women who traveled on their own to seek out family members or request admission and other forms of government assistance) and their knowledge of relief options.[53]

Without more exact information on the total numbers of petitioners from outside Cairo, it is difficult to ascertain the full extent to which the rural poor of Egypt made use of the shelter when other options for care were unavailable. Judith Tucker has documented the ways in which economic changes under way during this period weakened the peasant family's ability to support its nonproductive members.[54] It is likely that some of the shelter's residents, lacking family care, had initially made their way to Cairo either to beg (as is discussed in the next section) or to seek aid from the Dabtiyya. Conclusive determinations about the role the shelter played in assisting the rural poor will have to await further study. Toledano's accounts of migration to Cairo and the precarious life of individuals who lacked networks of support further suggests that Takiyyat Tulun, for some recent arrivals, could have served as an essential safety net. Many of the individuals who claimed they had "no one to care for them" or who indicated that they were "strangers" could have been new arrivals to the city. Migrant women whose husbands had either died or been conscripted into the army were sometimes far from other forms of care and hence were dependent on state aid. As mentioned earlier, women who made this shelter their home generally stayed longer than men, thus indicating the absence of other alternatives for assistance.

The families whom Duff Gordon encountered in November 1862 were not only individuals who had requested admission to the shelter. Among the poor who made Takiyyat Tulun their home were but also beggars who had been apprehended in the government's periodic sweeps of the streets and markets of Cairo. Like the Maristan before it, Takiyyat Tulun had a dual purpose: those who requested assistance from the state were given refuge in this institution if they were deemed deserving. At the same time, the shelter admitted individuals who had not come of their own free will. The next section addresses the second role of the Takiyya, and explores in greater depth the multiple meanings of the expression "the charity of the khedive."

Haqq/Mustahiqq (to have the right, to be deserving)

In addition to determining the status of applicants to Takiyyat Tulun, doctors at agencies charged with managing relief efforts for the poor were responsible for assessing the eligibility of beggars who had been arrested. From of the 1850s onward, as in the 1830s and 1840s, able-bodied beggars who had been arrested were put to work; although non-residents were sent back to their villages of origin, residents of Cairo deemed fit for work were employed in government projects. Government records portray admission to Takiyyat Tulun as a haqq, or right. The idea that the state's charity was a "right" is most clearly illustrated in the numerous run-ins Qasim Yusuf had with the Dabtiyya and Civilian Hospital in the winter of 1853–54. Arrested for begging in 1853, Qasim was dealt nearly the full range of experiences befalling individuals who had transgressed government prohibitions on begging. Luckily for him, he could prove that he was a resident of Cairo, thus avoiding expulsion from the city. But, perhaps unfortunately for him, when he underwent an examination, or kashf, at the Civilian Hospital, the doctors determined that he was strong and capable of earning a living. As a punishment for begging, Qasim was sent to work at the government bakery.[55]

Nearly two months later, claiming to be ill, Qasim was subjected to another examination at the Civilian Hospital. On this occasion, the doctors determined that he was indeed sick. Qasim's illness, added to his poverty, earned him admission to Takiyyat Tulun, where, as the account recording the circumstances of his second interaction with doctors of the Civilian Hospital stated, "he will be admitted to the Takiyya to be cared for out of the charity of *al-Janab al-Asfa* [his compassionate Highness], as is done for those who have rights like him."[56]

Qasim was only one of the hundreds of beggars apprehended on the streets of Cairo in the 1850s. As in the 1830s and 1840s, officials who carried out their arrests were complying with laws prohibiting begging and used the space of the shelter to enforce these laws. Although Muhammad Ali's various industrial and military projects had proven unsuccessful and had been dismantled,[57] the legacy of his actions — the consolidation of landholdings and continued efforts to tax and conscript the peasantry — pervaded the economic and political landscape of Egypt long after his death. Attempts to clear public spaces of beggars and loiterers were one consequence of the continued hold the state sought to have on the peasantry; in 1853–54, for example, extensive accounts of the arrest and deportation and the arrest and internment of beggars were recorded.[58] At this juncture, the use of Takiyyat Tulun, like the Maristan before it, was intended in part to assist in controlling the mobility of the poor. At the same time, the shelter helped clear the streets of the beggars whose activities were described as "inappropriate" while they themselves were coming to be described as "unsightly." But at the same time, as with the admission of the poor to the Maristan, the government's apprehension of beggars, as well as its admission of the poor who petitioned for care, was presented as a form of charity. Records concerning the processing of these two categories frequently noted that they were admitted to the shelter "out of the charity of the khedive."

The reigns of Abbas I (1848–54) and Said (1854–1863) witnessed the continuation of many projects initiated during the first half of the nineteenth century. Infrastructure was one area that developed at a rapid clip during their rule. Railways were built and roads and irrigation networks improved. Officials of the police department continued to patrol public spaces and arrested those found begging or loitering in an effort to control migration to Cairo, just as they had in the two decades before.[59] As in the era of Muhammad Ali, peasants' evading taxation and their absconding from military conscription were two key concerns. For these reasons, government roundups of beggars continued unabated during the first half of the 1850s as did attempts to track down individuals who might have sought refuge in Cairo. The records of the arrest and deportation of individuals recount how groups of men and women from the same village, as well as individuals found to be nonresidents of Cairo, were sent back to the villages from which they had fled.[60]

Government prohibitions on begging, restrictions that also applied to loitering from the 1850s on, justified the arrest of individuals and their deportation to their places of origin. Such restrictions reflected suspicions about the potential of the homeless committing crimes. Concerned specifically with issues of public order and security, in August 1858, for example, the police arrested three men—two of them were identified as being from Malatya (in Asia Minor)—for loitering and deported them from Cairo.[61] In prior years, individuals might have been transported to their place of origin by boat along the Nile or by foot, but from the 1850s on, with the introduction of a rail line between Cairo and Alexandria, the arrest and deportation of loiterers was easy and quick.

Policing the streets and markets of cities such as Cairo and Alexandria could serve benevolent ends as well. For example, when homeless young boys wandering around without work in Alexandria were discovered to be residents of Cairo or to have guardians there, they were sent back to family members who could take care of them. Muhammad Farg, whose father was a *qahwaji* (a coffee seller) in Cairo, was returned to Cairo upon being arrested for wandering in the streets of Alexandria, an activity deemed "inappropriate" for a young boy.[62] Shahhata, another young boy, had accompanied his father, the livestock dealer al-Hagg Shahhata, to Alexandria; but when his father died suddenly, the boy could not return to his home in Cairo. Police picked him up when they found him wandering "without work or residence" and sent him to Cairo, where he was handed over to his brother Salih.[63]

At the same time that they were apprehending and deporting nonresidents arrested in their periodic sweeps of Cairo and Alexandria and working to reunite families, the Dabtiyya's officials were rounding up beggars found in the streets and marketplaces of Cairo. The invalid and elderly, whether residents of Cairo or elsewhere, were admitted to Takiyyat Tulun. Ali al-Qafas from Hasaniyya, Musatir Ibrahim from al-Kayt Shubrakhayt, and Ahmad Salim from Tanta, for example—all identified as being invalid—were admitted to the shelter.[64] Other beggars identified as residents of Cairo were also admitted to Takiyyat Tulun. The day following the arrest of the non-Cairenes, the guards of the neighborhood of Al-Sayyida Zaynab arrested another group of invalids, this time consisting of seven beggars (one was a woman), all from Cairo. Although one person was released upon proving that he had not been begging, the other six were admitted to Takiyyat Tulun.[65]

Takiyyat Tulun was not the only institution sheltering beggars who had been rounded up in Cairo's public spaces. Since religious and ethnic communities were required to care for their poorer members, the Dabtiyya also called on the heads of these communities both to provide for and to discipline their own members when they had been arrested for begging. A week before the arrests of Ali al-Qafas and others, the Dabtiyya informed the heads of the Levantine, Armenian, Syrian, and Coptic communities that numerous people from their respective communities had been arrested for begging. These beggars were then sent to the heads of their communities, who were told to ensure that their members would never beg again. Among those who received a severe reprimand from a religious leader was the Armenian Christian Ibrahim al-Fayan, who had been previously confined to Takiyyat Tulun but who upon release was caught begging again.[66]

Due to the centralization of government involvement in poor-relief activities, members of religious and ethnic communities were to some extent differentiated. Police documents and other records affirm that care for non-Muslims was usually relegated to religious communities, although non-Muslims were also, on occasion, found among shelter inmates. Lists of shelter residents for the period of 1859–61 include at least one Coptic Christian, named Girgis Abd al-Masih.[67] Being a member of a minority religious or ethnic community, however, did not exempt a person deemed "fit for work" from working, as in the case of Yusuf Shami, whom the guards of Muski (where the Dabtiyya was located) apprehended for begging and engaged in labor.[68] Foreign beggars and vagrants were also arrested during the nineteenth century. In 1864 when the Greek Georgi Shalur was arrested for loitering and inappropriate behavior, he was sent to the Greek consul for punishment.[69]

As in the 1830s and 1840s, putting an end to begging was intended as a way of clearing the streets of the poor. On one hand, the prohibition on begging ensured that nonresident and resident sturdy beggars would not be allowed to gain subsistence through charity; instead they would be forced to work. On the other hand, the government ensured that the poor would be taken care of and kept out of the public eye. While the government did not question the fact that the deserving poor merited charity, prohibitions on begging and later loitering restricted charity to those whom the government deemed deserving of assistance. Sturdy beggars or those capable of earning a living in the countryside who sought subsistence by begging in major cities faced expulsion; and sturdy beggars from the major cities could be put to work in government projects such as Cairo's government-run bakery or Alexandria's tanneries. Seeking to put a stop to vagrancy, the Egyptian government also enforced policies that stipulated the military or agricultural training of vagrants.[70] Repeat offenders, able-bodied persons who continued to beg, were sent to the army.[71] In this way, the government continued to impose a political economy of poor relief and simultaneously endeavored to preserve public order. The able-bodied were to be put to work, while those deserving of care merited the charity of the state.

The government's prerogative to dictate who was deserving of charity and how they would be provided for reflected an attempt to gain a monopoly over benevolence. The ruler's obligation to care for his populace was manifested not only in the admission of petitioners to Takiyyat Tulun but also in the admission of beggars found seeking the charity of the Cairene populace. By admitting those deemed deserving of care to Takiyyat Tulun, officials in Cairo assured that those in need would be cared for. Yet beggars, once admitted — or rather confined — to Takiyyat Tulun, would not be released until the government was reassured that either the residents could take care of themselves and their families, or someone else could provide such care, with the idea that the beggars were not to return to begging. In many cases inmates of Takiyyat Tulun could gain release from the shelter only when someone promised to take care of them and guaranteed that the person would never beg again. Some records show that inmates could petition for their own release by declaring that they were able to care for themselves. In other instances, inmates escaped from the shelter.

Cairo authorities' attempts to control beggars' presence in the streets and markets and the use of Takiyyat Tulun as both a shelter and a place of confinement show how policies toward the poor in the second half of the nineteenth century continued to represent both benevolence and social control. To understand how state charity could perform these two functions at the same time we must more minutely analyze how people procured the release of inmates from the shelter and return, once more, to the people who residing in Takiyyat Tulun.

A Guarantee

By prohibiting begging, successive governments in Egypt endeavored to clear the streets of the itinerant poor. These policies served multiple goals. First, public spaces were monitored in the interest of public health. Second the able-bodied poor were put to work, particularly in the 1830s and 1840s, when labor demands in agriculture and industry were acute. Third, Cairo authorities had assistance in controlling access to the geographic space of Cairo. Behind the policy of interning the "deserving poor" was the idea that rather than having to resort to begging, an individual would be supported by the state or a relative. In this way, the state maintained a safety net ensuring care for those in need, as in the case of petitioners for assistance.

Beggars who were being apprehended did not necessarily feel that they were receiving state benevolence. Instead they found their autonomy severely curtailed by the government's restrictions on their movements. The arrest records of Iskili Husayn, "a Turkish dervish" who was arrested for engaging in various acts of begging in 1854, and of

Muhammad Ibrahim ibn Muhammad, a resident of Darb al-Hadr in Cairo who was arrested for begging in the streets in 1863, noted that each was to be sent to Takiyyat Tulun, "never to be released."[72] What were Cairo authorities' intentions in confining such men? Certainly, in the case of an unnamed mute man arrested in October 1863, we learn how Takiyyat Tulun functioned to exclude individuals displaying behavior that threatened public order. This unnamed man had already been confined to the shelter for having "wandered around in an inappropriate manner" and was, upon being caught again, sent to Takiyyat Tulun to ensure that he would not harm anyone.[73] Hence we might assume that both Iskili Husayn and Muhammad Ibrahim had prior begging infractions. The fact that Iskili Husayn was a "Turkish" dervish, at a time when Ottoman authorities in Istanbul and Anatolia were seeking to regulate the movement of dervishes, furthermore, might have implied that Cairo authorities had been instructed to keep an eye on these individuals.[74] Yet the internment of beggars, as illustrated in friends' and relatives' attempts to gain their freedom, also served other ends.

It is clear that one of the government's biggest concerns was care of the poor and a desire to keep beggars out of public spaces. We can see this in policies pertaining to beggars whose place of residence was outside Cairo. Nonresident beggars could gain their release if they promised to return to their villages. Yusuf Nagm and his wife, Bihana, after having stayed in the Takiyya for six and a half months, requested release. The Dabtiyya granted their request after obtaining "the necessary guarantee" (al-taʿahhud al-lazim) that they would not stay in Cairo and would head straight for their village.[75] Husayn Hasan, arrested for "wandering in the streets of Cairo, demanding charity of all of God's creatures," had been sent to Takiyyat Tulun out of the charity of al-Wali al-Niʿam (the Supreme Benefactor) in December 1858; but in March 1859, Nafisa, a relative of his, arrived at the Dabtiyya and requested that Husayn Hasan be released, given that he was from Kafr al-Shaykh and his children were there. The Dabtiyya and administrators of Takiyyat Tulun complied with her request, releasing him with the stipulation that he immediately go back to his village and never return to Cairo.[76]

We also find numerous requests made by individuals to have a Cairene family member or relative released from Takiyyat Tulun. Accompanying each request were statements attesting to the petitioner's ability to take care of the person being released and assuring the central authorities that the person would not continue to beg. These promises, as well as confirmations from authorities in the petitioner's neighborhood (attesting to his or her good standing), served as the taʿahud or daman (guarantee).[77] Qamir bint Abdul Rahman had spent only ten days

in Takiyyat Tulun when her brother Al-Hagg Hasan al-Sirgani requested
to have her released. He promised officials at the Dabtiyya that she
would never beg again and provided proof from the sheikh of Azbakiyya, the sheikh of Darb Mustafa, and his neighbors that he was finan-
cially able to support her.[78] When Hadiya petitioned for the release of
her son Hasanayn from Takiyyat Tulun, she presented proof from the
Sheikh of Azbakiyya that Hasanayn was able to support himself.[79] Istayta gained the release of her husband, Gama' Mustafa after he had
spent at least seven months in the shelter.[80] Records for Takiyyat Tulun
from the year of 1859–60 indicate that individuals arrested for begging
could stay for quite some time before a relative or friend arrived to seek
their release. Shamir bint Ali spent at least eight months there before
her mother, Nayna, presented a petition for her release, stating that she
was capable of providing for her daughter.[81] Aysha bint Muhammad
presented the proper guarantees to have her son Hagazi released from
the Takiyya after he had been there for at least seven months.[82]

People unrelated to the inmates of Takiyyat Tulun also sought their
release. Sheikh Abd al-Wahhab Dhuwaq al-Sulaymaniyya from al-Azhar
mosque requested the release of Sheikh Abd al-Karim al-Sabiq. In procuring Abd al-Karim's release, Abd al-Wahhab swore that Abd al-Karim
would never beg in the markets again.[83] Al-Hagg Muhammad, the *wakil*
(manager) of an *izba* (agricultural estate) in Al-Jawani, came to Takiyyat Tulun seeking Al-Hagg Hasan, one of the peasants from his izba.
He was successful in procuring Al-Hagg Hasan's release and had him
brought back to the izba.[84] Without mentioning their relationship,
Muhammad Sa'ad al-Fayani petitioned for the release of a blind man,
Ali al-Naggar, who had been in the shelter for at least seven months.
Ibrahim Abd al-Al gained the release of Fatma bint Salam (again, no
mention was made of their relationship) after she had been in the shelter for only two weeks.[85]

Residents of the shelter could also petition for their own release, and
in many cases records demonstrate that they were required to provide a
guarantee of their future good conduct. Ali Miyt and his wife, Ayda
bint Khalil, petitioned for their release after having lived in the shelter
for at least seven months.[86] Al-Hagg Ibrahim Hadir, who had petitioned
for admission, informed authorities after staying in the Takiyya for
eight and a half months that he could now take care of himself, and he
was released.[87] Groups of women also petitioned to get into Tulun and
later requested release. Khadra bint Muhammad, her daughter Nasra,
and her sister Latifa stayed perhaps just long enough to shore up their
resources. Just seven months and one week after their arrival, they petitioned to be released.[88] To obtain their release, they provided authorities
with a daman testifying to their good behavior.[89] Istayta bint Muham-

mad and her son were also able to procure their own release from the shelter after promising not to beg.[90]

The frequent release of residents from this shelter, either permanently or for short periods during which they were allowed to return to their villages of origin, is further indication of the mobility of Egypt's poor. But it also illustrates the fact that the poor used this shelter as just one among many options for assistance. Individuals might have sought admission during times when their families could not provide for them — for example, women whose husbands were in the army — or when a family's resources were limited. That the poor's residence in the shelter was punctuated by travel to their villages of origin, sometimes over great distances and occasionally at the government's expense, indicated close ties with families and relatives. Such mobility also draws our attention to the unreliability of poor people's accounts that they had "no one" to care for them. In many cases, individuals petitioning for state assistance presented their need within criteria that the state dictated. But perhaps for some, such accounts were fictional.

Two groups of individuals, arrested beggars and poor petitioners, lived side by side within the walls of Takiyyat Tulun. Yet although Cairo authorities intended to use the shelter, like the Maristan before it, as a means of clearing the streets of Cairo of beggars, the confinement of beggars was never absolute. Nor, as we will see in the next section, did the state have the means to provide care for (much less confine) all beggars found in Cairo's public spaces.

The Extent of Charity

Among the poor at Takiyyat Tulun who might have been aware of Duff Gordon's visit in the fall of 1862, or at least heard the mad scramble for the sixpence she had given to one of the Arab women, were Ibrahim al-Misiri and his wife, Ayda bint al-Murshidi. Just four years before Duff Gordon's visit, Ibrahim had requested that he, his wife, and their child, Sayada, be admitted to Takiyyat Tulun, noting that he was an invalid, needy, and poor. In their assessment of Ibrahim's request, doctors of the Civilian Hospital confirmed that he and his family deserved (*yasta-haqqu*) to be admitted to Takiyyat Tulun. Ibrahim and his family, it appears, made the shelter their home. With the exception of a twenty-five-day period when she received permission to return to their village, until her death in the autumn of 1860, their young daughter Sayada lived with them in the shelter. Ibrahim and Ayda lived there at least into the fall of 1861.

The fact that Sayada had been required to gain permission to leave the shelter for her brief journey to the family's home village illustrates the restrictions imposed on the residents. We had seen how such *accounts of arrest* sometimes included stipulations that once admitted, a beggar could not leave the shelter. Frequently, petitions for the release of a relative or acquaintance show that beggars were released only upon the receipt of a guarantee of their good behavior and of abstinence from begging. Yet even petitioners' freedom to leave and return to the shelter was hindered by other means of control.

Sayada's having to ask for permission to leave the shelter was also undoubtedly due to a particular restriction placed on her family. The final section of the record of Ibrahim and his family's admission stipulated that the family "is admitted to Takiyyat al-Fuqara like others like them to live out of the charities of al-Wali al-Niʿam al-Khidiwi [the Supreme Benefactor, the khedive] with the understanding that they will not be released." We can only speculate about why the Dabtiyya specified that Ibrahim and his family would not be allowed to leave the shelter. Might they have fled the shelter on a prior occasion and been caught begging in the streets? This was the case of an invalid man named Burli Uthman Agha, who, residing in the shelter in 1863, had escaped and subsequently been arrested for begging and sent back to the shelter. On this occasion, Dabtiyya officials as in the case of Ibrahim and his family, resolutely forbade Burli Uthman Agha to leave the shelter again.[91] Ibrahim's family's circumstances, and those of Burli Uthman Agha, draw our attention to the fine line that may have existed between petitioning and being arrested: did petitioning for admission normally imply the petitioner's freedom to leave the shelter? If so, did arrested beggars ever have the option of requesting admission (that is, of presenting a petition) and thereby guaranteeing themselves more opportunities to leave and return to the shelter?

In addition to specific examples of Dabtiyya officials notifying the shelter's administrators that a shelter inmate was not allowed to leave, another way in which the shelter authorities made sure that residents would not leave was requiring those who left to reapply for admission. Leaving the shelter could expose a needy person to the likelihood that he or she might be turned away; which is why many residents of Takiyyat Tulun, like Sayada, were careful to apply for permission to leave. One person who failed to get the required permission but left the shelter anyway was Khalukha bint Khalil, who lived in Takiyyat Tulun with her husband Hasanayn. She left the shelter to go to Alexandria without obtaining permission from the shelter's director. When she returned, she was required to request readmission. The director of the shelter granted her request, and Khalukha went on to stay in Takiyyat Tulun for at least two more years.[92] When Fatma's husband, Abdul Aziz, who had formerly been living in the Takiyya, returned from the Hijaz, he was initially refused admission to the shelter. He entered it only after Fatma petitioned on his behalf.[93] The same strictures on leaving were applied at a poorhouse established after the closure of Takiyyat Tulun. The act of leaving Takiyyat Tura, which housed up to three hundred indigent people, meant that a resident's name could be "scratched off" (*shataba*) the list of the deserving poor who were allowed to reside in this shelter. Because the number of applicants at shelters such as Takiyyat Tura exceeded the number of persons who could be accommodated, petitioners had to present their cases in a way that would gain them entry or reentry.[94]

The case of Ibrahim and his family, as well as of Khalukha, Fatma, and Abdul Aziz, indicate that petitioners stayed—either of their own free will, or because of a stipulation—for long periods. One way in which shelter inmates' right to leave the shelter was controlled was the formulation of readmission policies that meant the potential for difficulties when being readmitted. Since I have discovered only one record pertaining to the use of guards in this shelter, and no budget-related documents referring to salary allotments for such employees, it seems evident that readmission restrictions served to keep Takiyyat Tulun's inmates within its walls. Other records indicate that many of this shelter's residents either fled or went through the formality of requesting a release.

Many were also dismissed without a record of their having been released into the care of a friend or relative. In the same way that the flight of inmates reveals that the shelter was incapable of completely restrictions its residents, the dismissal of shelter residents, as well as other difficulties Cairo authorities encountered in trying to maintain control over the poor who made Takiyyat Tulun their home, indicates how the "confinement" of beggars in this era was never absolute.

Takiyyat Tulun did not have the capacity to intern the poor for an unlimited length of time. As evidence of this—alongside individuals who gained their release after the intercession of a friend or relative—we have accounts of petitioners who, after being considered deserving of admission, were dismissed after only one year. When Mansur Khalaf Allah requested to be admitted to Takiyyat Tulun, the head doctor (*hakimbasha*) of the Dabtiyya determined that Mansur was deserving. Mansur made his request in June 1859, but he was dismissed at the end of September, having stayed in the Takiyya for only three months.[95] Izmirli Husayn Agha, deemed deserving because he was poor and unable to earn a living, was admitted to the shelter and stayed for thirteen months before he was dismissed.[96] Sulayman Khalil, also considered deserving because he was an invalid, stayed for more than two years before he was released by order of a "screening" (*daman al-mafruzin*).[97]

Shelter administrators also released groups en masse. When a young

girl named Khadra and others found themselves among those being expelled in a *farz* (a screening or dismissal), they petitioned for readmission and were granted it.[98] Re-admittance requests made by groups of
people, coupled with initial petitions for admission made by hundreds
more, demonstrate how desperate circumstances forced people to seek
the state's charity, even if in so doing they were required to forgo some
of their freedoms.

The application of a screening process indicates how necessary it was
for the shelters' administrators to prioritize the needs of inmates because of the lack of space and resources. Whereas initially the Maristan
had served as a means of enforcing prohibitions on begging, in the case
of Takiyyat Tulun, with the passage of time and an increase in the demands the poor made on the state, shelter administrators saw that they
did not have the means to confine (and provide for) the poor who
sought admission and possibly even those who were confined following
arrests for begging.

Within the shelter, people who had requested admission lived side by
side with those who had been arrested, indicating that no distinctions
were made which may have stigmatized some inmates or subjected them
to different treatment. Groups of unrelated men shared some sections of
the mosque, and women and children were relegated to rooms in other
sections. Duff Gordon's ignorance of why the Turkish and Arab families
she had visited had made this shelter their home indicates a lack of such
distinctions. This can also be seen in the paucity of references to the
circumstances of their admission, and of more detailed information on
the physical layout of the shelter, which would have demonstrated how
residents' movements were restricted.

Other features of the shelter provide us with further information
about its permeability in relation to the world beyond its walls. The
space of the shelter and the lives of its residents were not entirely cut off
from the outside world. It is likely that residents acquired food from
beyond this shelter's walls. Though the salary records of employees at
Takiyyat Tulun indicate that the shelter had a cook, the young boy
whom Duff Gordon had met had explained, while gesticulating wildly,
that his family slept, ate, and cooked in the rooms of their dwelling,
thus indicating that at least some of the residents cooked their own
meals. Further proof that many families cooked for themselves comes
from the preservationists' complaints that the "cooking fires of the
poor" had permanently damaged the ceilings in some areas of the
mosque.

The space of Takiyyat Tulun was also permeated by people like Duff
Gordon and other tourists and foreign residents of Egypt who, although
they might have come with the express purpose of looking at the archi-

tecture of the Ahmad ibn Tulun mosque, could not help remarking on the presence of the residents. Given that Egypt's poor were such a topic of interest for foreigners, the next chapter explores European perspectives of the poor and poor relief in Egypt during the nineteenth and early twentieth centuries to show how the poor and the alleged lack of care provided for them fitted within European discourses of Egypt's inability to govern itself.

Seeking Assistance from Multiple Sources

Records of the Dabtiyya showing admissions to and releases from Takiyyat Tulun and the lists of residents demonstrate how Takiyyat Tulun came to be used by the poor of not only Cairo but also other locales throughout the Middle East. Records of petitions are the best indicators of how the poor actively sought the help of the state; but the range of documents detailing the interactions between the Dabtiyya and the poor most importantly illustrate how this shelter, and the government's assistance as a whole, figured into the popular knowledge of not only Egypt's poor but the poor in areas as far away as Mecca and Istanbul. Although the shelter located in Ahmad ibn Tulun Mosque had been established as a means of confining the poor, the poor of Egypt, like the poor of England discussed by Lynn Lees, made use of this shelter for their own purposes. Mothers gave birth to children in this structure and later left it; men, women, and children stayed temporarily or for longer periods of time, and many people came to die there. Although it represented just one option (hence illustrating that contrary to the proverb "If menticity should unfortunately be thy lot, knock at the large gates only,"[99] the poor clearly made use of multiple forms of relief, knocking on many doors), its use by the poor indicates that while the state attempted to impose its own benevolence, the poor also demanded it. However, in the years to come, the poor would find themselves knocking not only at the large gates of the state — for the state found itself increasingly unable to address their needs — but also at the doors of private organizations.

Just a year after Hekekyan and Lady Duff Gordon visited Takiyyat Tulun, Khedive Ismail convened a meeting of government officials. On the agenda were questions about the dwindling funds of Takiyyat Tulun. Demands placed on the shelter's administrators by the sheer number of poor people seeking assistance there, as well as a loss of revenue in various government offices that had previously provided for its financial security, forced Ismail to turn to other ways of funding this establishment. He called for the diversion of funds that had previously financed other institutions (including the religious endowments his grandfather Muhammad Ali had established in his homeland of Kavala) toward the care of the poor at Takiyyat Tulun.[100]

That Ismail could have been so concerned with ensuring the continuous functioning of Takiyyat Tulun speaks, as we have seen in previous instances, of a ruler's obligations toward his populace. Indeed, Ismail's charitable contributions were not limited to his own subjects but included the poor of France and Istanbul. He frequently responded generously to the solicitations of missionary and philanthropic groups in Europe, some of which served Egypt's poor and others which operated in Istanbul.[101] In this manner he demonstrated his benevolence to his Ottoman cousins as well as to the European audiences whom he sought to please. Yet Ismail was interested in maintaining this shelter for aesthetic purposes as well. Takiyyat Tulun could be used to assist the government in clearing the streets of the itinerant poor just at the time when Ismail and his government sought to present Cairo as a modern and fashionable city.[102] In this respect, clearing the streets of beggars was necessary, for their presence was deemed inappropriate and their actions unsightly. Similar efforts were made at this time in Alexandria, where growing numbers of Europeans lived. Orders calling for the removal of beggars from public spaces in Cairo and Alexandria included descriptions of their activities (begging, laundering, and cooking in public spaces) as "unsightly," "inappropriate," and "unhealthy."[103]

Accounts of arrests, records of petitions, lists of shelter residents, and correspondence pertaining to policies toward Egypt's itinerant poor (from the 1850s through the 1870s) demonstrate an important tradition of state involvement in poor relief and illustrate the ongoing use of modern institutions and policies established in the reign of Muhammad Ali. The reigns of Abbas and Said—the middle decades—were not years of decline, as Toledano has shown. Rather, bureaucratic institutions, policing apparatuses, and institutions such as hospitals continued to function.[104] During the reign of Ismail, through the rule of his son, Tawfiq (1879–92), and during that of his successors during the British occupation, managing the public presence of the poor remained a concern.

The government's abilities to care for the poor, in shelters such as Takiyyat Tulun or in hospital facilities such as Qasr al-Ayni, however, were severely hampered by the financial difficulties Egypt faced in the 1870s. By 1879, the Ministry of Awqaf, which had assumed the purview of establishments such as Takiyyat Tulun, had to turn away the poor who sought assistance.[105]

In the early 1880s, Takiyyat Tulun had ceased to serve as a poor shelter as well. In the interest of conservation, preservationists and art historians (members of a khedival committee entrusted with ensuring the conservation of Arab art and architecture throughout Egypt) began to put forth plans for the repair of the mosque.[106] In the place of this shelter, subsequent *takaya* (state-run shelters) were established: Tura (which housed up to three hundred indigent persons) and Abdin (which was established in the early twentieth century and provided care for twenty five indigent women). Neither was adequate in terms of responding to the demands of the poor. In the absence of sufficient poor-relief efforts by the state during the British occupation, a broad range of private organizations, both European and indigenous, stepped in to provide assistance.

IV

THE SPECTACLE OF THE POOR

VISITORS TO EGYPT as well as Westerners residing there were struck by how frequently beggars and street peddlers accosted them. In front of Shepheard's Hotel, and in the fashionable shopping districts of Cairo and Alexandria, and at historic sites such as the pharaonic ruins and mosques, they were met with cries of "baksheesh" from Egyptian children and adults demanding alms. Beggars were not only a nuisance but they also spoiled the very historic sites that Europeans had come to see. In the case of Ahmad ibn Tulun Mosque, European visitors might not have been prepared to be as sympathetic as Duff Gordon was when she toured the mosque in 1862. Baedeker's 1878 guide to Egypt, for example, warned tourists that "paupers and cripples" who made this mosque their home "pester the visitor for alms." The guidebook also noted that the poor who had taken up residence there had damaged the architecture of this mosque, which once had been beautiful and harmonious.[1]

A number of Europeans traveling in Egypt and the Ottoman Empire in the first half of the century had remarked on a religious ethos permeating these societies' attention to the poor. Edward Lane, Baroness Minutoli, and Reverend Walsh, for example, recognized the degree of tolerance for beggars in the region and commented on the care that the poor received. However, as more and more Europeans arrived in Egypt, their depictions of Egypt's poor and Egypt's poverty became increasingly condemnatory. The British in particular, who had played an advisory role in the administration of Egypt's finances in the 1870s and then occupied the country in 1882, regarded Egypt's beggars as an eyesore, a nuisance, and carriers of filth and disease.

The figures of beggars and other needy persons symbolized the "impoverished" and "dependent" status of Egypt. Caricatures depicting them made Egypt synonymous with beggars or other needy individuals. In the British satirical journal *Punch*, Egypt's relationship to Britain was represented by the body and actions of the street peddler, the beggar, and the convalescent. The street peddler represented Egypt's subordination to England and its dependence on creditors. In 1876, *Punch* featured a cartoon of the Ottoman sultan Abdul Hamid II as a street peddler accosting England (symbolized by the figure of John Bull) with sponges (figure 4.1). The sponges, representing the successive loans that

Figure 4.1. During the mid-to-late nineteenth century, both the Ottoman Empire and Egypt acquired a number of loans from European banks and creditors. By the 1870s each government found itself unable to pay its debts. The depiction of the sultan and khedive as street peddlers reflects their subordination as well as their beleaguered attempts to acquire money in any way possible. (Reproduced from *Punch*, May 20, 1876, with permission of Punch, Ltd.)

the Ottomans had received, illustrated the Ottoman Empire's insatiable desire to soak up all the European creditors had to offer. The Egyptian khedive Ismail, harassing John Bull, was portrayed in an equally unattractive light. His attempts to sell Bull balloons represented the Egyptians' "floating debt," their forestalling on the repayment of loans, and their inability to manage their own finances. After the British occupied Egypt in 1882, Egypt's dependence on and subordination to the British were depicted as a convalescent patient (figure 4.2): throwing off the "crutches" of the Dual Control, the patient gratefully received a walking stick, namely a British financial advisor, to support and assist him in managing Egypt's economy and repaying Egypt's loans. During this period, the Suez Canal, essential to British imperial interests, was portrayed as an infant, safe in the arms of John Bull after being saved from the impending anarchy of the Urabi revolt. Egypt's gratitude for Brit-

JANUARY 27, 1883.] PUNCH, OR THE LONDON

MUCH BETTER!

Dr. Dufferin (to his Egyptian Patient). " HERE, MY 'INTERESTING' CONVALES-
CENT, YOU WILL FIND THIS SMALL STAFF MORE SERVICEABLE TO YOU THAN
THOSE OLD CRUTCHES!"

Figure 4.2. Due to Egypt's desperate financial situation, Khedive Ismail sought assistance from the European powers. In 1876 they established the Caisse de la dette publique; as part of this arrangement, the "Dual Control" — two comptrollers, one British, the other French, who oversaw state revenues and expenditures — was created. With the British occupation of Egypt in 1882 — an occupation predicated on, among other things, concern that Egypt was incapable of repaying its loans — British advisers began to oversee Egypt's financial affairs. In this cartoon Egypt, depicted as a convalescent, expresses its gratitude to the British. (Reproduced from *Punch,* January 27, 1883, with permission of Punch, Ltd.)

ain's financial assistance was represented by crocodiles posing as begging dogs and happy to receive the medicine that Rothschild financiers provided (figures 4.3 and 4.4).

Similarly, Egypt's subordination, following the commencement of the British occupation, was not lost on Egyptian satirists. In 1883 Yaqub Sannu', publisher of *Abu Naddara Zurqa*, featured a cartoon of Egypt's newfound subordination to the British. In this caricature, occupied Egypt (the khedive Tawfiq) groveled at the feet of Lord Dufferin, beseeching him for assistance (figure 4.5).

In the same way that Egypt was depicted as a beggar in cartoons, for Europeans, specifically for the British in the late nineteenth century, beggars became a trope for Egypt and its poverty in many other publications. The spectacle of the poor, their pestering public presence, their "diseased" nature, and their beseeching cries of "baksheesh" were aspects of Egypt that European tourists and residents had come to expect. Egypt's poor were featured in travel guides: their images built on nearly a century of travel writing and, by the end of the nineteenth century, their depiction entailed, much like *Punch*'s criticisms of Egypt's rulers and finances, a focus on the benevolent role of outsiders, particularly Britain, in improving Egypt.

Travel guides routinely included warnings about the large number of beggars who assailed tourists throughout Egypt. Such depictions fitted into established tropes of Egypt's poverty and the omnipresence of the poor. As this chapter will demonstrate, European tourists and residents of Egypt frequently came into contact—and *expected* to come into contact—with beggars. In some cases, they tried desperately to avoid them, seeking refuge from their cries in the comfort of the Thomas Cook steamers.[2] In other instances, they gave alms and made contributions to numerous missionary and other charitable organizations in Egypt.

Whatever the extent of their real interactions with the poor, tourists arrived in Egypt prepared for any contact. In published guides they learned that begging was a "favourite" occupation in Cairo and that "[v]ery little food and raiment are necessary in this climate, and starvation is a thing almost unheard of. Blind people, and those on whom nature has bestowed some disfigurement of person, are certain of gaining a subsistence by begging."[3] The guidebooks also instructed tourists on how to deal with beggars:

Sir Gardner Wilkinson has justly observed that the cry Bakshish, bakshish ya khawagah (oh sir! a gift!), with which Europeans are invariably assailed, is an insulting substitute for the good-day of other countries. The Arab reserves his pious benedictions for his own countrymen, but never hesitates to take advantage of what he considers the folly of foreign travelers. The

"SAFE!"

JOHN BULL, A.B. "LOR' BLESS YOU, MY DEARS, YOU NEEDN'T WORRIT YOURSELVES. I'LL LOOK AFTER
'IM AS IF HE WAS MY OWN CHILD!"

Figure 4.3. In the years following the cotton boom of the 1860s, growing numbers of European investors and businessmen came to Egypt. Egyptian frustration concerning the privileges these foreigners enjoyed, coupled with anger toward unfair promotion practices in the military and animosity toward Egypt's new khedive, Tawfiq—installed by the British in 1879—resulted in a widespread rebellion known as the Urabi revolt. Afraid that this movement would threaten Britain's hold on Egypt and its access to the Suez Canal, of which Britain was a principal shareholder, and would result in the creation of a gov-

best reply to such applications is ma fish, ma fish (I have nothing for you), which will generally have the effect of dispersing the assailants. Or the beggar may be silenced with the words "Allah ya'tik" (May God give thee).[4]

Even advertisements for Egypt's health resorts in Helwan, just south of Cairo, included discussions of how European visitors should respond to beggars. The author of *Helouan: An Egyptian Health Resort* discouraged the giving of "baksheesh," because giving one coin would inevitably lead to more entreaties. The government of Egypt, he noted, had issued "earnest appeals" requesting that visitors not heed beggars' requests.[5]

The information provided in these guidebooks (whether on the climate, cities, transportation, historic treasures, hotels and living arrangements, or prices) prepared tourists for what to expect when they arrived in Egypt. These succinct guidebooks were portable and, like guides of today, were passed around from tourist to tourist. Yet visitors shared lore and information they had gathered from other sources as well. Their perceptions of Egypt and its people — even before they opened Baedeker's or Murray's — were colored by the writings of travelers and residents who had gone before them. These portrayals of Egypt's poor were repeated in subsequent publications, to the point that the poor, their condition, and the reasons for their poverty became a preconceived entity.

In his analysis of the portrayals of poverty in Calcutta, John Hutnyk remarks that "a politics of poverty" is "rehearsed" through the casual discourse of travelers (their conceptions mirroring guidebooks that have already "enframed" the poor) as well as in novels, monographs, and travel literature.[6] A "politics of *Egypt's* poverty" — represented first in the early nineteenth century in travel literature and re-represented in varying ways throughout that century and into the next — also succeeded in creating a "known" entity, or spectacle, of the poor (and their public presence) as well as recognizable tropes of Egypt's inability to manage its own finances (as represented by Egypt's street-peddler khedive) and care for its poor.

Although the poor were ubiquitous in European descriptions of Egypt,

---

ernment hostile to the repayment of Egypt's loans, the British invaded Egypt. The British "occupation" would last until 1952, with the last British troops removed from the Canal Zone in 1956. This cartoon, reminiscent of the pharaoh's daughter's rescue of the baby Moses, shows that Britain has assumed responsibility for the safety and well-being of this infant (the Suez Canal). Surrounding John Bull are wet nurses dressed in the national costumes of other European countries. (Reproduced from *Punch*, September 2, 1882, with permission of Punch, Ltd.)

LORD DE ROTHSCHILD'S EGYPTIAN SOOTHING-SYRUP.   FEEDING-TIME; A LITTLE TREAT ALL ROUND.

Figure 4.4. Egypt (as begging crocodiles) receiving medicine from creditors. While the crocodiles' smiles reflect Egypt's gratitude, their bared teeth also represent the dangers that European creditors' and governments' involvement posed there. Such fears held particular resonance for the British public following the death of the famed General Charles George Gordon in the Sudan in January 1885. (Reproduced from *Punch*, August 8, 1885, with permission of Punch, Ltd.)

by the beginning of the twentieth century, the nature of discussions of who the poor were as well as who should be held responsible for them, had changed. The word *poor* came to mean primarily women and children, and the obligation to provide for them was the domain not only of Egypt's government but of private philanthropy as well. A "politics of Egypt's poverty" became essential to how the British, as a colonial power, saw their role in Egypt and how European residents there found

Figure 4.5. Depictions of the Egyptians when Europe treated them with respect and, following the British occupation, when Egyptians were subordinate to Europeans. The satirical journal *Abu Naddara Zurqa* was critical of European imperialism and Khedive Tawfiq's policies. (Reproduced from *Abu Naddara al-Zurqa*, March 4, 1883, courtesy of Princeton University Library.)

opportunities to introduce their own philanthropic and medical projects. Whereas British medical personnel and residents in Egypt depicted Egypt's poor as a nuisance and a source of disease, by the early twentieth century, Egypt's philanthropists came to portray care for the poor in a different light: as a national duty.

Depictions of Egypt's Poor in the Era
Preceding the British Occupation

Guidebooks were essential for travelers to acquire knowledge about the country they were planning to visit. These texts became available for visitors to Egypt after 1847, when the publisher John Murray invited the Egyptologist Sir Gardner Wilkinson to write the first guide to Egypt.[7] Two other guides, Baedeker's *Egypt* and *Egypt and the Sudan*, went through seven editions between 1878 and 1914.

Yet books other than travel guides also provided extensive information on Egypt's history and culture and served as important resources for travelers and the writers of guidebooks. Lane's *Manners and Customs of the Modern Egyptian* and similar books were read by and shared among travelers such as Duff Gordon.[8] The information these texts provided enframed Egypt in a particular fashion that, in turn, colored travelers perceptions.[9] Travelers to Egypt might have arrived with preconceived notions of what to expect, but not all of them left with the same impressions. Living among Egyptians (Duff Gordon, for example, lived in Egypt for seven years) and learning Arabic gave Europeans insights that built on and, in some ways, corrected these preconceptions. However, many travelers employed the same tropes and ideas repeatedly, and visits to places of interest (such as, for example, Cairo's insane asylums located in the Maristan and later in a converted warehouse in Bulaq) included in their itinerary became a part of their commentary. In their portrayals of Egypt's poor and insane, European visitors focused on two concepts: the omnipresence of Egypt's indigent in public spaces and the lack of regard that Egyptians and their government had for the poor and others in desperate need. These portrayals lasted well into the early twentieth century as visitors, medical doctors, missionaries, and statesmen repeated similar litanies.

When describing Cairo's public spaces, those traveling to Egypt in the first half of the nineteenth century frequently mentioned presence of the poor. William Yates, a British medical doctor, related how the streets were full of "water carriers, peddlers, beggars, saints, and women, naked children grubbing in the dirt, charm vendors . . . fakirs, lepers, jugglers and mountebanks, all passing and repassing in pursuit of their particular business."[10] Cleanliness in Cairo "is altogether disregarded . . . there are so many disgusting sights, and so much sickness, blindness, and real misery."[11] Although, as Yates pointed out, Muhammad Ali had made many improvements in Cairo—such as widening the streets and encouraging public hygiene—he had done nothing for the insane. Yates noted that "not withstanding the talked of doings of Clot Bey on medical subjects," little was being done to alleviate the conditions in the Maristan Qalawun, which housed the insane as well as the indigent at the time of his visit.[12] Using his discussion of the lack of care for the insane, the aged, and the poor as a means for launching a broader condemnation of the despotism of Muhammad Ali's rule in Egypt, Yates mirrored the perceptions of other British residents and statesmen who vilified Muhammad Ali's actions. Such critiques also reflected British animosity toward the French (as represented by Clot Bey) and emphasized that Christian countries guaranteed (in addition to providing protection through their law and systems of justice) care for the sick, destitute, and insane.[13]

For political purposes, Yates intended to contrast Egypt's treatment of the insane and poor with their treatment in Christian countries. Other authors also frequently highlighted the state of Egypt's poor, attributing, like Yates, their poverty to Muhammad Ali's conscription policies and economic projects: Edward Lane remarked that conscription had forced men who lost their sons to resort to begging to survive; Bayle St. John noted that conscription had increased the number of paupers in the cities; and James August St. John claimed that many women had turned to prostitution during their husbands' absence. Many British observers argued that economic desperation forced parents to sell their children and that the monopoly system had led to government-created famines.[14] Madden and other travelers also asserted that conscription had emptied whole villages of their inhabitants.[15]

Such descriptions of decimation, noted by observers of the actions of Egypt's subsequent governors, continued throughout the nineteenth century. Bayle St. John and Jerome von Crowins Smith pointed to the continued effect that conscription in the 1850s had on Egyptian families, as well as to the impoverishment of the peasantry owing to taxation policies. W. H. Bartlett noted how the presence of a large number of blind people throughout Egypt was attributable to conscription policies and remarked that poverty emerged out of the arbitrary taxes imposed on the peasantry.[16] In later decades, the corvée system was also targeted as a cause of destitution.[17]

Cultural traits where also given as an explanation for the suffering and destitution of Egypt's inhabitants. Egyptians' superstitions were allegedly the reason behind unsanitary habits such as their lack of cleanliness.[18] In Europeans' nineteenth-century depictions of Egypt's poverty, similar descriptions are offered repeatedly. Although Marsot argued that the negative commentaries about Muhammad Ali emerged within the context of British industrial competition with and contempt for Muhammad Ali's policies, their continued use illustrates that such representations were not confined to Muhammad Ali's reign but fitted into a larger literary genre that served to distinguish the (despotic) Orient from the (enlightened) West.[19]

Travelers and residents admonished the Egyptian government for its impoverishing economic practices, such as taxation policies, conscription, and corvée, and they condemned the government for its neglect of the insane. Their remarks on the latter confirmed that Egypt's rulers were oblivious to the suffering of Egypt's most destitute and needy. The Maristan Qalawun and subsequent buildings used to confine the insane were frequently the object of European condemnations. After a visit to the Maristan in 1826, R. R. Madden remarked that the "poor wretches within were chained by the neck to the bars of the grated windows. The keeper went round as he would do in a menagerie of wild beasts, rattling the chain at the windows to rouse the inmates, and dragging them by it when they were tardy in approaching." Madden tried to persuade "the keeper" to introduce more humane treatment, but his advice was ignored.[20] Visiting the Maristan in the 1830s, J. A. St. John acknowledged that madhouses were terrifying anywhere in the world but that "nowhere, perhaps, on earth, can anything so terrible, so disgusting, be witnessed as the madhouse of Cairo, where, as may be certainly inferred from the ferocious aspect of the keepers, and appearance of the victims, lacerated and covered with wounds, scenes of cruelty and suffering occur not elsewhere exhibited out of hell. "[21] J. Moureau noted how all of the insane, regardless of their degree of insanity, were chained in the Maristan. Yates, visiting this institution at approximately the same time, likened the Maristan to a prison because all of the insane were kept in cells. The indigent, who were kept in other sections of the building, "were to be seen crawling about, or declining despondingly, on the bare stones."[22] Sophia Lane Poole, who visited the Maristan while touring mosques in the area, also commented on the conditions in which its inmates were kept, noting that the insane had more than enough to eat thanks to government provisions and food donations provided by visitors to the asylum. Like Moureau and Yates, however, Lane Poole remarked on the "wretchedness" of the institution but hoped, with the insane's imminent transfer to another institution (the Civilian Hospital of Azbakiyya), that their situation would improve.[23]

Other than accounts by Clot Bey, we do not have details of the conditions of the insane in the Civilian Hospital; but visitors to an institution that was renovated to house former residents of the Civilian Hospital described their treatment there as still inadequate.[24] The only exception to the numerous negative descriptions is an account by W. H. Bartlett. In the late 1840s, Bartlett visited the new asylum in Bulaq and noted that "thanks to European influences upon the naturally humane feelings of Muhammad Ali, [it] has replaced the old 'Morostan,' with its horrors, which was so long a standing subject for description with Egyptian tourists."[25] Within thirty years, however, visitors noted that the inmates there were again in a wretched state.[26] Medical doctors A. R. Urquhart and Grant, who visited in the late 1870s, remarked on the absence of trained physicians and attendants, the presence of "decaying" bedding, and the continued use of chains for some inmates. Grant and Urquhart estimated the number of inmates at 250, though their translator guessed that the number was substantially higher, between 500 or 1000. Dr. William liam Samuel Tuke, visiting the asylum one year later was better able to assess the population in this institution, fixing its number at 200; he was also much more forgiving of the attempts that Dr. Muhammad Tagroi, the principal medical officer, made to care for the insane. Budgetary constraints, explained Tagroi, limited efforts to effect improvements. Like his grandfather William Tuke, an English philanthropist devoted to improving facilities for the insane, W. S. Tuke was interested in the construction of hospitals for the insane and in promoting care without excessive physical restraints. Some of W. S. Tuke's questions for Tagroi regarded the use of restraints. On his visit to the asylum in 1878, he was told that the only restraints employed were strait waistcoats.[27]

When told about the relatively low number of insane people housed in Cairo's asylums, nineteenth-century European visitors reported that harmless lunatics were allowed to "go at large."[28] Similar observations were made during the British occupation, when the freedom afforded to the "quiet" insane was looked upon with scorn rather than being perceived as the degree of tolerance with which the insane were accepted in the society at large. During that period, the presence of the insane in the public spaces of Egypt's cities was considered indicative of the lack of care provided to the insane by their own families.

The frequency with which travelers made reference to the poor and the ease with which travellers entered institutions such as the insane asylums of Cairo speak to a particular privilege enjoyed by European men and women who had the freedom to transgress the boundaries between the public and private realms. The insane asylum was included in Wilkinson's 1847 travel guide for Egypt, suggesting that visiting this institution was considered feasible for tourists arriving even for a brief time.[29] Like the women and men of London's West End who easily crossed the boundaries between the rich and the poor, travelers to Egypt commented on the activities of a group of people whom they identified as belonging to a separate category of humans. As the upper classes in Victorian England set forth their own ideas about how the poor could best learn to improve themselves, travelers to Egypt arrived with fixed ideas about the proper care of the poor and appropriate treatments for the insane.[30]

Instead of directing their critiques toward the poor themselves, travelers to Egypt criticized the government for its despotism, its conscription policies and corvée, and its lack of regard for the poor and needy. Such criticism largely implied an inability of Muslims to care for their own poor. Frequently, as visitors to the insane asylums of the Maristan Qalawun and Bulaq noted, it was only thanks to Christian countries' interventions (for example, at the urging of Clot Bey) that the insane of Egypt received better treatment.

Yet travelers to Egypt in the era preceding the British occupation recognized that *private* charity also existed; they saw that care for the poor was an important feature of Islam. Von Crowins Smith noted that "[a]ll systems of religion enjoin alms giving. Charity is encouraged in Egypt, and the pious in their lifetime, often make provision for the necessities of the poor."[31] Whatever large charitable endowments had previously existed had been usurped by greedy managers or by the government, according to Europeans' descriptions.[32] Western travelers holding Egypt's government and rulers responsible for the treatment of its poor and insane, identifying religious endowments as sites of corruption and abuse, and alluding to the civilized manner in which those in need were cared for in Christian countries launched specific condemnations against Islamic forms of charity and the actions of Egypt's Islamic government. In their remarks on the lack of care for the poor in the years following 1882, however, visitors redirected their criticism away from a sole focus on the government toward censure of Egypt's upper classes, berating them for not assuming responsibility for the poor. Prior to the British occupation, European travelers recognized the potential role Christian countries could play in improving the conditions of the Egyptian poor. During the occupation, when they criticized Egypt's upper classes for shirking their obligations toward the poor, British officials and residents in Egypt made a place for themselves as promoters of philanthropy.

Inherent in the pre-1882 condemnation of the Egyptian government's inability to take care of its own populace was a more profound critique of Egyptians' ability to govern themselves. Compounded by the government's bankruptcy and the Urabi revolt, this notion helped pave the way for the British occupation of Egypt.[33] Although modern scholars acknowledge the racism in the comments of European observers such as Yates, we cannot entirely disregard these critiques. Their portrayals of Egypt must be read with an eye toward the political impact the commentaries were intended to have in diplomatic circles and among private citizens; but they are also valuable in other ways. First, read alongside archival materials (and corroborating these materials, as Fahmy has done),[34] they enrich our understanding of social history, for they give readers descriptions of what indigenous people living in that period saw as ordinary and unnoteworthy. Second, read as a historical record, the descriptions of foreign observers show how particular tropes of Egypt — such as the lack of cleanliness and poverty — became so internalized that they came to be expressed repeatedly in travel writing.

During the nineteenth century, the perceptions travelers had of Egypt's poor built on preconceived notions of the country and its population. On their arrival in Egypt, tourists visited its ancient monuments and, in addition to describing the sites they visited, provided commentary on the inhabitants of the cities and rural areas, frequently remarking on their impoverished state. Contributions made by the tourist agency Thomas Cook and Son, together with fees charged to tourists designated for the restoration of numerous historic monuments, ensured that Egypt would remain an "open air" museum for Westerners. Boxes next to monuments into which charitable donations to the poor — themselves an "attraction" — were placed appealed to tourists' humanitarian impulses.[35] Yet these contributions simultaneously confirmed the tourists' moral and economic superiority and echoed portrayals of Egypt's dependency as represented in the satirical journal *Punch*.[36]

Egypt as "Diseased": Perceptions of Egypt Following the British Occupation

Humanitarian ideas about the treatment of the insane in England (where, beginning in the late eighteenth century, restraints in some asylums were no longer used) colored the perspectives of travelers to Egypt who visited the insane asylums in the Maristan and in Bulaq. The comparisons they made between treatment in Egypt and treatment in England reinforced attitudes about the superiority of Western methods of care. Visitors' portrayals of the Egyptian government's lack of interest in the poor contributed to Europeans' notions about the inability of Egyptians to govern themselves or care for their own poor.

Similar perceptions were introduced within a discourse on the "diseased" conditions of Egypt which emerged in the aftermath of the British occupation in 1882. Just as criticisms about the treatment of the insane or ideas about Western superiority must be understood within the context of the development of humanitarian and empire-centered ideas in Europe, notions of sanitation and cleanliness that the British brought to Egypt emerged out of movements and discussions in England concerning fears of infection, cholera, and the role of the poor in spreading disease. Whereas in England these anxieties were played out the poorer sections of major cities, in Egypt they were transposed to the country as a whole.

Ironically, at the same time that Egypt was being portrayed as diseased, growing numbers of middle-class Europeans, including many British citizens, were traveling to Egypt to experience what they considered a healthy climate. British citizens wintered or resided there year-round. Thomas Cook and Son described Cairo as a winter suburb of London, and they advertised the city as "the chosen winter playground for the whole fashionable world."[37] Many Europeans came specifically to health resorts and *maisons de Santé* (houses of health). Every year more than six thousand and as many as eight thousand "searchers after health and pleasure" visited Cairo.[38]

The fact that Egypt could serve as a "first rate health resort" for Europeans even though it was portrayed as a site of disease for Egyptians was due to the gift of climate, according to *The Lancet*; yet "[m]an has, on the other hand, done but little to improve and much to diminish . . . these climatic advantages." Overcrowded and unsanitary towns, villages, and dwellings, together with a lack of colonial expenditures for the Egyptian Department of Public Health and "ignorance and indifference of the population to all matters of hygiene," resulted in the unhealthy conditions prevalent in Egypt.[39] An unspecified but "well known medical work" published in 1911 labeled Cairo as one of "the most unsanitary spots in the world."[40] Diseases abounded because of the unsanitary conditions of the country and the purported absence of government investment in public health projects. The importance of ensuring the health of Egypt's population *should be* the concern of health professionals and the British government, for, as Andrew Balfour, the former president of the Egyptian public health commission and director of the Wellcome Bureau of Scientific Research, stated, Egypt was "the hub of the wheel of Empire" and acted as a great filter, protecting Europe from the diseases of the East.[41]

Medical practitioners writing for *The Lancet* were critical of British colonial officials' meager expenditures on public health projects. Yet in occupying Egypt with the ostensible intention of "balancing the books," colonial officials constantly struggled to show how cost-efficiently they could operate in Egypt and were compelled to assuage the British publics and parliamentary members' fears that the British commitment to Egypt would be too costly. Trimming the Egyptian government's budget early in the British occupation required disengagement from as many public welfare programs as possible and a shift in the appropriation of a greater part of the responsibility for education, medical assistance, and other social welfare programs to private organizations. Lord Cromer, the consul general of Egypt from 1883 to 1907, noted that the need for medical facilities was indeed acute, but he emphasized that the funds for such institutions were unavailable. In an 1895 report, he remarked that "[d]emands are now constantly made for the creation of new dispensaries and hospitals throughout the country, and it is a matter of the deepest regret that the resources of the (Sanitary) Department should be so limited as to prevent these demands being complied with."[42] A larger outlay of money for public health and educational facilities was budgeted only after the first years of the occupation when investments had been made in hydraulic engineering and agriculture, intended to be profitable to the state coffers, European investors, and the Egyptian elite.[43]

Thus, British colonial officials keep expenditures in Egypt at a minimum so that those critical of the occupation would have less ammunition for their grievances. This is not to say that the British did not undertake any reform efforts whatsoever. In fact, they focused on a number of programs deemed essential to maintaining stability. As Tignor has argued, discussions of the Egyptian question in the British press and in Parliament remained contentious, and colonial officials attempted to keep Egypt "calm" to avoid drawing attention to it.[44] During their first years in Egypt, the British directed their reform efforts toward programs that would immediately ensure order and security, specifically the courts, the police, and the military.[45] Relying on his experiences in India, where "low taxation is the panacea for British rule," Lord Cromer endeavored to reduce the land tax and other financial obligations of the Egyptian peasantry to prevent them from becoming a "dangerous" class.[46] Tignor notes that British health professionals and contributors to *The Lancet* and the *British Medical Journal* urged colonial officials in Egypt to work toward improving public health. However, only after the appointment of Horatio Herbert Kitchener as proconsul of Egypt and after Egypt had reached financial solvency were greater expenditures made in public health.[47] Even in the initial years of the occupation, however, some money was spent on public health and numerous improvements were made in health care provision and the care of the insane.[48] Paying attention to health care, according to one British observer, could win the gratitude of the Egyptian populace.[49]

British budgetary priorities, shaped by colonial experiences in other areas of British Empire, also had a negative impact on education. Cromer, for example, chose not to foster education, based on his experiences in India, where nationalist feelings had emerged among the educated class.[50] In response to insufficient educational opportunities, as will be discussed in greater length in the next chapter, members of Egypt's population joined together to create free educational opportunities for students and dispense scholarships.

From the perspective of the British, insufficient finances were partly to blame for the unsanitary and diseased conditions in Egypt; but this situation was also were the fault of the Egyptians themselves.[51] Here, Egypt's financial mismanagement and dependence on the British to provide a "walking stick" (a financial adviser) and the Egyptian population's dependence on British medical expertise overlap. All classes of Egyptians, in the view of *The Lancet*'s Egypt correspondent, were "indescribably dirty in their houses and their habits and have not yet learned the rudiments of domestic sanitation."[52] Children's eye diseases were the fault of Egyptian mothers who were indifferent to flies and allowed infected children to sleep with the uninfected ones.[53] The health of the Egyptian populace, remarked Andrew Balfour, the director-in-chief of the Wellcome Bureau of Scientific Research and the former president of the Egyptian Public Health Commission, would have to depend on British medical personnel, for it was "hopeless to expect a disease-ridden people to play their proper part in furthering the welfare of their country."[54] One British medical observer, noted that the extent of diseases in the country caused a "shocking waste of life and waste of labour" and that he was "not sanguine enough to believe that the native in the country can be persuaded, or taught, or induced within many generations, to observe European ideas of cleanliness."[55]

Some health officials did believe that the Egyptian population could be taught the importance of cleanliness. They argued that Egyptians had great respect for British health practitioners, who could keep them docile during epidemics and similar health crises.[56] British public health officials argued that although it may be difficult to educate mothers and adults about hygiene, like European children who "took the gospel of cleanliness" back to their parents, Egyptian children who were "docile, receptive, and imitative" could be taught to keep their eyes clean and trained in other hygienic practices.[57] The "backward civilization" and ignorance of Egyptians, especially evident in the high rate of infant mortality, could also be easily addressed through the introduction of maternity schools and children's dispensaries.[58] *The Lancet* described infant mortality—one in three children died before the age of one—as a "holocaust," which in "civilized times" could not be allowed to continue.[59]

Egyptians, particularly women and children, respected British health professionals (a point that Duff Gordon remarked on as well) and came to British-established clinics and dispensaries "fearlessly." Correspondents writing for *The Lancet*, as well as colonial reports on policies in Egypt, accentuated the Egyptian populace's "growing willingness to go to hospitals," the fact that the "native populace appreciated the advantages of hospital treatment," and that ophthalmic hospitals had "secured the confidence of the Muhammadan population."[60]

Health authorities also called attention to the improvements they were making in the insane asylums of Cairo, frequently contrasting their actions and practices to the conditions of the asylums prior to the occupation. They depicted changes made in the care of the insane as bringing civilization to Egypt. John Warnock, director of the Abbasiyya insane asylum, who improved the ventilation into the principal building and employed inmates in such activities as gardening and carpentry, was described as carrying out a "peaceful revolution."[61] Reports on the progress made in public health and medicine noted that the period of British rule had witnessed the eradication of the use of chains and mechanical restraints in the principal insane asylum of Abbasiyya, the separation of the "dangerous" insane from the "quiet" insane, and more conscientious care.

Time and again, Egyptians were found guilty of neglect and abuse of those in need. Families themselves were to blame they neglected them at home or subjected them to torture, and they allowed insane family members to go "adrift" in the streets.[62] Regulations, not the Egyptians' sympathy for the insane, accounted for Britain's success in "civilizing" Egypt. Warnock remarked that overcrowding in the Abbasiyya asylum and the construction of an additional asylum in Khanqa were indicative not of growing numbers of insane persons but rather of a "growing civilization, for public policy now demands that more and more potentially dangerous lunatics shall be detained in the asylum instead of allowing them to be continually discharged and readmitted."[63]

The discourse about public health and medicine served to affirm the racial and medical superiority of the British and to accentuate the necessity of the British presence in Egypt.[64] Accounts of health conditions in Egypt emphasized diseases and infections as the key features of the rural and urban landscape. Unlike advertisements portraying Egypt as a health resort, in discussions of mortality rates, sanitation in the urban and rural areas, and inadequate and unhygienic public health facilities, shortcomings were attributed to Egyptian ignorance. Just as Egypt's khedive had been portrayed as as devoid of sound financial management skills, Egyptians were seen as lacking an understanding of the rudiments of medicine, the importance of supplying clean drinking water and providing adequate means to drain sewage, or using any preventive measures for fighting infection and disease. British medical specialists and colonial officials blamed the lack of concern with cleanliness on Egypt's "diseased" nature, its "backward civilization," and its "poverty and ignorance." Colonial officials, medical personnel, and members of charitable organizations emphasized that "teaching" the Egyptians about "civilized" sanitation and hygiene (much like "teaching" the lower classes of Britain about these issues) should be part of their reforming and civilizing mission in Egypt.[65]

Egyptians' Indifference to the Poor

British colonial officials and medical personnel in Egypt condemned the inadequacy of so-called traditional forms of medical care in Egypt, asserting that Britain had brought progress and health to Egypt. British health officials, such as Dr. Bonté Sheldon Elgood, medical officer of the Ministry of Education, were condemnatory towards native practices of health care, noting that the high infant mortality role was due to women's insistence on seeing native *hakima*s (female medical specialists) and *daya*s (midwives), whose training and practice were not supervised by the British.[66] They also belittled the existence of indigenous institutions established to care for the poor, both claiming that none existed, *and* arguing that those in place were inadequate. Those considered most culpable for Egypt's lack of care for the poor were officials in the Ministry of Religious Endowments, who "did their utmost" to obstruct progress.[67] The Takaya of Tura and Qabbari, which became the responsibility of the Ministry of Religious Endowments, were criticized as being insalubrious, with their residents being kept in dismal conditions. Remarking on the 1893 report of the Egyptian Sanitary Department, *The Lancet* described Takiyyat Tura as being in a "wretched" condition, emphasizing that "[t]he condition of this 'Te-Kia' [*sic*] . . . is enough to show us what care the Egyptians take of their co-religionists, and we tremble to think what would be the conditions of the hospitals of the country if it were not for the handful of English medical men attached to the sanitary service of Egypt."[68] A correspondent for *The Lancet*, visiting Takiyyat Tura in 1902, noted a marked improvement in the shelter compared with its condition in 1884. In 1884, the inmates were "half-starved, and sometimes put in chains," and one man had been reported as walking "stark naked" among the women in the shelter. Yet, the correspondent noted by 1902, some improvements had been made. A new hospital had been built, replacing a series of huts that had sheltered the poor, and unmarried patients were separated from one another by gender.[69]

Numerous accounts in the annual reports of the consuls general accused the khedive and members of the Ministry of Religious Endowments of misappropriating funds. The poor cared for through the ministry's institutions, consequently, allegedly suffered neglect.[70] In writing of the medical services provided by this office, Sir Valentine Chirol noted that since the Department of Public Health "has no rights of inspection over these institutions, one can only infer from the meagre pittances allowed to them that they form no exception to the general rule of inefficiency and worse for which the Wakf [*sic*] administration is notorious amongst Egyptians themselves."[71]

Concerns about waqf mismanagement were not limited to the period of the British occupation. Prior to its centralization in 1851, the management of individual awqafs had already been the object of criticism; institutions funded through endowments frequently fell into disrepair owing to the negligence of their supervisors (*nazir/nuzara*). Rulers in the central Ottoman lands, like those of Egypt, struggled to ensure efficiency and combat graft.[72]

During the British occupation, charges of corruption and the inadequacy of facilities leveled at the Ministry of Religious Endowments represented issues of public health, but they also reflected a struggle between Egypt's khedive and British comptrollers. Accusations of endowment mismanagement and decrepit facilities were as much about the struggle between Muslims seeking to maintain control over a religious (and pious) institution as they were about real concerns about public health. From the British perspective, as long as the khedive maintained control over this office, he could use its funds for his own ends. During Abbas Hilmi's rule (1892–1914), waqf profits were directed toward political purposes, including the nationalist cause. Such actions proved to be the death knell for Egypt's attempts to maintain absolute control over this ministry. During Kitchener's rule as proconsul — a reign that included much tighter restrictions on the Egyptians, particularly Egyptian nationalist activities — the British finally succeeded in wresting control this office.[73]

Despite the criticisms leveled against it, under Egyptian management the Ministry of Religious Endowments had been prolific in its attempts to assist the poor in Cairo, Mecca, and Medina. It shouldered numerous financial and administrative responsibilities in areas of poor relief and medical care. The poor shelters of Mecca and Medina, which the ministry helped finance, provided food and shelter for nearly 6,000 people in one year alone: 4,000 were cared for during the months of the Hajj, and 2,000 in the remaining eight months.[74] This office also administered two shelters in Cairo: Takiyyat Tura, established in 1884 and intended to provide shelter to up to 300 persons, and Takiyyat Abdin, established in 1904 and providing shelter for 30 single women. In Alexandria, Takiyyat al-Qabbari, another shelter under the ministry's management, contained 120 beds for men and women.[75] Throughout Cairo and the provinces of Egypt, clinics funded and run by the Ministry of Religious Endowments treated 105,916 patients in just over one year (1906–1907). From October 1906 through December 1907, the ophthalmic clinic at Qalawun had 64,463 patients, the Mustashfa al-Azhar (Hospital of al-Azhar) had 8,128, the Mustashfa Manshiya had 28,739, the Ayada Bulaq (Clinic of Bulaq) had 18,902, the Ayada Misr al-Qadima (Old Cairo) had 21,975, the Ayada Tanta had 2,870, and the Ayada Iskandariyya 843.[76] Under British control, this ministry also financed and administered an orphanage, located in Bab al-Luq, Cairo, which provided beds for 96 boys and 35 girls. In the orphanage, the children received elementary education; boys were trained in trades, and girls were taught cooking, ironing, and sewing.[77]

Alongside British condemnations of the actions (or lack of actions) of the Ministry of Religious Endowments, Egypt's elite were portrayed as being unresponsive to the needs of poor Egyptians, particularly in private philanthropy. Combined with ideas of the absence of Egyptian initiatives in health care and sanitary efforts, perspectives on indigenous forms of health care and poor relief served to justify the necessity of a continued British presence in Egypt. The American writer Elizabeth Cooper noted how "[t]he question of almsgiving is very great in all Moslem lands. One-twentieth of a man's income is to be given to charity, yet there are no organized charities in Egypt, no poorhouses, no homes for the aged, nor the sick, nor the insane."[78] Sir Valentine Chirol, writing on Egyptians' desire for freedom from British rule, portrayed the Egyptians as unfit for independence since, among other reasons, they had no sense of social duty to their fellow Egyptians. Chirol claimed that philanthropy was "almost unknown" among the Egyptian educated classes and, using as an example the large number of street children in Cairo, argued that only through British rule and the examples set by missionaries did Egyptians understand the importance of caring for their children.[79] Cooper echoed this perception of indigenous philanthropy:

> It is only lately that women seem to be awakening to their social obligations, regarding their unfortunate sisters, in activities other than the sending of food or the dropping of money into outstretched hands. To-day in Cairo, a band of generous women are carrying on a home for helpless women and babies, the patronesses of which are members of the well known and influential families of Egypt.[80]

Lord Cromer recounted how the princesses in the Khedival family established this society for the protection of infant life (the Mabarat Muhammad Ali), "taking their lead" from the initiative of founders of the Lady Cromer Dispensary.[81]

Within the medical discourse about the unhealthiness of Egyptians, even the upper classes were targeted as not knowing the rudiments of health care; yet by the early twentieth century, writers for *The Lancet* began to recognize the important role the upper classes could play in disseminating information about health and diseases.

In many realms, British medical professionals had reason to deplore the lack of proper medical services available to Egyptians. Since the late 1850s, the Egyptian government had made less of an investment in this field and the quality of care might have diminished.[82] The quality of services may well have suffered, but the government did not entirely ignore the medical or poor-relief needs of Egyptians. As will be discussed in the next chapter, philanthropy was already an important aspect of various religious communities' programs and was increasingly, in the early twentieth century, coming to be the domain of multireligious and multiethnic associations as well. Egypt's philanthropists, in part responding to European critiques of negligence toward the poor, but also grounding their actions in religious traditions, appeared center stage at this time.

Whose Responsibility Are the Poor?

Queried by James Galloway Weir about the extent of services provided for orphans and the destitute of Egypt, Under-Secretary of State for Foreign Affairs Earl Percy denied the need for such services:

Lord Cromer has reported that the Mussulman [sic] religious foundations in Egypt dispose of considerable revenues for the maintenance of the poor and aged, and large sums are granted yearly by the Mussulman Benevolent Society. There is also a foundling home which receives children irrespective of creed, and various religious communities have funds devoted to the relief of the poor. There is, at present, no need of any further institutions of this character.[83]

Lord Cromer, colonial officials, and numerous travelers to Egypt such as Cooper, Chirol, and medical correspondents writing for *The Lancet*, however, denied the existence of private philanthropies such as the Muslim Benevolent Society in their accounts of Egyptian's inability to care for the poor. At the same time, they criticized the care that Egyptian institutions provided to the indigent. But when questioned by members of Parliament, Percy argued that the poor-relief facilities were adequate. However, contrary to his claims, there was clearly a need for institutions to provide poor relief during the late nineteenth and early twentieth centuries. Institutions for the blind, infirm, and elderly had to turn away people who petitioned for assistance. Insane asylums often had to discharge the "quiet" insane to the streets.[84]

Although medical correspondents for *The Lancet* and public health commissioner in Cairo were critical of the Ministry of Religious Endowments, they also frequently looked to this office to assist in caring for the poor. For example, in 1918 Warnock, the director of the Abbasiyya asylum, requested that this office assume responsibility for the quiet insane when other Egyptian government facilities proved inadequate, and the Department of Public Health called upon the Ministry of Religious Endowments to take charge of creating more almshouses for the elderly and others in dire circumstances. The growing number of people in need of assistance, he argued, only swelled the numbers of beggars, who became "foci of infection."[85]

The Ministry of Religious Endowments' efforts in poor relief were broad ranging, yet they were insufficient. Cities such as Cairo were faced with a growing public presence of the poor (particularly during World War I), and, most alarmingly, in the eyes of Egyptian and European philanthropists, the number of street children was increasing rapidly. Although British colonial officials recognized their responsibility to deal with matters of public health—as indicated, for example, by their concerns about conditions in asylums and infant mortality—it was up to the Ministry of Religious Endowments to care for the truly indigent.

As in the period of 1848 and on, when records indicate that the Dabtiyya received petitions made to the khedive requesting admission to Takiyyat Tulun, in the early twentieth century the ruler of Egypt continued to receive requests for admission to the shelters of Tura, Abdin, and

Qabbari. Simultaneously, however, philanthropic organizations were entering the arena of assisting the poor. Some of these organizations, such as the Muslim Benevolent Society (to which Percy had referred when he mentioned that there was no need to provide further means of assistance to Egypt's destitute) and the Coptic Benevolent Society provided for the poor of both religions, although they had been established with the initial aim of assisting only coreligionists. A number of other multidenominational associations came into being at that time and in the years following World War I. Their efforts, directed toward the care of children, took place within a discourse of national duty and citizenship rather than necessarily within a framework of religious obligations to the poor. In the course of their formation, these associations recognized the poor and particularly indigent children as the future of the nation; but these associations also also made a space for the elite of Egypt to contribute toward to the creation of the nation and increase their role within it. Within such a scenario, Egypt — particularly its elite — had the responsibility of caring for its own poor.

V

THE FUTURE OF THE NATION

IN DECEMBER 1910, Dr. Abd al-Aziz Nazmi gave an address to members of the Royal Society in Cairo on the topic of children's health. Nazmi argued that although caring for the elderly and the poor was an important attribute of any civilized nation, saving the young ensured its future. Saving children, he said, was an act of national defense:

> It is in the interest of everyone, as well as their obligation, to participate in actions to save children and protect the general health, to fight infant mortality which annihilates the nation, and to reduce the number of infirm, invalids, and criminals who are miserable parasites living at the expense of society and constituting a permanent public danger.[1]

Nazmi's call for the full involvement of Egyptians in taking care of the poor—and most importantly their essential role in caring for children—was indicative of a transformation in attitudes toward the poor and the introduction of new actors to the field of charity and philanthropy. The Royal Society and its monthly meetings were one example of forums in which members of Egypt's professional classes addressed such concerns as the protection of children—with "protection" entailing measures to ensure children's health and promote their ability to make productive contributions to society—and the reasons behind mendicancy and increases in crime rates. Members of the Royal Society came from a range of professions in the judiciary, in education, in publishing, and in business. Their ethnic and religious identities also reflected the cosmopolitan features of early-twentieth-century Egypt. Membership lists comprised established families of Muslim, Greek, Jewish, Coptic, and Armenian origin.[2] The overall platforms of this society included a focus on modernizing Egypt and bringing it up to par with Western countries.[3]

The forums of the Royal Society included discussion of economic and political issues as well as calls for the upper classes to become involved in social concerns. Egypt's commitment to—and particularly Egyptian elites' investments in—such social issues as protecting children, eradicating juvenile delinquency, and clearing the streets of the indigent was portrayed as a barometer of Egypt's ability to conform with Western standards and to be considered Western and "civilized." To this end, members of the society engaged in studies of Egypt's social problems and developed projects to ameliorate them. Nazmi's activities outside the lecture hall exemplified the application of the Royal Society's ideas and the unique role the upper classes believed they should play in improving Egypt's social problems. Alongside his other "nationalist" projects, Nazmi founded children's dispensaries and health clinics and sponsored the establishment of a shelter for Cairo's street children.[4]

Nazmi's actions, and the discussions and activities of the Royal Society, were part and parcel of a new era in Egypt's history: the rise of an associational movement and the development of civil society. Numerous associations — geographical clubs, antiquities societies, workers' organizations, a variety of professional syndicates, and, most important for our purposes, groups committed to the care of the poor and children — came onto the scene in the late nineteenth and early twentieth centuries.[5] This chapter explores the rise of philanthropic associations in late-nineteenth-century Egypt and their activities during the first half of the twentieth century to demonstrate how their actions served multiple purposes and how philanthropy can never be divorced from politics. For their external audiences, the numerous charitable projects that Egypt's upper classes established were intended to counter British accusations of Egypt's negligence toward the poor. Through their proposals and their programs, which frequently alluded to or utilized scientific discourses, members of the Royal Society (many of whom were involved in philanthropic organizations) sought to prove Egypt's rightful inclusion among other Western nations. On the domestic front, Egypt's upper classes created a space for themselves in Egyptian society through their philanthropic activities, including programs for improving the lives of children, the promotion of hygiene, and efforts to make Egypt's poor into productive citizens. Their actions thereby represented their paternalistic role in improving Egypt. Through the institutions that they established, they endeavored to steer Egypt's poor toward becoming productive citizens. The activities of these associations and discourses on the poor and the future of Egypt's impoverished children underscored their belief that Egypt's lower classes were essential members of the Egyptian nation. The actions of various philanthropic groups were imbued with political meaning on yet another level as well: the institutions they established challenged the traditional role of Egypt's ruler as the primary benefactor of large-scale benevolence projects.

The Advent of Associations in Late-Nineteenth-Century Egypt

From the late nineteenth century on, philanthropic groups were increasingly involved and visible in establishing orphanages and educational and medical facilities for children. While they grounded their activities and goals within the religious imperative of caring for the poor, members of these associations utilized the press and other public forums to advertise their activities and call for contributions to their causes. As they brought their activities to the attention of the Egyptian public, they posited their actions within a framework of national duty and in this manner laid claim to the elites' role as the vanguard in fulfilling a national obligation. The actions of these groups, their use of public venues (newspapers and meetings), and their calls for the involvement of other members of Egyptian society across ethnic and religious divides demonstrate how these associations constituted a vital element in the development of Egypt's civil society at the end of the nineteenth and beginning of the twentieth century. The poor themselves became politicized, as the numerous organizations engaging in philanthropic work at this juncture in Egypt's history sought to prove their own abilities to best provide for them.

The introduction of philanthropic associations in late-nineteenth-century Egypt can be attributed to the convergence of several factors: the inadequacy or absence of state-sponsored services; a religious, ethnic, or national community's collectively felt threat; the increasing presence of an educated elite; and avenues of communication such as the press and forums in which organizations advertised their actions and efforts and solicited donations. A move away from indiscriminate charitable giving and toward the creation of vocational and educational opportunities for the poor was central to the activities of the associations founded in Egypt during this period.

Until the late nineteenth century, communally based care in Egypt had been an important feature in the lives of both Muslims and religious and ethnic minorities. For many groups, religious endowments, together with community and familial obligations toward the poor, had ensured a safety net for the destitute for centuries. Providing assistance to one's coreligionists built on the *millet* system, in which each community had the obligation to take care of its own members and police their actions.

The second half of the nineteenth century witnessed the rise of charitable associations even though communally based care continued to exist. Members active in the philanthropic movement had been influenced by the success of associations in Europe. From mid-century on, Egyptian study missions in France gained exposure to associations there and were impressed by the ideology and projects of these groups. Many of these students, who went on to play influential roles in Egyptian society, concluded that associations were "among the main catalysts of the success and development" of European cultures, and they hoped to introduce similar associations in Egypt. Many took part in the Freemasonry movement. A number of those who joined the Freemasons in later years, in turn, went on to found or become members in charitable associations. Butros Ghali, Muhammad Abduh, and Sa'd Zaghlul were all such members.[6]

A commitment to associational forms of giving involved collective decision making on the part of members — in terms of outlining projects and determining need — and the pooling of resources by fund raising efforts and calls for donations. Joining together in associations allowed individuals to carry out charitable projects on a grand scale: for example, groups such as the Muslim Benevolent Society and the Coptic Benevolent Society established schools, medical facilities, and orphanages. Such projects replaced, and constituted a threat to, a ruler's monopoly over large charitable works.[7]

As early as 1879, Muslims in Egypt began founding their own charitable associations. In that year, the journalist Abd Allah Nadim established the first Muslim Benevolent Society in Alexandria. The primary goals of this association were providing free education to poor Muslim children and orphans and giving moral and religious guidance.[8] Just thirteen years later, in 1892, prominent Egyptian nationalists established an association also named the Muslim Benevolent Society. Its founding members included various statesmen and reformers such as Muhammad Abduh, Talat Harb, Sa'd Zaghlul, and Mustafa Kamil. This second Muslim Benevolent Society, like that of 1879, worked to provide education and medical assistance and established branches throughout Egypt.

The nationalist and reformist programs of organizations such as the Muslim Benevolent Society presented their care of the poor and the vulnerable (such as infants and children) as proof of their nationalist and charitable devotion. In addition to care, the society endeavored to provide industrial training and other necessary forms of education to orphans, the poor, children of workers, and foundlings.[9] The Malga' al-Abbasiyya, an industrial training school and orphanage in Alexandria, was one such institution founded by the Muslim Benevolent Society to fulfill these ends. A commitment to improving the moral and religious education of boys admitted to this school lay behind the Malga' al-Abbasiyya's educational mission, but the institution also served practical ends. During a time when unemployment benefits and workers' compensation were unavailable, such institutions functioned as a source of aid for the families of workers who had been injured in industrial accidents. Such was the case of Ahmad al-Bahiri, a disabled former employee of the railway company, who presented a request for the enrollment of his sons in the Malga' al-Abbasiyya. In his petition (addressed to Egypt's ruler, Abbas Hilmi), he explained that he had once worked for the Egyptian railroad, but after losing his leg in an accident he was no longer able to earn a living. Since he had no income, he could not provide for his two sons, Ahmad (nine years old) and Muhammad (six years old). At the Malga' his two sons would have the opportunity to learn a trade and one day to provide for their father.

Hilmi Ahmad Shalabi argues that the work carried out by the Muslim Benevolent Society was in great part prompted by the government's lack of involvement in education as well as the overall impoverishment of Egypt's population during the early decades of the British occupation.[10] Muhammad Shawqi al-Fangari, like Shalabi, views the actions of the Muslim Benevolent Society as a nationalist response to the British occupation, particularly colonial officials' neglect of important services such as education and medicine. Further, the free education provided by the Muslim Benevolent Society, as well as by Coptic Christians, served to counter the actions of missionaries in Egypt.[11]

Insufficient funds and a lack of care for the poor were certainly features of British colonial rule in Egypt. However, as I have been noted, Britain's involvement in public health, sanitation, and the medical services illustrates that the British were not as negligent as Fangari and Shalabi contend. Education was one area where Egyptian philanthropists saw a great need for funds. Their desire to contribute toward educational projects arose as much out of fear of missionary inroads as from concern about the inadequacy of state funds. Finally, the creation of associations was not only in response to a threat or a way to rectify a shortcoming. Establishing schools and other services for one's community helped strengthen ethnic and religious cohesiveness.

By 1900, Western missionaries had been participating in charitable and humanitarian projects in Egypt for more than half a century. Active primarily in education, missionary groups established numerous schools during the 1830s and 1840s. The British Church Missionary Society educated Copts in schools established in 1839–40; the French Maison du bon pasteur founded a Catholic girls' school in Cairo in 1845; the Lazarists established a school in 1847; the Filles de la charité founded a day school for girls, a *pensionnat*, and an orphanage; and the American Protestant missions became increasingly active in establishing schools during 1855–66.[12] Abandoned or orphaned children also received attention from missionary groups; in 1850 the Pères de Terre-Sainte brought in two children who had been left at their church, and the Dames de la charité began to assist the poor and take in orphaned and abandoned children. In 1860 the Orphanage of St. Vincent de Paul in Alexandria also began to provide care and education to orphaned and abandoned children.[13] Although these organizations assisted primarily Christian groups, and although Muslims were wary of missionary actions, some schools, like those of Mary Whately, were attended by Muslim children.[14]

The activities of missionaries were felt most acutely by the Coptic community, among whose poor the missionaries proselytized aggressively. One way of responding to the missionary threat was through the establishment of Coptic schools for the indigent. Another, more extensive avenue through which the Copts provided for their own indigent was the founding of the Coptic Benevolent Society in 1881. This society provided scholarships and medical assistance, and it distributed food and clothing to poor Copts and Muslims.[15] Religious endowments, yearly membership dues, and fund-raising parties financed these projects. Building on the religious principle of a community's obligations toward the needy, the society reinforced the bonds between Copts and ensured assistance to those in need. Yet underlying the society's actions, and alongside its religious principles, were — in the words of its founder, the legist Butros Ghali — humanitarian (*insaniyya*) goals.

The actions of Jewish and Greek philanthropic groups are another example of denominational-centered aspects of charitable giving. By the late nineteenth century, members of Egypt's Jewish community were active in the establishment of a range of institutions, including schools, hospitals and medical dispensaries, orphanages, and clubs.[16] As Shalabi had argued for the Muslim community, the early twentieth century witnessed increased efforts to establish a range of services and institutions for the Greeks of Egypt. Alexander Kitroeff argues that the absence of state welfare services necessitated the development of large-scale charitable institutions. But he also shows how these institutions served purposes beyond charity. They enhanced ethnic pride and increased Greek residents' sense of a common identity and a common bond with one another.[17]

A broad range of services established in the late nineteenth and early twentieth centuries — whether schools, hospitals, or social clubs — emerged in tandem with the development of civil society and the institutions that made the success of civil society possible. Public forums (talks, meetings, publications, and the press) through which society members could communicate needs, raise funds, and advertise their efforts reinforced a collective identity and allowed members to assess and discuss needs and accomplishments. These avenues also permitted discussions of problems plaguing society as a whole, not just those of particular religious communities.

Three aspects of Egyptian society came to the attention of Egypt's elite across ethnic and religious divides: the increased public presence of the urban poor, infant mortality and the poor health and hygiene of children, and growing numbers of street children in cities such as Cairo and Alexandria.[18] To address these social problems head-on, members of Egypt's elite formed numerous organizations that at times crossed religious and ethnic lines. In the period following the First World War and in the era of Egypt's 1919 Revolution, a rhetoric of nationalism and national duty permeated the activities of groups that later developed into multiethnic and multireligious organizations. The associations founded during this period geared their projects toward the improvement of the health and morals of the poor. Whereas religious obligations had been a catalyst for the establishment of sectarian organizations such as the Muslim and Coptic Benevolent Societies, new concepts of nationhood and citizenship lay behind the actions of these associations, which crossed religious and ethnic divides. The agendas of a number of associations founded during this period included new perceptions of hygiene and new ideas about the possibility of "improving" the condition of the poor through education, vocational training, and health care initiatives.

Conceptions of the Poor

In his presentation on the need to suppress mendicancy in Egypt — given before the same Royal Society where Nazmi had spoken five years earlier — Kamel Greiss recounted how he daily encountered a poor woman soliciting alms near a church in Faggala, a Christian quarter of Cairo.[19] Greiss expressed his amazement at how, having passed this woman over the course of ten years, the children who were clustered around her never grew older. Greiss presented this story alongside numerous accounts of beggars whom he had observed plying their trade in Cairo, all of whom, he believed, were not actually poor, but rather were impostors. The existence of "armies" of beggars and vagrants in Cairo and other Egyptian cities represented, in Greiss's view, a threat to society.

Greiss was not alone in condemning the public presence of the poor and the potential criminality of beggars and vagrants. Beginning in the early twentieth century, Egypt's police punished adult able-bodied males caught begging or wandering in the streets of urban areas as well as in the countryside. The first begging infraction was punished with fines, but subsequent violations led to imprisonment and even transport. Police regulations stipulated that vagabonds and suspect persons had to have their anthropometric measurements taken. Even those who had found temporary work were considered suspect persons: in the rural areas village watchmen (*ghafir*) supervised temporary workmen closely, and contractors hiring laborers for public works projects were required to inform local police stations of the names and home villages of their workers.[20] Legitimate beggars (*les mendiants valides*) were not crimi-

Figure 5.1. Beggars requested alms from Egyptians and foreigners alike. (Reproduced from *Al-Lata'if al-Musawwara*, February 10, 1919, courtesy of the President and Fellows of Harvard College.)

nalized to the same extent as able-bodied men, however. Restrictions were made as to where they were allowed to beg. Soliciting alms in some areas of Cairo, for example, was resolutely prohibited, but in other areas those activities were allowed. Charitable persons, such as tourists, were reminded by public placards that giving alms to beggars was praiseworthy but that charity served only to encourage beggars who presumably were able to work.[21] Egyptian caricatures portray the widespread impression that beggars frequently assailed both indigenous inhabitants and British residents (figure 5.1).

Greiss's condemnation of begging best illustrates a decided shift in perceptions of the poor and the responsibilities of charitable persons; it also represents the apogee of new discourses about Egypt's poor. His stance was one of absolute intolerance. He accused beggars of being lazy peasants pursuing a career of begging instead of the more difficult work of the countryside; and, in his presentation to the Royal Society, Greiss attempted to dissuade people with charitable impulses from giving alms to the poor. His comments on the dangers that the poor posed to society were repeated in other forums before the Royal Society and were echoed—albeit in a language of disease and hygiene—by such medical officers as Dr. Bonté Sheldon Elgood, who described beggars as foci of infection and called for their removal from public spaces.[22]

Greiss's remarks to the Royal Society represent one person's perception of how begging and the charitable acts associated with it were divorced from prior religious connotations. Even those who were considered the deserving poor, such as women with small children, were not to be trusted as being truly worthy of assistance. As Greiss looked for precedents for the treatment of the poor, he referred to the papyri of pharaonic Egypt and practices in ancient Greece and the Roman Empire; then he discussed the actions of Muhammad Ali, specifically Muhammad Ali's establishment of a *dépôt de mendicité*. Greiss's omission of references to either the Judaic-Christian tradition or to Islam highlighted his disavowal of any religious obligation toward the poor and underscored the profoundly rational and secular distancing he sought to achieve in his portrayal of the public poor and the needs of Egyptian society's most vulnerable.

The absence of religious references in Greiss's remarks represents a myopia; yet such omissions can be understood in light of the multi-ethnic and multireligious membership of the Royal Society and the new and more secular approaches to care for the poor coming to the fore in early twentieth-century Egypt. The papers that members presented frequently avoided any mention of religion, instead promoting rational and secular ideas. Specifically, their presentations and papers about the treatment of the poor included European precedents of caring for them as their key points of reference. With the exception of Greiss's paper, which focused primarily on adult beggars and vagrants, society members' presentations and essays that dealt with the topic of the poor highlighted the plight of children. Their papers emphasized the reformability of children and preventive measures, such as education and vocational training, to be taken against poverty; they also illustrated how a discourse of hygiene and eugenics (though to a lesser extent) permeated perceptions of poverty and the poor.

The speeches presented by Royal Society members echoed ongoing scientific discourses and discussions of societal concerns as well as ideas of improving the poor evident in European discussions of poverty and children and youth. But they also represented emerging discourses of nationalism and posited that the involvement of Egypt's elite was imperative in ensuring that Egypt's wealth—namely, the potential productivity of its citizens—would not be wasted. Issues such as the unequal distribution of wealth, landlessness, and the causes of poverty were absent from members' proposals. Instead, children and their physical and moral health became the centerpieces of society members' efforts and the activities of associations.

The Family and the Nation

More than three decades before Greiss's speech at the Royal Society, another forum engaged in questions of the protection of children. In the 1880s *Al-Muqtataf*, a magazine devoted to science and progress, published an article exploring infant mortality in cities. The article explained that cities, crowded and polluted as they were, were detrimental to the health of mothers and young children. In addition, life for city infants was precarious because urban mothers, unlike mothers in the countryside, depended on wet nurses and cow's milk to feed their babies. The solution was to be found in education, knowing the rules of hygiene, and sending nursing mothers to the countryside with their children. The article proposed that the children of the poor and abandoned children should be cared for in homes established through charity.[23]

Al-Muqtataf's subject matter was international in its scope; its proposals for improvements in health frequently drew from scientific findings in Europe and North America. Hence, on one hand the subject matter of this article could be read as a contrast between the health of cities and that of the countryside in various parts of the world. On the other hand, the juxtaposition of the countryside and the city and the condemnation of the use of wet nurses must be read as criticisms of the habits of Egyptian better-off mothers who could afford wet nurses and as emphasizing the health and purity of the Egyptian countryside with its ability to ensure its residents' health. The article—while drawing attention to practices in other areas of the world—also set forth a blueprint identifying the institutions and people who would be responsible for Egypt's needy children.

Such discussions of infant mortality and child health were prevalent in the Egyptian press at the turn of the century. The forums held on these topics reflected real concerns about the Egyptian health community and reformers, given that, in the statistics provided by British medical officers, one in three Egyptian children did not survive infancy. Yet at the same time, discussions of infant and child health reflected a commitment to a new understanding of the link between the nation and its citizens and the creation of a new set of relationships between the elite and the lower classes. The iconography of the relationship between the nation and its children (or citizens) was best represented in cartoons following the 1919 Revolution which depict Egypt as a mother nursing her infant, but the idealization of the Egyptian countryside harked back to Egyptian efforts to attain self-sufficiency and financial independence as well as freedom from dependence and foreign intervention (figure 5.2). In later years, depictions of the family were solidly grounded in representations of Safiyya Zaghlul, the wife of Sa'd Zaghlul, leader of the Wafd party, who was portrayed as Egypt's "mother."[24] Egypt's elite played a unique role in ensuring the strength of this nation; for they, in their self-depictions, were responsible for inculcating in the lower classes a better understanding of health and hygiene and the proper way to raise children.

Among their other projects, Egypt's elite recognized the dire problem of infant mortality and worked to make child health and welfare a priority of the Egyptian government and Egyptian philanthropists. Whereas British health officials blamed infant mortality on the ignorance and unclean habits of Egyptian mothers, Nazmi and other advocates of child health were less condemnatory in their critiques. Nazmi, who received his medical training in France, began practicing medicine in Egypt in 1903 and went on to become the director of the medical division of the Ministry of Religious Endowments and a member of the Royal Society.[25] As a proponent of child health, Nazmi published numerous articles on the importance of proper hygiene for mothers and infants. In the periodical *Majalat al-Abbasiyya* and other forums, Nazmi promoted preventive techniques of medical care—such as cleanliness of the child and his/her clothing and surroundings—and encouraged proper nutritional habits. He stressed that the education of young

Figure 5.2. Iconography of Egypt as a nursing mother. The infant represents the newly established Egyptian National Bank (Bank Misr), who will survive thanks to the love, care, and nourishment provided by its mother, Egypt. The children crowded around the nursing mother and infant represent the foreign banks active in Egypt, who question whether the baby will live. (Reproduced from *Al-Lata'if al-Musawwara*, August 2, 1920, courtesy of the President and Fellows of Harvard College.)

girls in housewifery and proper child-care techniques was imperative for the health of subsequent generations and ultimately for the health of the nation.[26]

Nazmi did not only discuss child health in intellectual forums such as scientific magazines or the halls of the Royal Society. As a member of the Société pour la protection d'enfance (SIPE, Society for the Protection of Childhood, established in 1907), he applied his ideas, promoting the education of Egyptian mothers in matters of hygiene and cleanliness.[27] The hospital of this society provided periodic checkups for infants of the poor as well as lessons in proper child care and nutrition. Among his other duties for the society, Nazmi delivered lectures in the hope of "popularizing among the native inhabitants what modern science teaches in regards to saving infant life."[28]

Nazmi brought his medical expertise to the inhabitants of popular quarters such as Cairo's Darb al-Ahmar, where he had established a medical dispensary. He believed that sharing medical knowledge was an obligation of Egypt's elite, and he saw this responsibility as being directed especially toward children. In Nazmi's view, a nation without healthy children was a weak nation, and hence it was the obligation of Egypt's elite to promote child health and welfare.

Other members of Egypt's elite also used the language of duty when referring to their own efforts to promote care for Egypt's needy children. In the case of one group of women's involvement in the creation of a children's dispensary, the idea of "obligation" was placed within a discourse of responsibility and shame. Just as members of the Coptic community countered the activities of missionary groups by establishing their own institutions, female members of Egypt's elite, from a range of ethnic and religious groups, found it incumbent to engage in philanthropic projects as a way of offseting the activities of the wives and families of British officials in Egypt.

In 1911, when Princess Ayn al-Hayat proposed the idea of establishing a dispensary along the lines of the Lady Cromer Dispensary, she commented to Huda Sha'rawi that "It is, indeed, shameful that we in Egypt do not undertake such projects ourselves. It is our duty to be at the head of charitable works in Egypt. I intend to sponsor a dispensary." The Mabarat Muhammad Ali, as the dispensary and school founded by the princesses of the royal family was called, provided medical services and a school that offered classes on infant care, hygiene, and home management. Donations made by the royal family and fund-raising events such as the sale of stamps (depicting a woman embracing a poor girl) and annual charity fetes held in the palaces of the Egyptian royalty and the homes of the elite financed the dispensary and school. Both European and Egyptian medical doctors volunteered their services in the dispensary.[29]

In the years that followed the Mabara's establishment, elite Egyptian women became key participants in emerging philanthropic associations. In a society that discouraged women's participation in public forums and political affairs, women's involvement in charitable associations was considered a legitimate activity. As in Europe and North America, where maternalist welfare activities were seen as a "natural" domain for women, in Egypt women's participation in infant and child health advocacy and children's education was considered an acceptable sphere of influence. Egyptian women's participation in maternalist activities brought women increasingly into the public sphere and "served as a path to professions and an entry into the world of politics."[30]

Most importantly in the case of many Egyptian women, an ethos of piety also legitimated their actions. Muslim women throughout the Islamic period in Egypt and in other Islamic countries had been the founders or overseers of religious endowments. Their participation in charitable endeavors at the turn of the century was an extension of a role they traditionally played. Egyptian women further confirmed and justified their participation in the public realm of charity as actions carried out in the service of the nation.[31] Margot Badran has argued that women's participation in philanthropy changed the dynamics of charitable relations between the rich and the poor. Whereas the poor had previously come to the rich to seek assistance (through facilities such as awqaf), the advent of philanthropic efforts at the beginning of the twentieth century now meant that the rich went to the poor and exposed themselves to the harsh environment in which the poor lived.[32]

Women extended their charitable efforts to other women and girls, concentrating their efforts in vocational training, helping girls find work in viable trades, and calling for reforms that would improve their social status.[33] Advocacy of women's education and concern for the welfare of Egyptian girls and women, as with concern about health and infant mortality, increasingly drew upper-class women together in charitable associations. Their collective concerns also brought them into the public sphere. One proponent of girls' education was the leading literary figure Malak Hifni Nasif. Although she could not be present at a national congress held in 1911 because it was attended by men, she sent a list of demands, including making primary education mandatory for girls, providing instruction on hygiene and proper child care for girls and young women, training girls and young women in nursing and medicine, and promising greater equality for women on divorce issues.[34] Platforms such as those Nasif formulated became a rallying point for women whose associations grew increasingly visible in the years following the nominal independence of Egypt.[35]

In Egypt, beginning in the first decades of the British occupation, concern for children, their health, and their well-being was always discussed within an international and comparative framework. In the 1880s the international aspect of child health, particularly proposals for how Egyptians could gain from the knowledge of medical experts in Europe, was promoted in scientific and literary magazines such as *Al-Muqtataf*. In the early twentieth century, attention to infant mortality and the role of hygiene in the health of children and mothers increasingly became the domain of governmental departments responsible for the promotion of health care, such as the Ministry of Religious Endowments, and associations, such as the SIPE and the Mabarat Muhammad Ali. In each forum in which child health was discussed, an underlying discourse implied that the future of the nation depended on the health and well-being of children. A language of national obligation posited that Egypt's elite were responsible for promoting health projects such as dispensaries, as well as educational facilities for teaching the lower classes about hygiene and nutrition. Yet as children grew older, they too had a responsibility to the nation in that they were required to make positive contributions to society. Just as the elite supported charitable projects for teaching mothers how to best care for their infants and children, the Royal Society urged Egypt's elite to take on the tutelage of juveniles. Through this paternal care, juveniles were to be taught the importance of work, steered away from a life of potential crime, and engaged in efforts that made positive contributions to Egyptian society. Such *national* efforts were intended to supplement existing communal care for Egypt's poor.

The Reformability of Egyptian Juvenile Delinquents

Private initiatives in social services, such as parole surveillance and efforts to ensure the moral welfare of Egypt's youth, were one means by which the elite were called upon to reform Egypt's poor. Appeals for more involvement of the elite in this realm paralleled state actions in crime prevention and law enforcement. Fighting crime was a high priority during the British occupation, and each year saw increased expenditures for prison construction and maintenance, the establishment of reformatories and vocational centers for convicts, the training and employment of police officers, and the development of anticrime techniques such as anthropometric measurements and fingerprinting.[36] Although the treatment of adult offenders was viewed as the preserve of the state, members of the Royal Society and other associations, particularly after World War I, expressed greater interest and began to intervene more actively in efforts to curtail juvenile delinquency. Their actions included the promotion of parole programs for children convicted of crimes, but they also placed great emphasis on crime prevention through vocational training opportunities for street children (specifically street boys).

Together with discussions of prison expenditures, colonial officials and crime experts included in their annual reports lengthy discussions of the successes of the improved prison system and other crime-deterrent programs. Initial British policies in prison reform were intended to reduce crowding in prisons and introduce training and other projects to ensure labor for public works projects. Colonial officials oversaw the building of new prisons and the introduction of various programs intended to ensure that imprisonment would deter crime. They also claimed to reduce the severity of punishments. Yet prisons continued to be overcrowded. Arguments for the reasons behind prison overcrowding included the idea that Egyptians did not consider a prison term a social disgrace. The British also argued that the fact that prisons were too comfortable and provided food and shelter accounted for many Egyptians' *desire* for incarceration.[37]

Reported cases of violent crime, such as brigandage and murder, were numerous during the British occupation, and British officials continually sought to explain the increase in crime. Mr. Machell, a police inspector, argued that increased prosperity resulted in crime because "[t]he extraordinary prosperity of the fellaheen has whetted their appetite and created in them a lust for gain. This breeds envy, malice, and hatred. The amount of crime in Egypt to-day can be directly traced to these causes."[38] Machell asserted that crime and criminal acts were simply indicative of a society where little value was placed on human life.[39] At times, officials drew attention to the fact that poverty actually increased criminal behavior.[40] On other occasions, they argued that the law and prisons were not harsh enough.[41] Whatever the "cause," statistics for the late nineteenth and early twentieth centuries indicated a sharp rise in crime. A number of factors led to rising incarceration rates, including more thorough record keeping and the intensified criminalization of a multitude of activities. By expanding its police forces and introducing more precise criminal identification techniques such as fingerprinting and anthropometric measurements, British colonial officials sought to increase surveillance of the Egyptian populace.[42]

British colonial officials emphasized how the prisons served to reform criminals and taught them the value of industriousness. With the goal of ensuring gainful employment after release, some of the larger prisons emphasized training in manual skills such as metalworking and carpentry.[43] To this end, an adult reformatory was established at the turn of the century. Prisoners received training in skills as well as instruction in reading and writing; their conduct determined the length of their prison term. Monetary incentives, specifically weekly wages and rewards for good conduct and progress in schoolwork, were an important aspect of the reforming nature of this institution.[44]

Although Coles Pasha, Egypt's prison inspector at the turn of the century, could not — or chose not to — measure the success of his adult reformatory, his discussions of the juvenile reformatory that he developed provide more information on the institution's role in "reforming" young boys and girls. Established initially in Alexandria as a "philanthropic institution" with funds coming from private subscriptions and government subsidies, the reformatory was intended to separate youth sentenced to prison in government jails from incarcerated adults.[45] Shortly after Coles Pasha was appointed prison inspector in 1897, he ordered the reformatory in Alexandria closed and established a new reformatory in Giza, initially housing this facility in abandoned prison buildings. In 1898 the Egyptian government built an entirely new reformatory along the lines of juvenile reformatories in Europe, modeling it after the County Council School for Waifs and Strays near London and the Belgian Reformatory at Ypres.[46]

Designed to house both boys and girls, the reformatory had two separate sections, with workshops and classrooms in each. The inmates' schedule included schoolwork and workshop time for boys, training in domestic crafts for girls, and drills, gymnastics, and musical band rehearsals. As with the adult reformatory, Coles attempted to instill discipline through the use of monetary rewards. In addition, children went on weekly outings as a reward for good conduct.[47]

Although originally intended to punish juvenile offenders for theft, murder, and minor criminal infractions, in 1908 another function was added to the reformatory: punishment for "street boys and waifs." For nearly a decade, municipal officials had identified street children in the urban areas of Egypt as a problem. European officials commented that these children, who sold small items, shined shoes, or begged, were either orphaned, abandoned, or had been sent out by their parents to earn a living. Coles Pasha had proposed to punish "waifs and strays" with confinement in the juvenile reformatory in 1900, but this legislation was not implemented until 1908.[48]

The number of street children visible in cities such as Cairo had prompted the use of the juvenile reformatory as a way of incarcerating them, and, ultimately, the reformatory was intended to ensure their employment by means of vocational training programs. But World War I impoverished both rural and urban families and resulted in the growing numbers and increased visibility of poor children. Anxiety about the presence of these street children was expressed in new terminology, which depicted them, increasingly, as a threat to society. In Cairo juvenile vagrants were described as "armies"; the police commissioner of Cairo was reported to have said that on any one night it was possible to arrest five hundred juvenile vagrants in one section of Cairo alone.[49]

According to members of the Royal Society, "saving" or protecting children by ensuring their health care and by training juveniles necessitated the participation of the entire Egyptian society, particularly the elite. Speakers at numerous forums on the protection of children called for philanthropists and benevolent societies to participate in their care and training.[50] Just as individuals in Western countries "took the initiative in the study of the question of juveniles and it was they, again, who incurred considerable expenses to attain their end," noted Ahmed Sami, the director of the Industrial Farm School of Gabal al-Asfar, it was "now time that our wealthy countrymen should follow suit and take the matter up seriously, so as to save the country from the overwhelming dangers."[51]

The role of the elite in curbing juvenile delinquency, like their role in endorsing programs to combat infant mortality, was set within broader, more international discussions about the protection of children in European cities and the United States. By situating the actions of Egypt's elite within a larger framework of projects under way in Western nations, contributors to the Royal Society placed Egypt among "civilized" countries and set a course so it could attain the same status and efficacy as the Western elite.[52] Members of the Royal Society frequently referred to efforts to create and improve reformatories and to introduce parole programs under way in Europe and the United States, arguing that Egypt could benefit from similar projects. Egypt's participation in international conferences on the protection of children, in 1913 and again in 1923, gave speakers a European point of reference for discussing the successes of programs in other regions of the world and comparing these efforts with projects under way in Egypt. *How* Egypt took care of its delinquent or potentially delinquent youth set it on par with Europe and the United States and the modern and rational techniques of youth intervention practiced there.[53]

The comparisons that presenters such as the legists Hassan Nachat and Ahmed Sami made with the problem of street children in Europe influenced their and their audiences' perceptions of this phenomenon in Egypt. They showed how European parents were to blame because they frequently sent their children out into the streets to earn a living. Charitable organizations, in Sami's view, were also culpable, because they had the power to save a neglected child who "tomorrow would become their *concitoyen* [fellow citizen]."[54] Yet the accusations made by Nachat and Sami were intended only for Egypt: Egyptian parents were guilty of letting their children go unsupervised in the streets, and Egypt's philanthropic organizations had the responsibility of assuming the tutelage of those very children who, if left unprotected, might pursue a life of crime. As in the case of late imperial Russia, where the press played an ever greater role in propagating ideas of crime and introduced a concept of "hooliganism" to Saint Petersburg, Egypt's press, particularly the illustrated press (*Al-Lata'if al-Musawwara*), brought into public discourse discussions of Cairo's street children and possible solutions to the problem.[55]

Just as Badran's argument that charitable work exposed the elite to the living conditions of Egypt's poor, the press, especially photography, brought Egypt's upper classes into greater contact with the poor and the conditions in which they lived. In the media (and photography), members of the elite drew attention to their charitable activities and called upon other Egyptians to make similar contributions. Images of children were frequently included in *Al-Lata'if al-Musawwara*; they were an important aspect of advertisements for medical practices as well as for food items, featuring light-skinned European children in poses accentuating their health and well-being. But children in dire circumstances were also portrayed: *Al-Lata'if al-Musawwara* included photographs of Lebanese children dying in the streets of Beirut during World War I and, particularly following the 1919 Revolution, featured exposés on street children in Cairo.

In 1917 discussions of responsibility accompanied photographs of street children, with the article chiding Egypt's elite for not doing more to ensure their care. To remind readers of the persistence of this problem, *Al-Lata'if al-Musawwara* reprinted the same article in 1919 in an issue that included discussion of a new shelter to be established for boys called the Malga' al-Hurriyya (Shelter of Freedom). The repeated commentaries on the conditions of these street children (referred to as *mutasharidun* [vagrants], *ibna' al-shawari'* [children of the street], *ibna al-sabil* [street waifs], a play on the term *ibn al-sabil* [wayfarers], just one of the groups of individuals depicted in the Quran as being deserving of charity) forcefully asserted that care for these children was part of the national duty.[56]

Unlike Victorian photographs of street children, those in *Al-Lata'if al-Musawwara* do not appear to be staged or "fictionalized" with the intention of evoking the readers' sympathy or fear. Photographed in broad daylight, the cheerful, smiling children radiated innocence and hope, a portrayal contrasting sharply with images of the "ragged child" in British philanthropists' tracts on the criminality of the poor (figures 5.3 and 5.4).[57]

Where photographic effect does resemble depictions of street children in Britain is their demonstration of poverty, however. One example of this performance was staged at a fund-raising event for the Malga' al-Hurriyya in 1919. There, Nazmi, a strong proponent of infant and child health in Egypt who was also one of the founders of this new shelter, brought a number of street children dressed in rags before the audience as he discussed how the "children of this dear nation" (referring to the street boys) could, if neglected, turn to crime. As the boys stood beside him on the stage, Nazmi continually referred to their potential criminality and compared their dismal state to the predicament of animals, which, more fortunately, were protected by associations such as the Society for the Protection of Animals. However, while Nazmi wished to impress upon his audience these boys' potential criminality, he also intended to show that there was hope for them. With this end in mind, he presented to the audience former street children who, having learned trades in reformatories, were now well dressed, and holding the tools of their newly acquired trades, were prepared to make a productive

Figure 5.3. Street children in Cairo (reprint of article from August 2, 1917). In the photo on the left, the young girl and boy hold cans in their hands. Photographed in broad daylight, their smiles reflect both cheerfulness and comfort in front of the camera. The photo on the right depicts a boy dressed in rags. He appears to be standing in front of a European café; behind him to the right sits a man dressed in European clothes. (Reproduced from *Al-Lata'if al-Musawwara*, May 26, 1919, courtesy of the President and Fellows of Harvard College.)

contribution to Egypt. Nazmi's intentions, and the goals of subsequent speakers and poetry reciters at this event, were to convince Egypt's elite of the importance of contributing to the cause of the Malga' al-Hurriyya and to impress upon them the idea that their contributions benefited the nation and therefore constituted a national duty.[58]

Such "before and after" scenarios (street waif versus productive citizen) were rehearsed in other venues as well. The publications of the Malagi al-Abbasiyya, for example, presented photographs of boys upon their arrival at the shelter as well as their engagement (upon redressing) in vocational trades and participation in musical bands. An article on the creation of another shelter in 1921, the Malga' Abna al-Shawari'a (Shelter for Street Boys), included photographs of young boys' physical

Figure 5.4. Street children in Cairo, 1919. On the page facing the newspaper article about street children in Cairo is a second photo exposé of street children. As in the photographs of two years previously, the children are photographed in broad daylight, with many of them smiling. (Reproduced from *Al-Lata'if al-Musawwara,* May 26, 1919, courtesy of the President and Fellows of Harvard College.)

deformities and their disheveled appearance upon their admission and their clean and neat appearance later (figures 5.5 and 5.6).

Advertisements for government-run reformatories presented boys in formal attire and showed them taking part in various sports and musical events. Such depictions attested to the reformability of boys and their potential health and vitality, and, as in the case of shelters funded by philanthropy, they illustrated the essential role the elite could play in ensuring children's (and hence the Egyptian nation's) productive future. The SIPE also made use of "before and after" photographs to advertise its efforts in providing medical assistance to indigent children so as to drive home the point that health care ensured productive (and nondelinquent) children.[59]

The press was an important medium for publicizing the fund-raising efforts of Nazmi and other philanthropists. Articles highlighted Nazmi's efforts to create the Malga' al-Hurriyya and posited his actions within the context of his other "national" projects.[60] Yet the press also became a forum for expressing public displeasure when, after more than two years of fund raising, the Malga' al-Hurriyya remained only a blueprint. In an atmosphere of growing distrust and condemnation of the slow pace of Nazmi's efforts, *Al-Lata'if al-Musawwara* became a sounding

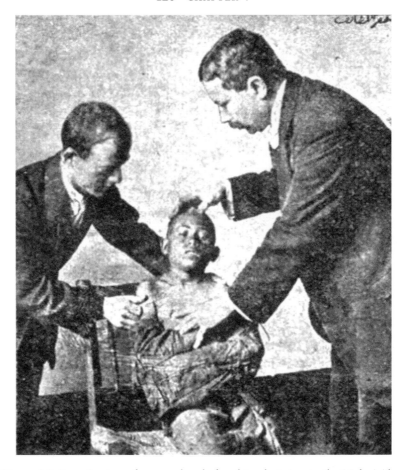

Figure 5.5. Examination of a street boy before his admission to the Malga' Abna al-Shawari'a. The doctors examining the boy might have been Europeans. (Reproduced from *Al-Lata'if al-Musawwara,* February 21, 1921, courtesy of the President and Fellows of Harvard College.)

board for discussing numerous more successful projects to assist orphans and street children, initiated by other publicly minded Egyptians and by Europeans and Americans residing in Egypt. Because many of these projects had minimal budgets, writers chided Nazmi and his cofounders for their insistence that the six thousand Egyptian pounds they had raised were insufficient. One example of *Al-Lata'if al-Musawwara*'s challenge to Nazmi's claims was an article on an orphanage founded by Lilian Tisher, an American woman in Asyut. The article described how she began the orphanage in a rented house in 1911 with

Figure 5.6. Photograph of benefactors and boys enrolled in the Malga' Abna al-Shawari'a. This shelter was founded by Egyptian and European philanthropists. The boys' ages appear to range from five to fifteen years. All are dressed in matching *galabiyya*. (Reproduced from *Al-Lata'if al-Musawwara*, February 21, 1921, courtesy of the President and Fellows of Harvard College.)

only twelve Egyptian pounds but eventually came to care for more than one hundred Christian and Muslim children, providing young girls with training in sewing, cooking, and housekeeping and apprenticeships for boys in shoemaking, carpentery, and blacksmithing.[61] Cartoons and poems also provided a biting critique of Nazmi and his cofounders' waste. One caricature depicted the proponents of Malga' al-Hurriyya looking for street children. Yet they were unable to find any because members of a rival association, which had founded the Malga' Abna al-Shawari'a, had already rescued them (figure 5.7).[62]

A growing emphasis on the activities of various associations in the aftermath of the 1919 Revolution, while drawing our attention to the numerous charitable efforts and the ways in which the press and the public condemned Nazmi's wastefulness, also highlights a key feature of charitable associations in this era: namely, the manner in which the rise of associations occurs not only due to increased demand but also as a result of competition among elites.[63] The pages of *Al-Lata'if al-Musawwara* in the era following the 1919 Revolution included a variety of advertisements for religiously based organizations as well as groups whose efforts were directed toward children regardless of religious affil-

Figure 5.7. The press, in addition to promoting the work of philanthropists, could also be a barometer of public criticism. In this cartoon, a critique of the Malga' al-Hurriyya Committee's slowness in establishing a shelter, the founders of the Malga' Abna al-Shawari'a have already "rescued" all the street boys to be found. (Reproduced from *Al-Lata'if al-Musawwara*, February 28, 1921, courtesy of the President and Fellows of Harvard College.)

iation. Many of these groups couched their actions in a rhetoric of national duty, implying their own role in building and fortifying the Egyptian nation.

Once it was finally founded, the Malga' al-Hurriyya exemplified the multidenominational aspect of attention to the poor. Its financial sponsors came from a range of ethnic and religious backgrounds, and its resident boys included Christians, Muslims, and Jews.

An implicit language of shame mobilized the Egyptian elite to take part in charitable efforts and made clear the necessity of Egyptians' caring for the poor. An article in the Coptic newspaper *Al-Watan* called upon wealthy landowners to care for the rural populace by establishing rural health dispensaries. The development of the country would be advanced, argued this article's author, only by improving the health of the rural populace.[64] While *Al-Watan* put forth proposals for the amelioration of rural poverty as a whole, Muslim groups adopted a language of shame and obligation in the print media to draw attention to the actions of missionary groups in the city of Tanta. A Muslim father who had enrolled his two children in a missionary school after the death of their mother attempted to pull them out from the school when he learned that they were receiving a Christian education; he was nevertheless charged the full tuition. When he was unable to pay, a public subscription was raised in Tanta. Whereas the Arabic-language newspapers reporting this event praised the benevolence of prominent citizens and officials in Tanta for taking charge of this matter, one of them, *Al-Ahali*, condemned the negligence of rich Muslims who had allowed such a situation to develop. The *Al-Ahali* article expressed hope that the actions of the missionaries had, at the very least drawn the attention of the rich to the plight of the poor and that wealthy Muslims would now take it upon themselves to open their hearts to the destitute.[65] In this case, the Muslim community, which had allegedly neglected its obligations to its poor, was impelled to respond to the missionary threat. Such a case was similar to the events surrounding Princess Ayn al-Hayat's establishment of the Mabarat Muhammad Ali when outsiders' intervention had catalyzed the royal family into action.

Yet alongside shame being a factor in the creation of associations and the resulting greater attention to the needs of poor children, the discourse of nationalism with which poor relief (and again, poor relief directed primarily toward children) was imbued served as an impetus for numerous groups to also found associations. All associations at this time included some reference to the way in which they served the poor, and, in this manner, implicitly and explicitly, served the nation.

The print media were important forums for discussing the plight of the poor. In addition to calls for landowners to provide for the rural peasantry, newspapers' front-page stories drew the literate public's attention to issues pertaining to the takaya (for example, concerns about the embezzlement of funds and complaints by the poor that their rations were inadequate), the efforts of the White Slavery Society in rescuing girls from prostitution, and the plight of the impoverished in Egypt's rural areas. Newspapers such as *Al-Watan* also criticized the Egyptian government for introducing harsher restrictions on vagrancy and called for more compassionate and humane treatment of Egypt's destitute. Many questioned the policies of the Egyptian government, but none challenged the status quo. Discussions about children were nonthreatening, and articles on how to ameliorate their situation did not call into question wealth disparities, landlessness, and the economic privileges of Europeans residing in Egypt.[66]

✻

From the last decades of the nineteenth through the first decades of the twentieth centuries, children appeared center stage in discourses of charity in Europe, North America, and Egypt. In Egypt attention focused on children's vulnerability in a variety of venues, including child labor, prostitution, and their presence in the streets. To address the issue of child labor, British groups called upon the foreign secretary and colonial officials in Egypt to ascertain children's working conditions.[67] Prostitution was not addressed directly by associations, although the efforts of women's groups to help young girls find viable trades was one way in which they attempted to protect them. White slavery societies, whose membership was international, also condemned the practice of prostitution.[68] Concerning street children, various philanthropic organizations were increasingly active in this area. The nationalist and patriotic discourse surrounding the topic of children and the family enabled Egypt's elite to use their actions in the field to make a positive contribution to the nation and, simultaneously, draw attention to their own importance in helping to constitute and construct that nation.

Philanthropic groups were just one form associations took in early-twentieth-century Egypt. This period also witnessed the emergence of professional syndicates and political organizations whose activities the Egyptian government eyed with suspicion. During the 1920s and 1930s, when successive governments attempted to legislatively restrict the actions of these syndicates and political organizations, philanthropic groups also found themselves under scrutiny.[69] Beginning in this era, the government required that associations involved in charitable activities indicate that their aims were entirely charitable in order to continue to function. By the last years of the 1930s, intervention in the actions of philanthropic associations became even more direct. Prime Minister Ali Mahir established the Ministry of Social Affairs, an office that endeavored to control both private voluntary organizations and the educational and charitable activities of labor unions.[70]

Constituting a Nation

A range of philanthropic associations emerged during the last decades of the nineteenth and the first years of the twentieth century. These groups, in addition to providing medical assistance and educational stipends or facilities to the poor, had another issue in common: increased attention to children. Concurrent with Egypt's struggle for independence from British Rule in the first decades of the twentieth century, an emphasis on children as the future of the nation led numerous organizations to help in poor relief. To advertise their efforts, call attention to the plight of street children, and accentuate the importance of fighting infant mortality, these organizations' rhetoric included the idea of children as an essential element of the Egyptian nation. The rhetoric of saving children also served to affirm the paternalist role of the Egyptian upper classes: in the absence of "proper" care from the children's own parents, Egypt's elite assumed the tutelage of children. A focus on poor children and the argument that their health and productivity would guarantee the future of the nation served to unite many members of the elite (regardless of their religious background) in attempts to "save" and "reform" children and make an investment toward their care. Children from a variety of ethnic and religious backgrounds were cared for together in some of the institutions established at this time.

The Malga' al-Hurriyya best represents the multidenominational aspect of care for poor children in this era. The boys enrolled in this institution included Christians, Muslims, and Jews. The average age of boys admitted to the Malga' was ten, and, interestingly, very few of the boys were street children without parents: of 104 boys admitted in 1923, only 3 were identified as *abna' al-sabil* (boys of the street). A number of boys were identified as having no parents and of having been transferred from other orphanages. In many instances, admission records indicate that a parent had requested that a son be admitted to receive care and training because he or she did not have the means to raise the son. Fifty-seven cases mention that the father was deceased and note that the mother was "poor," and 13 cases refer to the poverty of the mother but do not mention the father's status. The requests parents submitted to administrators of the Malga' frequently noted that the parent (either the father or the mother) was incapable of earning a living, often because he or she was invalid. In one case, the father was in prison; in another, the father was insane. Like the two sons of Muhammad al-Bahiri, who were enrolled together in the Malga' al-Abbasiyya, it appears that on occasion brothers were admitted together.[71]

Boys admitted to this institution received training in carpet weaving, sewing, carpentry, and shoemaking. Parents hoped that the training their children received would one day enable their children to take care of them. Enrolling their children in the Malga', where students were given room and board, also improved the finances of a family in desperate circumstances. Just as sending a child into the streets to shine shoes or perform other tasks brought in money, enrolling a child in any one of the industrial training programs established by charitable associations (which frequently covered room and board) reduced a family's expenses in the short term. The child's ability to earn money after acquiring a trade, in the longer run, was also an essential component of the family's income. For this reason, as in the instances of mothers who requested that their children be admitted to orphanages and industrial training programs in San Juan, Puerto Rico, the parents of applicants to schools such as the Malga' al-Hurriyya made sure to present petitions emphasizing their poverty and desperation to ensure their children's admission.[72] As with state-sponsored shelters such as the Maristan, Takiyyat Tulun, Takiyyat Tura, Takiyyat Abdin, and Takiyyat Qabbari, the poor made use of the assistance philanthropic groups provided. For the poor, these institutions, vocational training centers, and educational projects represented a viable means of relief.

The projects of the numerous associations founded after the 1919 Revolution were geared toward children, specifically street children and orphans. Through vocational training, these associations hoped to steer children away from a life of potential crime. Simultaneously, underlying the associations' programs were commitments to improving the health and well-being of children. Whereas associations founded in the late nineteenth century had been religiously based and had been geared, at the time of their establishment, toward assisting the poor of particular denominations, a number of societies founded in the late 1910s and the 1920s were multidenominational and included a focus on children (regardless of their religious or ethnic backround) as "the future" of the Egyptian nation. Apart from the rhetoric of nationalism pervading the publications and agendas of these various associations, the activities of each resulted in the forging of a national identity among its members. Membership lists, publications, and activities served to confirm their participation in a nation-building project.

On one level, the projects of each association brought members together for a common cause, which they saw as being of immediate or long-term benefit to themselves, their community, and the larger national body, but in social — and socially exclusive — milieus. However, associations also advertised their efforts in specific newspapers geared toward particular audiences and extended invitations to a broader range of people who subsequently could be considered as "belonging."[73] The Arabic-language print media and accompanying photographs of Egypt's indigent children brought these very ideas of inclusiveness to a broader range of people and, in this manner, reaffirmed that efforts to ameliorate the lives of poor children could be done only through the contributions of other members of the nation. Newspapers and other publications thus created a sense of inclusiveness that in many cases transcended religious divides. The issue of children's health and well-being was portrayed as a national rather than a community problem, necessitating the whole country's financial and moral commitment. Fund-raising events, lottery tickets, and calls for subscriptions in newspapers such as *Al-Ahram* and periodicals such as *Al-Lata'if al-Musawwara* further served to promote the inclusiveness of members of a nation and their active involvement in improving the lives of society's more vulnerable members.

Nevertheless, signs of exclusiveness were still evident. Language served to exclude individuals from participating in events and denied some groups access to information about the activities of other associations. Advertisements to palace dances and charity bazaars in the English-language newspaper the *Egyptian Gazette*, for example, were intended only for the expatriate community and the English-speaking elite of Cairo and Alexandria. Some aspects of the socialization of children were also delineated by religious affiliation; for example, from the 1920s on, organizations whose efforts were geared toward youth and their moral upbringing were religiously segregated. Medical concerns for infants and small children could cross religious divides, but adolescents' exposure to religious morals and ideals could not.

While elites sometimes competed as each group sought to prove its abilities and commitments toward the poor, on a more profound level the inclusion of discussion of the poor in Arabic-language journals was essential for creating a new discourse of the poor as members of the Egyptian nation. In discussions of Egyptians' responsibilities to their compatriots and in cartoons depicting a range of Egyptians representing the nation (rich and poor alike, as well as children), newspapers and a new national language about national problems and concerns affirmed the inclusion of the poor as members of the Egyptian nation (figure 5.8).

A Proliferation of Associations and the Return of the State

During the 1920s, the number of associations concerned with the needs of poor children increased. In part, this proliferation was a result of a demand for services. However, in the late 1910s, this increase also indi-

Figure 5.8. The Egyptian nation parading before Lord Milner. Despite their promises to leave Egypt once the financial situation had stabilized, the British continued to occupy the country. In 1919, Egyptians rose up in revolt, calling for an end to the British presence there. Lord Milner was sent as the head of a British commission established to investigate the basis of their grievances. This cartoon illustrates how all Egyptians, rich and poor, old and young, demanded *al-istiqlal al-tamm* — complete independence. (Reproduced from *Al-Lata'if al-Musawwara*, October 13, 1919, courtesy of the President and Fellows of Harvard College.)

cated competition between elites and religious denominations. From the 1920s on, discourses of the nation and patriotism (discourses that had resonance with the charitable goals of associations founded in the immediate aftermath of the 1919 Revolution) were often replaced with emphases on religious obligation and denomination-centered charity. Associations that continued to be multidenominational were more frequently concerned with the rights of women or the medical welfare of children; but they were outnumbered by those which dealt specifically with the education of children of a particular religion.

As in the late 1910s, associations raised funds through private subscriptions and fund-raising events such as lotteries and celebrity performances. These organizations also solicited funds from Egypt's ruler, King Fuad.[74] In their requests to the king, they sought to impress him with the breadth of their charitable endeavors and the vast number of poor who were fed, clothed, and sheltered as a result of their efforts.

Associations of this era also continued to have direct contact with the poor. The poor who sought assistance, for example, from the Jam'iyyat al-Muwasah al-Islamiyya (the Society of Islamic Benevolence) presented their requests to a committee who determined whether they were deserving.[75]

Another similarity between associations of the 1920s and 1930s and those of the period of the 1919 Revolution was their emphases on the health and well-being of children. Providing training in industrial training schools continued to be a priority, as did the health of children in general. Organizations such as the SIPE continued to inspire charitable giving by tapping into the anxieties of the wealthy; as in the speeches of Nazmi in 1919, SIPE fete invitations included dire warnings that a failure to contribute to efforts to combat tuberculosis, for example, would expose the children of the wealthy to this disease. Failure to stop the spread of tuberculosis, warned the SIPE, potentially exposed society at large to an army of criminals, as tuberculars were unable to make positive contributions to society and would succumb to criminality to survive.[76]

Efforts to improve the health of children in this era included not only medical assistance but also an increasing focus on sports and moral fortitude. These two foci merged in the programs of various denominational associations. One example was the Muslim Youth Association (established in 1928), which identified itself as modeled on the YMCA but emphasized Muslim religious instruction alongside sports activities.

Distinctive to this period's associations was their conscious disavowal of political agendas. The Egyptian National Archives contain pamphlets of Muslim and Coptic associations that refer to the goals of each association, noting how each was, for example, intended as a way to "care for the poor, heal their sick, and bury their poor." Yet each pamphlet clearly proclaimed — frequently on the cover — that the organization had no political goals. Invitations and lottery tickets state that the organizers have received permission from the Ministry of the Interior to hold a fund-raising event or lottery. This distancing from political agendas became necessary from the 1920s onward due to the government's continued efforts to curtail political activities.[77]

The extent to which associations sought to prove their disavowal of politics draws our attention to organizations whose actions, although charitable, also had political goals. The Muslim Brotherhood best reflected the dual (and effective) role an association could play. The Muslim Brotherhood's activities included assistance to the poor, medical services, and educational opportunities. This organization's attempts to create jobs for the poor and the unemployed as well as their industrial and commercial enterprises — which were free from foreign ownership and management — illustrated their success.[78] The involvement of labor activists in literacy drives and the success of these programs were another example of how an organization's involvement in education could simultaneously meet political objectives.[79]

In an effort to counter and preempt the political activities of charitable associations, and in the hope of drawing more popular support from the Egyptian population, King Farouk's government went a step further than his father. Whereas King Fuad had contributed to a variety of organizations and allowed them to exist, provided they did not engage in political activities, King Farouk's government assumed control over all associations in 1939. In that year, Egypt's government, led by the pro-Axis prime minister Ali Mahir, established the Ministry of Social Affairs. With the establishment of this ministry, associations were required to register their activities. The ministry assumed responsibility for a variety of charitable enterprises and initiated numerous projects of its own. The justification for these actions was that

> [i]t was felt at the time that it was no longer wise to leave the various social problems to be dealt with by haphazard efforts curtailed by opposing currents and conflicting opinions. It was a supreme duty of the State to observe and record social conditions and their development, to diagnose social diseases and defects and to study the methods of treatment; to plan, in light of these observations and studies, a comprehensive and permanent policy of social rehabilitation with a view to uplifting the poor classes, raising the standard of living of the individual as well as the family, and finally assuring the biggest share of social justice to the people.[80]

The Ministry of Social Affairs began to supervise all varieties of charitable work, including associations such as the Muslim and Coptic Benevolent Societies and homes for juvenile delinquents, the aged, the poor, and beggars. The ministry planned to provide social services, housing, and soup kitchens throughout Egypt; up to 14,050 meals to be served daily — 3,300 meals to be provided in the poorer sections of Cairo.[81] Many of these projects were never carried out.[82] The state did not only supervise charitable work but also subsidized select charitable societies. According to government statistics compiled in the late 1940s, societies operating in Egypt numbered nearly three thousand. As in previous decades, their attention was directed primarily toward the needs of children, medical concerns, and education.

One important achievement of the Ministry of Social Affairs was the placement of King Farouk at the center of welfare activities. The king frequently visited homes for the aged, the poor, and orphans to observe their activities and to have his photograph taken with them. The king's intense involvement in public health projects dated from World War II, when an outbreak of malaria devastated Egypt. As Nancy Gallagher shows, within the context of ongoing rivalries between the palace and politicians, King Farouk attempted to use the campaign against malaria to his advantage.[83] The poverty of rural Egyptians during this era also came to the forefront of political discussions as politicians and the press proposed remedies. National attention to the rural poor also led to competition between political parties and personages, both eager to prove their concern for malaria victims. The Wafd, for example, made extravagant public displays of benevolence by distributing food, clothing, and blankets in malaria-stricken areas.[84]

Although King Farouk's efforts to draw attention to his own benevolence and interest in the poor began during World War II, his actions can be set against the backdrop of Egypt's defeat in the 1948 war. With each benevolent action, the king attempted to improve his image in the eyes of the populace. Government involvement was not only for reasons of public relations however; it also arose in response to communist agitation among the rural and urban poor. As Jean Garrison argues, "[P]ublic assistance was considered counterrevolutionary because it both enabled the government to deflect criticism by pointing to its reform efforts and to give discretionary grants to the very poorest who might also be the most likely to be swayed to radical ideologies."[85]

The Egyptian government's oversight of welfare work, like the actions of Ottoman sultans in previous centuries, had come full circle. The state had become directly involved in charitable enterprises during the nineteenth century. Then, philanthropic associations had proliferated at the end of the nineteenth and beginning of the twentieth centuries. By the third decade of the twentieth century, however, the state had begun to intervene more directly. Of particular political import in the 1940s and early 1950s was the way in which King Farouk took advantage of the media (including government publications, such as photographs and advertisements of the Ministry of Social Affairs) to draw attention to his activities.[86] Ottoman sultans had used the strategic placement of mosques and mosque complexes and the choreographing of ceremonials to advertise their efforts and bring them face to face with their needy subjects. King Farouk personally visited the programs and institutions founded by benevolent societies active during this era. His visits and the Ministry of Social Affairs' oversight of their activities were meant to emphasize the fact that the King himself was, like rulers before him, the true source of beneficence.

During the first decades of the British occupation, private groups came to play a greater role in the arena of poor relief. Private initiative in charitable endeavors in Egypt was not new: throughout Islamic history charity and pious endowments by private individuals ensured some measure of care for the poor. Yet the exemplary aspect of private involvement in poor relief in this era was the fact that charitable endeavors took the form of philanthropic associations established by Egypt's upper classes, allowed for greater participation of women in the public sphere, and served charitable goals. By presenting themselves as individuals responsible for the welfare of the poor (particularly children), Egypt's elites affirmed their membership in the nation and at the same time fulfilled a number of political objectives. These included presenting Egypt as an equal among Western nations (in terms of reforming and improving the plight of poor children, as well as in demonstrating the extent to which Egypt's elite were capable of caring for their poor). For Egyptians, these strategies served to counter prior depictions of the poor as suffering from neglect.

During the British occupation, the government's social priorities were sidetracked by political exigencies such as gaining independence from foreign rule.[87] Associations arose, in part, to fill voids left by the state. Religious organizations, such as the Coptic and Muslim Benevolent Societies, as well as multireligious and multiethnic associations, were some examples of the new actors in the field. These groups, in addition to providing medical assistance and educational stipends or facilities to the poor, had another issue in common: increased attention to children. Simultaneous with Egypt's struggle for independence from British rule in the first decades of the twentieth century, an emphasis on children as the future of the nation brought numerous indigenous organizations onto the scene of poor relief. These organizations employed a rhetoric of children as essential elements in the Egyptian nation to draw attention to themselves and to the import of their activities. The rhetoric of saving children also served to affirm a paternalist role for the Egyptian upper classes. And a focus on poor children and the argument that their health and productivity were essential to the future of the nation served to unite the upper classes (regardless of their religious background) in their attempts to "save" and "reform" children and invest in their care.

In the late 1930s, the Egyptian government returned to poor relief through its forceful appropriation and oversight of private organizations' charitable activities. Its motivations were multiple. Among other reasons, the government of King Farouk sought to prove the king's (and the government's) commitment to improving the conditions of the poor. Yet his actions were not successful in legitimating him in the eyes of the Egyptian populace. The defeat of 1948 and a growing dissatisfaction with the monarchy, as well as the government's inability and unwillingness to redress Egypt's social and economic disparities and other difficulties (such as landlessness and wealth disparities in rural areas), led to the overthrow of King Farouk in 1952.

Key to the domestic programs of the new generation of politicians such as Gamal Abdul Nasser were efforts to improve the conditions of Egypt's rural inhabitants through programs such as land reform (a topic that, alongside other discussions about the reasons for impoverishment, had remained taboo for the philanthropic groups active in the first decades of the twentieth century). Egypt's constitution, promulgated in 1956, promised the abolition of imperialism and feudalism and the establishment of a strong army, social justice, and a democratic society. Price controls on food and rent were intended to aid the poor. The socialist revolution of 1961, which included the nationalization of most large-scale industries, also prioritized social insurance for workers and put forth a new rhetoric of rights for the poor and the government's commitment to ensuring a decent living for all of Egypt's inhabitants.[88]

VI

CONCLUSION

FROM "THE POOR" TO "POVERTY"

IN HIS ACCOUNT of the reasons behind the establishment of the Ministry of Social Affairs in 1939, its minister, Dr. Ahmed Hussein, noted that Egypt's social problems could not be left to "haphazard" initiatives and that it was "a supreme duty of the State" to ameliorate the conditions of the poor, raise the standard of living for individuals and families, and ensure social justice for Egypt's inhabitants. The creation of the Ministry of Social Affairs, however, reflected more than the benevolence of the state. Intended to counter and monitor the activities of potentially political groups (such as the Muslim Brotherhood and communist organizations, which were responsive to the needs of Egypt's poor) and bring the state back to the center of charity, its establishment was a political move on the part of the Egyptian government.

However, at the same time that the foundation of the Ministry of Social Affairs served secular and political ends, the Egyptian government's involvement in poor-relief projects represented a continuation of charitable state activity—traditions steeped in Islam and in an Islamic ethos of care for the poor. King Farouk's efforts to put himself center stage in charitable activities built on the actions of Ottoman statesmen and rulers throughout the Middle East. In the Ottoman Empire, the foundation and maintenance of mosques, poor shelters, soup kitchens, and hospitals had provided at least a safety net of care for many of the indigent. At the same time, these forms of charity had served political purposes. In addition to providing public services, rulers in previous eras had used religious endowments as "an instrument of public policy" to secure influence, prestige, and political legitimacy.[1] Nearly one hundred years before the establishment of the Ministry of Social Affairs, Muhammad Ali, fashioning his government's interventions in poor relief after Islamic and Ottoman traditions but also making use of new medical knowledge, had initiated numerous state projects including almshouses, free medical care for the indigent, and a foundling home and orphanage. Like the actions of the ministry and the goals attained through Ottoman rulers' establishment of religious endowments, Muhammad Ali's projects of poor relief, and those of successive governments and of individuals involved in charitable initiatives following his rule—as this book has shown—served more than just benevolent ends.

During the nineteenth century and the first half of the twentieth century, poor relief in Egypt underwent significant changes. Structural transformations involving the creation of new institutions and new and more interventionist methods of charity were representative of developments under way in this era. Both the actors and the targets of charity changed during this period as well: by the end of the nineteenth century, private associations—organizations with distinctive agendas and programs—arrived on the field of poor relief. At this time, the poor themselves and ideas about who constituted the deserving and the undeserving poor became a part of the state's policies. These distinctions were infused within the rhetoric of other organizations coming onto the scene of poor relief. Discourses about responsibility for the poor, and ideas about who was most capable of taking caring of them, also underwent changes in this era. In this final regard, the politicization of poverty brought professionals, politicians, and political parties to the field of poor relief and provided opportunities for them to demonstrate their own benevolence for political ends. Philanthropic associations' involvement in poor relief had constituted a decentering of benevolence. The state's takeover of this role demonstrated the centralization of charity.

Modern Bureaucracies, Modern Institutions

In the Middle East, the family, neighborhood, and religious community functioned as the most important sources of support and assistance to the indigent. In the society at large, the services of religious endowments, wherever they existed, were another form of basic care. In nineteenth-century Egypt, while religious endowments continued to provide for the poor and while the family and religious community continued to care for their destitute members, the Egyptian government became more directly and systematically involved in poor relief. During this era, the government established numerous institutions, including the Mahall al-Fuqara', located in the Maristan Qalawun, and Takiyyat Tulun. These facilities, of which the desperately poor made use, either involuntarily (as inmates) or voluntarily (seeking the state's assistance when they had exhausted other avenues of aid), were only two of the options available to the poor of Egypt and other areas of the Ottoman Empire. In records of petitions and actual petitions (petitions were available only for the early twentieth century at the time of this research), a language of benevolence accompanied records of the assistance afforded to the poor. At the same time, the poor utilized government-established criteria of deservedness to prove their eligibility for care. Although the ruler's obligations toward the poor fitted within a larger rubric of Islamic and Ottoman practices of social welfare, a *bureaucratization* and *depersonalization* of poor relief occurred through the actions of government-appointed officials and offices managing the public presence of the poor. These offices enacted prohibitions on begging and expelled the nonresident but able-bodied poor from Cairo, determined the eligibility of arrested beggars and petitioners for admission to to the shelter, and processed release requests made by the kin of shelter inmates.

The creation of specialized facilities and the bureaucratization of poor relief demonstrated key facets of the modern Egyptian state. Poor relief in Egypt as a whole and in Cairo most specifically, unlike in other locales of the Middle East where its practice was less systematic, became more centralized. At this juncture, policies toward the public poor were implemented to serve specific goals. The use of the Maristan as a place of internment and the conversion of the Ahmad ibn Tulun Mosque into a shelter for the poor fulfilled — coterminously — both pious and pragmatic purposes. The poor admitted into these shelters obtained food and a roof over their heads. But for many, a stay in these facilities came at the expense of their individual freedom. The number of persons who requested admission to the shelter, however, illustrates that the poor, perhaps out of desperation, were willing to forgo some of their independence. The government's goals to confine the poor were never completely realized. Shelter administrators occasionally expelled even individuals who were deemed deserving of assistance, and shelter residents, either on their own initiative or through the request of a family member or other acquaintance, were also able to gain their freedom.

The centralization of poor relief in Egypt, beginning in the first half of the nineteenth century, provides unprecedented perspectives on the Egyptian government's practices of managing the poor. The creation of various offices charged with monitoring the use of public spaces, the appointment of officials whose responsibilities included expelling the nonresident but sturdy poor (men as well as women), and the frequency of orders and decrees calling for the expulsion of the undesirable poor from cities such as Cairo indicate the Egyptian government's desire to find workers for Egypt's agricultural areas as well as infrastructural and industrial projects. Yet policies of removing the itinerant poor from Cairo's public spaces also brought police officers into contact with individuals who were unfit to work; and for these people, the government enacted a second set of policies. The Egyptian government never denied that the "deserving" poor merited charity — thus demonstrating that it respected religious tradition — but, through the establishment of poor houses and the enactment of prohibitions on begging, Cairo authorities endeavored to keep even the deserving poor out of sight. If these individuals had no one to provide for them, the government would assume responsibility for them. But if family members were willing to vouch for their good behavior, promise that they would not return to begging, and prove to the shelter's administrators that they were capable of taking care of their relative, the person would be released. The Egyptian government gave beggars two choices: either let their families take care of them or accept the charity of the state.

By establishing its own categories of those defined as "deserving" of charity and expelling able-bodied peasants from cities such as Cairo and forcing able-bodied residents to work, Muhammad Ali's government and subsequent regimes became more actively involved in poor relief. The charity of the state cannot be viewed solely as a means of social control or as an effort to restrict the mobility of Egypt's itinerant poor. Its actions served benevolent purposes as well. The services the state provided ensured that some of the poor would receive medical assistance, food, and shelter in state-sponsored facilities. The same charity also provided care for infants found in the streets of Cairo. The poor's dependence on the state is evident in the number of individuals who actively sought the assistance of the state.

Analysis of poor relief in the nineteenth and early twentieth centuries provides information on the comings and goings of the poor to and from state-run facilities, the range of options available to the destitute, and changing attitudes toward the poor. The documentation illustrates the enactment of government policies restricting the freedom of beggars, the poor's ability to take advantage of government initiatives and navigate through the various offices responsible for managing the poor, and the points at which state policies toward the poor were modified or even abandoned entirely. The shelters established during the rule of Muhammad Ali had served to remove (though not entirely) the itinerant poor from the streets; in the years following his death, they continued to serve that purpose. Their ongoing use illustrated the continued efficacy of this bureaucracy of poor relief and the continued viability of state institutions.

However, alongside the arrest of beggars, we find that the poor made increasing requests from the state for admission to shelters. Shelter administrators were unable to meet these demands fully, but accounts of individuals who made institutions such as Takiyyat Tulun their home reveal that the poor whose circumstances seemed the most desperate — mothers with small children, the elderly and invalid who had no other sources of care or shelter — succeeded in making this poorhouse their temporary or permanent home.

The Rise of Philanthropic Associations

After the closure of Takiyyat Tulun, other shelters housed the most desperately poor of Cairo and other areas who sought the state's assistance. At the same time, government correspondence concerning what to do with other issues, such as the quiet insane, and comments of British medical advisers and foreign visitors and residents describe the increased presence of the poor in Cairo's public spaces. Shelters such as Takiyyat Tura and Takiyyat Qabbari frequently rejected applicants; leaving one of these shelters, as Abd Allah Hasan had done when he sought medical treatment, meant that an indigent person might not be allowed back in. By the late nineteenth century, the number of desperately poor came to exceed the capacity of the state to care for them.

At this time new actors entered the field of poor relief to compensate for the inadequacy of government means to provide for Egypt's poor. Missionaries were one such organization. They provided medical assistance, care for orphans and abandoned children, and educational facilities, thus meeting some of the needs of the Egyptian populace. But their involvement at times came at a price. Copts and Muslims feared the proselytizing efforts of the missionaries and attempted to counter missionary activities by establishing their own facilities for care for the poor.

Private philanthropy, notably associations established by the British and Egyptian upper classes, served as an alternative. These associations, whose charity and philanthropic efforts were placed within an indigenous framework of religious piety, served multiple purposes. They were instrumental in establishing health care and educational facilities for the poor, and they brought the upper classes into greater contact with the poor. The poor took advantage of the services provided by these philanthropic groups: they requested medical assistance, received home visits (from the Coptic Benevolent Society), and enrolled their children in vocational training centers. In their interactions with one another, the elite who established these associations affirmed their role in caring for the poor. One feature of the changing relationship between the elite and the poor was a new sense of belonging to a national body. Focusing their efforts on poor children, considered indispensable members of the Egyptian nation, the elite advocated the importance of private initiative in their care. Predicating their actions upon a sense of moral obligation and framing their activities within a larger rhetoric of the Egyptian nation, Egypt's upper classes forged a place for themselves as participants in the effort to build and strengthen the nation. They viewed their efforts in tutelage of and care for the poor as rendering Egypt equal to other Western nations.

Their involvement in poor relief also represented a degree of self-consciousness. Prior to the British occupation, Westerners had depicted Egypt's government as despotic and negligent of the poor. When the occupation began, Egypt's elite were accused of being indifferent to the plight of the poor. As Egypt increasingly became the destination of tourists and a "health resort" for British vacationers, Egypt's upper classes grew more concerned with their image. They were also well aware of British portrayals of them: in October 1919 *Al-Lata'if al-Musawwara* reprinted a cartoon from the London paper the *Graphic*, which depicted, among other images of Egypt, "importunate guides" waiting for customers at the Shepheard's Hotel and "itinerant Arabs" plying "their trade" (that is, begging and peddling) in the streets (figure 6.1).

Egypt's monarch, King Farouk, concerned with his own image, sought to replace the beneficence of private associations and of the elite with his own. The establishment of the Ministry of Social Affairs illustrates how the Egyptian government made a forceful return to the field in the first half of the nineteenth century. King Farouk and government officials recognized the political import of charity. As a counterweight to the programs offered by societies such as the Muslim Brotherhood and the promises of communist agitators, the Egyptian government was compelled to demonstrate its own abilities to care for the poor. As Nancy Gallagher showed in *Egypt's Other Wars*, her book on the distribution of food and other services during the Second World War, competition developed between the palace and political parties, and among political parties themselves, as each sought to prove its abilities to best provide for the poor.

Policies of Inclusion and Exclusion

Among Muslims, a rubric of charity included the obligation of the family, community, and ruler to care for the weak and needy. How were determinations as to a person's need made? We do not have information on private charity and how private individuals distinguished between the deserving and the undeserving; but we do know that such distinctions were a concern of Islamic legists, as well as a problem that state officials in various eras and locales faced. Research on Istanbul illustrates that this city's authorities were, for reasons of public order, most concerned about the public presence of nonresident unemployed men who sought to migrate to the city. The able-bodied poor, men who had

Figure 6.1. Reprint of a September 20, 1919, cartoon published in the *Graphic.*
Among the scenes depicted are Egyptian tourist guides congregating at the Shepheard's Hotel and a beggar / street peddler accosting British soldiers. (Reproduced from *Al-Lata'if al-Musawwara*, October 13, 1919, courtesy of the President and Fellows of Harvard College.)

no connections or sources of support (from families, guilds, or other
social units), were also considered potentially troublesome.

In Egypt as well, we see that city officials sought to monitor the rural
poor's access to Cairo. As in Istanbul, maintaining public order and
security was one aspect of these policies. But city authorities also enacted prohibitions on begging so as to deny the sturdy poor access to
this form of subsistence and to clear the streets of the itinerant poor.
Individuals deemed fit for work constituted the undesirable and undeserving poor. If they were from the countryside, both men and women
in the period up to the 1850s found themselves back on the land from
which they had fled (or as Joseph Hekekyan describes, some of these
people were sent to work on the estates of Muhammad Ali and his
family). In the 1830s begging by even able bodied religious mendicants
was prohibited as a viable means of subsistence; instead, the beggars
were put to work in government-run factories. We also find that in the
1850s and 1860s, able-bodied residents of Cairo and Alexandria were

put to work in various projects. Vagrants found in the countryside were also rounded up and given employment or drafted into the army.

Such harsh punishments and control of the public presence of the sturdy poor, however, did not apply to individuals deemed deserving of assistance. Cairo authorities and shelter administrators established their own criteria about who was deserving of care. The deserving included the elderly and invalid, as well as single women and women with small children. Not all single women were considered deserving, however. Many women found wandering around the streets of Cairo on their own or women arrested among larger groups of peasants who had fled from the countryside were expelled from the city. Marcus has noted that a status of dependence served to distinguish the poor. In Cairo, authorities determined that these women's potential to earn a living (for example, as peasants in the countryside) meant that they were not among the deserving poor.

For individuals who were successful in proving their dependent status, state-run poor shelters provide information on their identities and circumstances. Unlike the records of institutions such as imaret in the Ottoman Empire or of facilities such as Sufi lodges, which also served as temporary homes for the poor, records of Takiyyat Tulun provide information on the gender of recipients as well as the circumstances that led them to seek state assistance. Most women and children stayed in the shelter longer than men, but men also frequently sought the charity of the state. Invalids, the elderly, and individuals who could prove that they were unable to provide for themselves and that they had no one to take care of them sought and received state care. They became residents — permanently or temporarily — of state-run facilities. Their requests for assistance illustrate how families in nineteenth-century Egypt were in many cases unable to provide for their own weak and destitute members.[2]

By the decades of the British occupation, the criteria for determining who was undeserving had become more sharply delineated. Able-bodied men, as in the decades preceding the occupation, were viewed with suspicion, and policies toward them became harsher and more restrictive. Sturdy male beggars were identified as vagrants and were subjected to fines, imprisonment, and transportation. The police and rural officials introduced pass laws and other methods of monitoring the movements of the laboring and migratory poor (such as seasonal workers) and kept track of their actions.

Fears of crime and brigandage lay behind the restrictions on the movements of able-bodied men. A language of criminality entered the parlance of the police and of indigenous and foreign reformers; vagrants were no longer simply individuals seeking casual work or a roof to sleep under; rather, in the first decades of the British occupation, they were described in ways that highlighted concern about their potential criminality. That adult male vagrants or the casually employed could constitute "armies" of criminals implied that younger men who had no familial or community ties could band together. Using language that served to heighten the fear of the potential criminality of street children and juvenile delinquents, prison reformers and association members emphasized the necessity of providing them with vocational training so that they would one day acquire viable trades. In fund-raising events and other forums at which street children were discussed, association members emphasized the positive potential of children. If raised properly and provided with education and training, they would make worthwhile contributions to the Egyptian nation. Key to their abilities to make such contributions, however, were the tutelage and actions of Egypt's wealthy classes.

Improving the Poor

In tandem with the growing restrictions on the sturdy poor (and suspicion of even the deserving poor, as was evident in Kamel Greiss's presentation to the Royal Society), new perspectives on the role of philanthropists and the uses of charity were introduced at the end of the nineteenth and the beginning of the twentieth centuries. The private individuals who merged their philanthropic efforts into the activities of associations supplemented traditional spontaneous forms of giving and the foundation of religious charitable endowments. They created institutions that served practical purposes: the poor deemed worthy of the charity that associations provided received vocational training, educational scholarships, and other forms of assistance geared toward their self-sufficiency and well-being. The Egyptian government adopted many similar programs. In the adult reformatories, as well as children's, reformatories, vocational training was introduced in the hope of helping former criminals begin a new life.

Beyond the focus that philanthropic associations had on street children in particular, other groups active in Egypt also provided assistance to poor families. One way was by providing educational opportunities for the children of single parents. Room and board eased financial strain on poor families and in the long run increased the child's potential to make a contribution to the family income. The Muslim and Coptic Benevolent Societies also provided financial and medical assistance, with each organization determining the poor's eligibility for care.

Although we have information on the numbers of families who received assistance from private associations, the ways in which these organizations determined the poor's deservedness are less clear. Lists of children enrolled in the Malga' al-Hurriyya show the status of their parents; these frequently included single mothers or families whose head of household was unable to work. Their petitions often highlighted their desperate economic circumstances. The category of the deserving poor in twentieth-century Egypt was nearly the same as that in the nineteenth century. Women, children, the elderly, and the invalid were objects of sympathy, but critics such as Greiss warned that even women and children beggars were "impostors"; and the Egyptian press promoted the idea that Cairo's street children could, at any moment, turn into armies of criminals.

New state interventions in poor relief, initiated in the first half of the nineteenth century, and the emergence of charitable organizations by the end of that century beautifully illustrate Egypt's encounters with the modern.[3] The bureaucratization of charity, made possible through the development of increasingly centralized offices, new institutions, and the employment of officials charged with overseeing public spaces and denying beggars access to these spaces, represented new state-societal relations and the introduction of highly specialized state apparatuses. Poor-relief projects and attitudes toward the itinerant poor, however, could not operate in a vacuum. Islamic and Ottoman traditions of charity and European advisers and observers influenced the development of institutions and practices. Aspects of these transformations demonstrated Egypt's proximity to Europe and the interplay of colonial encounters. But these developments also featured another condition of modernity: the internationalization of discourses concerning the poor and children's health and well-being—cross-cultural exchanges made possible through modern mediums such as the press and travel (tourism, educational enterprises, and international conferences).

❦

In the early nineteenth century Egypt's public poor had been a source of frustration for Cairo authorities seeking to rid the streets of beggars and other members of the itinerant poor. By the early part of the twentieth century, questions about who was responsible for taking care of the poor wandering in the streets and of other needy individuals entered in the public debate. Without assistance from their native countrymen, the poor were vulnerable to the proselityzing of missionaries, and without adequate training or education, they could turn to crime. Responsibility for caring for the poor, from the perspective of individuals such as indigenous reformers and journalists, lay with the Egyptians themselves.

The poor constituted part of the nation, and Egyptian society's investments and the institutions it established to care for them proved that
Egypt deserved to be considered among other civilized and modern nations.

Toward the middle of the twentieth century, political parties and the
king also entered the field of poor relief, this time due to their concerns
about the political influences charitable organizations might have on the
poor and, pragmatically, because of their interest in proving their abilities to care for the poor. Demonstrating their benevolence through the
bestowal of assistance, they sought to legitimate their rule and their
commitment to Egypt's populace. Their efforts, however, stopped short
of seeking solutions to poverty or raising questions about social justice.
Such political moves would be left to the platforms and agendas of their
successors. In the years following the fall of the monarchy in 1952,
discussions of Egypt's poor were replaced by debates about Egypt's poverty, proposals for strengthening the economy, and projects to lessen
Egypt's political and economic dependence on the West so as to create a
more viable future for Egypt.

NOTES

PREFACE
FINDING EGYPT'S POOR

1. In order of appearance, L 2/1/43/29/1142, 14 Rabi' I 1270 (January 14, 1854); L 2/1/43/168/1432, 14 Jumada I 1270 (February 12, 1854); L 2/11/17/48/20, 10 Rajab 1280 (December 21, 1863). I discuss the establishment and use of Takiyyat Tulun in my article "Getting into Takiyat Tulun." For distances between Cairo and its environs, I made use of Baedeker's *Egypt: Handbook for Travelers* (1914), 170.

2. See, for example, Dodwell, *Founder of Modern Egypt*; Rafi, *Asr Muhammad Ali*; and Marsot, *Egypt in the Reign of Muhammad Ali*.

3. Fahmy, *All the Pasha's Men*.

4. Toledano, *State and Society*. Also see idem, "Mehmet Ali Paşa."

5. Timothy Mitchell, *Colonizing Egypt*. Fahmy, *All the Pasha's Men*, 30–32.

6. Owen, *Cotton and the Egyptian Economy*.

7. Cuno, *The Pasha's Peasants*.

8. Tucker, *Women in Nineteenth-Century Egypt*.

9. Kuhnke, *Lives at Risk*.

10. On poor people's petitions for medical assistance, see Ener, "The Charity of the Khedive."

11. Tucker, *Women in Nineteenth-Century Egypt*, 103.

12. A number of authors mention benevolent associations that were active during this era. See Marsot, "The Revolutionary Gentlewoman in Egypt"; Kashef, "Egypt"; Shalabi, *Harakat al-Islah*; Ahmed, *Women and Gender in Islam*; Baron, *Women's Awakening*; and Badran, *Feminists, Islam, and the Nation*.

13. For policies toward the poor and the use of poor shelters in Europe, see, for example, Hufton, *The Poor of Eighteenth-Century France*. For an overview of poor relief and charity throughout England and the Continent, see Geremek, *Poverty*. An edited volume that brings the family and community to the forefront of research on the range of poor-relief options in various regions of the world is Peregrine Horden and Richard Smith's *Locus of Care*. A discussion of the roles that families and institutions played in caring for the insane is provided by the numerous contributors to *Anatomy of Madness*, ed. Bynum, Porter, and Sheperd. Analyses of the establishment of foundling homes in England and France, histories that include the ideologies of founders, moral pressures from society at large, statistics, and, in some cases, extensive information on the identities of mothers who abandoned their children, can be found in McClure, *Coram's Children*, and Fuchs, *Abandoned Children*.

In the case of the Middle East, there are new works by Miriam Hoexter, Adam Sabra, and Amy Singer, as well as a volume (Bonner et al., *Poverty and Charity*) comprising an analysis of poverty and charity across the geographic expanse of the Middle East from the seventh century onward. See Hoexter, *Endowments, Rulers, and Community*; Sabra, *Poverty and Charity in*

Medieval Islam; Singer, *Constructing Ottoman Beneficence*; and Bonner et al., *Poverty and Charity*. With the exception of chapters by Mark Cohen, Mine Ener, Eyal Ginio, Miriam Hoexter, Nadir Özbek, and Kathryn Libal, which seek to recover the voices of the poor who sought assistance, the contributors to the edited volume, like the monographs of Hoexter, Sabra, and Singer, examine primarily the founders of charitable works and their motivations.

14. Hoexter, "Charity, the Poor"; Singer, "Charity's Legacies."

15. Marcus, "Poverty and Poor Relief," and Ginio, "Living on the Margins of Charity."

16. Jean Deny notes that Cairo police records for the period preceding 1844 were destroyed in 1889 (*Sommaires des Archives Turques*, 31–32, 124, 443).

17. A team from the Centre d'etudes et de documentation economique, juridique, et social (CEDEJ), beginning in the early 1990s, conducted thorough research on an 1847 census. Prior to the British occupation of Egypt, this was the most complete census done in the nineteenth century.

CHAPTER I
BENEVOLENCE, CHARITY, AND PHILANTHROPY

1. Thornton, *The Present State of Turkey*, 2:155.

2. Fernea, "Children in the Muslim Middle East," 3–17.

3. For an overview of the impoverishment of women during different stages of their life cycles in the context of Europe, see Henderson and Wall, "Introduction."

4. Judith Tucker discusses how women received assistance from family members when they brought cases of divorce to court, for example. She also illustrates how the husband's family was responsible for supporting the wife and children if the husband was unable to do so. These, and other discussions of women's receipt of maintenance allowances, are found in Tucker's *In the House of the Law*, 113–47.

5. This is still true now. Andrea Rugh, "Orphanages in Egypt: Contradiction or Affirmation in a Family-Oriented Society," in *Children in the Muslim Middle East*, ed. Fernea, 126.

6. Stillman, "Charity and Social Services," 114.

7. Carol Delaney describes instances of nonrelatives giving support to needy neighbors in twentieth-century Turkish villages in *The Seed and the Soil*, 151–52. Marcus discusses neighborhood support networks in "Poverty and Poor Relief," 177. For forms of mutual assistance within Cairo's guilds, see Ghazaleh, "Masters of the Trade," 63–66.

8. Forster and Daniell, *The Life and Letters of Ogier Ghiselin de Busbecq*, 1:209.

9. Walsh, *Constantinople*, 2:457.

10. Minutoli, *Recollections of Egypt*, 50.

11. Thornton, *The Present State of Turkey*, 2:155–56.

12. For a discussion of the treatment of religious minorities during various eras of Islamic history, with a special emphasis on the Ottoman period, see C. E. Bosworth, "The Concept of Dhimma in Early Islam"; Robert Mantran, "For-

eign Merchants and the Minorities in Istanbul"; and "On the Realities of the Millet System: Jerusalem in the Sixteenth Century," in *Christians and Jews in the Ottoman Empire*, ed. Braude and Lewis.

13. Cohen, "Poverty as Reflected in the Cairo Geniza Documents."

14. Marcus, *The Middle East on the Eve of Modernity*, 216–17. Schlomo D. Goitein discusses various social services provided to Jews in tenth- through twelve-century Cairo in *Mediterranean Society*, vol. 3. For this era as well, see Cohen, "Poverty as Reflected in the Cairo Geniza Documents." Jacob Landau's book, *Jews in Nineteenth-Century Egypt* includes a discussion of provisions made for Jews in late-nineteenth-century Cairo and Alexandria.

15. Marshall Hodgson highlights the central role awqaf have played in Islamic society, noting that religious endowments were "the original means for financing Islam as a society" (*The Venture of Islam*). Since business enterprises (such as shops and other structures intended for commerce) were frequently established as awqaf, we find that such businesses were located in close proximity to mosque complexes. For the historical background on awqaf, see McChesney, *Charity and Philanthropy in Islam*.

16. See, for example, the range of services and institutions that individuals of various levels of social standing designated as awqaf in Trabzon, in Jennings, "Pious Foundations."

17. Hoexter, "Waqf Studies in the Twentieth Century," 479.

18. Hoexter, *Endowments, Rulers, and Community*.

19. Baer, "Women and Waqf," 21.

20. Petry, "A Paradox of Patronage," 192.

21. Sabra, *Poverty and Charity in Medieval Islam*, 99.

22. Sanders, *Ritual, Politics, and the City in Fatimid Cairo*.

23. Sabra, *Poverty and Charity in Medieval Islam*, 69–100, 134–68.

24. Bahaeddin Yediyıldız, *Institution du Vaqf au XVIIIe siècle en Turquie*, 248–58; Inalcık, *The Ottoman Empire*, 147–50; and idem, *Economic and Social History*, 47.

25. Forster and Daniell, *Life and Letters*, 1:136–39.

26. Inalcık, "Istanbul," 229. *Bayt al-Mal* was the term used for the central treasury of successive Islamic empires. For a discussion of its use in eras prior to the Ottomans, see Tourneau, "Bayt al-Mal."

27. Jomard, "*Description*," 584, 675, and 676; Winter, *Egyptian Society*, 34–35, 155. Also see DeJong, "Tasawwuf."

28. Schimmel, *Mystical Dimensions*, 120–24.

29. Wolper, "The Politics of Patronage," 40, and Dols, *Majnun*, 123.

30. Gallagher, *Medicine and Power*, 22–23.

31. Toledano, *State and Society*, 209. The term *takiyya*, in contemporary Egyptian parlance, is synonymous with "poorhouse." Nahid Hamdi Ahmad discusses how tekkes served as points of distribution for food and water for the poor but notes that only *members* of particular orders were admitted; see her "Watha'iq al-Takaya."

32. Çelebi, *Narrative of Travels*, 174. Amy Singer examines the creation of an imperial soup kitchen in Jerusalem in *Constructing Ottoman Beneficence*.

33. Inalcık, "Matbakh."

34. Marcus, "Poverty and Poor Relief."

35. Inalcık, "Matbakh," 810 and 812. For rituals of food distribution among inhabitants of the Arabian peninsula during the early Islamic period, see Bonner, "Poverty and Charity in the Rise of Islam."

36. Sabra, *Poverty and Charity in Medieval Islam*, 52–55.

37. Peirce, *Imperial Harem*, 202.

38. Sabra, *Poverty and Charity in Medieval Islam*, 62.

39. Inalcık, "Istanbul," 229.

40. Cuno, "Ideology and Juridical Discourse," 143–44.

41. Ibid., 156.

42. Horden and Smith, "Introduction," 9.

43. Thornton, *The Present State of Turkey*, 159.

44. Documents pertaining to the expulsion of beggars and vagrants are available in the Cevdet Zaptiye series, Başbakanlık Arşivi, Istanbul; see nos. 2637 (Rabiʿ I, 1144), 682 (22 Jumada I, 1217), and 1722 (Shaban 1237).

45. Bosworth, *Mediaeval Islamic Underworld*, 13–16.

46. Karpat, "Population and the Social and Economic Transformation," 89–90.

47. Tucker, *In the House of Law*, 78–112.

48. Toledano, *State and Society*, and Marcus, "Poverty and Poor Relief," 175.

49. A thorough examination of Ottoman Egypt's administrative history and a discussion of centralized practices prior to the nineteenth century is Stanford Shaw's *Financial and Administrative Organization*. Contributors to Hanna's *The State and Its Servants* also offer new findings on the administrative apparatuses of this era.

50. F. Robert Hunter describes features of the Egyptian state, namely bureaucratic centralization and the role of the household elite, in *Egypt under the Khedives*.

51. Sanders, *Ritual, Politics, and the City*; Amin, "Wathaʾiq Waqf al-Sultan"; Petry, "Paradox of Patronage"; Behrens-Abouseif, *Egypt's Adjustment to Ottoman Rule*; Afify, *Al-Awqaf wa al-Haya al-Iqtisadiyya*; and Sabra, *Poverty and Charity*.

52. From 1517 until the First World War, when the British designated it a protectorate, Egypt was a province of the Ottoman Empire. As Toledano and Fahmy have shown, Egypt's ruling elite were, culturally and politically, Ottomans. I do not, however, label the government "Ottoman-Egyptian." Although designating it as Egyptian implies a political independence that it did not achieve until the twentieth century, because my focus is on the government's domestic policies reflecting decisions made in Egypt for Egypt, I retain use of the terms *Egyptian government* and *Egypt's government* throughout.

53. I use the term *elite* interchangeably with *upper classes*. Although the middle classes were also involved in philanthropy (frequently they established philanthropic projects and invited elite members of society to serve as titular members), newspaper articles and other forums always called for the involvement of Egypt's "rich" or "wealthy classes" (what I translate, hence, as elites or upper classes) in philanthropic efforts.

54. Greiss, "La Mendicité en Egypte et sa repression," 207. *L'Egypte Con-*

temporaine was a publication of a society founded by Egypt's ruler and scholarly community; it was committed to the study of politics, society, law, and economics. Since at different periods the society was called the Sultanic Society and the Khedival Society, in later references I give it the more simple title of Royal Society.

55. Marsot, "The History of Muhammad Ali."

56. I discuss this hybridity, in terms of Ottoman, British, and French influences on practices of poor relief in Egypt during the first half of the nineteenth century, in "At the Crossroads of Empires."

57. In *Madness and Civilization*, Michel Foucault argues that seventeenth-century France witnessed "the great confinement." This confinement encompassed a new intolerance toward begging, the idle poor's imprisonment or forced labor, and the exclusion of society's marginal people (for example, the insane and lepers).

58. On the ways in which official and state-generated sources frequently provide information only on the goals of programs and not their actual outcomes, see Krieken, "The Poverty of Social Control," 8.

59. Lynn Lees examines how Benthamite ideals of surveillance were never put into practice in British poorhouses; see *The Solidarities of Strangers*, 107–9. The extent to which families depended on state and private agencies to assist them in caring for insane family members in seventeenth- and eighteenth-century England is discussed by Andrews in "'Hardly a Hospital,'" 63–81. Thomas Laqueur counters E. P. Thompson's argument that Sunday schools in England were one way in which the upper classes imposed work ethics and docility on the working classes; see *Religion and Respectability*.

60. Lees, *The Solidarities of Strangers* and "The Survival of the Unfit."

61. Skocpol, *Protecting Soldiers and Mothers*. Linda Gordon explores the rise of social work as a profession in the early twentieth century, the influence feminists had on the development of welfare during this era, and the demands of the needy; see *Pitied but Not Entitled*.

62. Koven and Michel, eds., *Mothers of a New World*.

63. Horden and Smith, *Locus of Care*, and Barry and Jones, *Medicine and Charity*.

64. Timothy Mitchell's *Colonizing Egypt* best represents the imposition of a "colonizing" and control model on the landscape of Egypt. In his book, Mitchell documents the advent of the increasingly interventionist state in nineteenth-century Egypt. He looks at the multitude of ways in which Muhammad Ali's regime and the regimes of his successors attempted to control, order, and discipline the Egyptian populace, bringing forth an analysis of a highly pervasive state apparatus that admittedly remained in many respects only a model or a blueprint. Fahmy, arguing that Mitchell's work limits itself to "enframing devices" and stops short of studying the actual effects and outcomes of these projects, in his own analysis of the Egyptian army seeks to understand when and why disciplining projects failed (*All the Pasha's Men*, 31–32).

65. Bruce Bellingham discusses the successes and failures of "child-saving" programs in New York City; see "Waifs and Strays."

66. Lees, "The Survival of the Unfit," and Lis and Soly, "'Total Institutions.'"

67. Adele Lindenmeyr examines how religious values and concern for the poor undermined attempts to criminalize begging and poverty; see her *Poverty Is Not a Vice*.

68. *Workhaus*, a combination of English and German words, is but one of the expressions used for the factory-type structure that was to be housed in Tak-iyyat Tulun. This structure was also referred to as a "maison de travail" in the correspondence between M. Pauchard and the Egyptian government. A discussion of this proposal (which included the hiring of Mr. Pauchard—from Lausanne, Switzerland—to oversee the creation of this "*workhaus*") is in DWQ Asr Ismail, box 56/1, December 20, 1875. Valérie Baqué discusses this project in "Approches de la marginalité en Egypt."

69. For an overview of the value and importance of this mosque as an Islamic monument, see *Comité de conservation des monuments de l'art Arabe*. Corbet, "Life and Works." Donald Reid discusses the mixed European and Egyptian membership of this committee in "Cultural Imperialism and Nationalism."

70. For an example of an association active in the early twentieth century, see Çiçek, "Asker Ailelerine Yardımcı Hanımlar Cemiyetinin Faaliyetleriyle Ilgili Bir Belge."

71. Nadir Özbek, "The Politics of Poor Relief."

72. Robert Bianchi discusses measures to curtail and restrict the actions of associations in early-twentieth-century Egypt; see his *Unruly Corporatism*.

73. Gallagher, *Egypt's Other Wars*.

CHAPTER II
DISCERNING BETWEEN THE DESERVING AND THE UNDESERVING POOR

1. Ali Bey, *The Travels of 'Ali Bey*, 1:391–92. Ali Bey al-Abbasi was a pseudonym used by the Spanish traveler Domingo Badia y Leblich.

2. Hillenbrand, "Masdjid."

3. Edwards, *A Thousand Miles up the Nile*, 22. In addition to serving as a place of worship, mosques in the medieval period were places where beggars and the insane congregated. Dols, *Majnun*, 473.

4. Despite accusations that Muhammad Ali's seizure of waqf land had negatively affected institutions funded by religious endowments, al-Azhar continued to provide food and assistance to ulema (religious clerics), students, and the needy throughout the nineteenth century. Yates, citing Van Egmont, noted that 2,000 people slept in al-Azhar each night, and between 5,000 and 6,000 received daily food rations. Yates, *Modern History and Condition*, 2:336. Also see James August St. John, *Egypt and Muhammad Ali*, 2:337. For information on the care of students and families of the ulema of al-Azhar, see Ruznama registers 224,176 (1227/1812), 1001, 6248, 6245, (1232/1817), 1361 (1243/1828), 3216 (1245/1830), and 4454 (1270/1854). Ali Mubarak discusses the functioning of the soup kitchen located in al-Azhar Mosque; see his *Al-Khitat al-Tawfi-qiyya*, 4:39. At the end of the nineteenth century, the government, through the Ministry of Religious Endowments, continued to provide assistance to the poor of al-Azhar. See S 11/1/10/148/52, 9 Jumada II 1290 (August 4, 1873), correspondence between the Majlis al-Khususi and the ministry. For the early twentieth century, information on provisions for al-Azhar can be found in a series of

registers entitled *Diwan al awqaf: majmu'at al-watha'iq mizaniya iradat wa masrufat diwan umum al aqwaf.*

5. Amin, "Watha'iq Waqf al-Sultan Qalawun."

6. For a discussion of the pious and simultaneously political functions of religious endowments in the Mamluk and Ottoman periods in Algeria, Egypt, and the central Ottoman lands, see Petry, "Paradox of Patronage"; Hoexter, *Endowments, Rulers, and Community*; Hanna, "Construction Work in Ottoman Cairo"; and Peirce, *Imperial Harem*, 198–209.

7. Marcus, "Poverty and Poor Relief," 171.

8. Toledano, *State and Society*, 103. See also Ross, "Survival Networks."

9. Minutoli, *Recollections of Egypt*, 50.

10. S 1/1/9/19/4, 7 Safar 1273 (October 7, 1856).

11. Edward Lane, *Manners and Customs*, 421–24. Sabra discusses how the Shi'ite holiday of Ashura, which gained importance as a holiday during Fatimid rule of Egypt, was commemorated in subsequent centuries.

12. Dols, *Majnun*, 460.

13. Edward Lane, *Manners and Customs*, 285–86.

14. Stillman, "Charity and Social Services," 114.

15. The Şeyhülislam, appointed by the sultan, was the chief religious cleric of the Ottoman Empire. The question before him read: What is the shari'a punishment for people who give alms to troublesome beggars at mosques? The answer: It is necessary to reprimand beggars and forbid troublesome begging, but those who give alms are virtuous. Düzdağ, *Şeyhülislam Ebüssuud Efendi Fetvaları Işiğinda 16. Asır Türk Hayatı*, 179. For the life and work of Ebu's-su'ud, see Imber, *Ebu's-su'ud*. For the medieval period and policies toward sturdy beggars, see Bosworth, *Mediaeval Islamic Underworld*, 13–16.

16. James August St. John, *Egypt and Muhammad Ali*, 1:138; Yates, *Modern History and Condition of Egypt*, 1:274, 331; and Edward Lane, *Manners and Customs*, 248, 327–28.

17. Mark Cohen, "The Foreign Jewish Poor in Medieval Egypt," in *Charity and Poverty*, ed. Bonner et al. Also see Rosenthal, "Stranger in Medieval Islam," 43.

18. Winter, *Egyptian Society under Ottoman Rule*, 292 n. 7. Abd al-Samad Diyarbakri, a Turkish chronicler residing in Egypt in the early to mid-sixteenth century, discusses policies toward peasants who had fled to Cairo during famines. Diyarbakri's observations are cited in *Egyptian Society under Ottoman Rule*, by Winter, 227.

19. Geremek, *Poverty*, 142–77.

20. Lis and Soly, *Poverty and Capitalism*, 92–93.

21. I discuss a number of these economic developments and their influence on attitudes toward the able-bodied poor in "Prohibitions on Begging."

22. L 2/1/7/14/11, 23 Ramadan 1262 (September 14, 1846) and Hekekyan Papers, 1843, vol. 2, fol. 120, British Library. The Ma'mur al-mutasahibin was also responsible for draft dodgers. See, for example, the capture of Abdul Fatah Khalil, a deserter, in L 2/1/8/233/367 23 Muharram 1263 (January 11, 1846).

23. Çadırcı, "Tanzimat Döneminde," 169–85.

24. Başbakanlık Osmanli Arşivi (the Ottoman Archives in Istanbul), Zaptiye (Police Records), no. 682, 22 Jumada I, 1217 (September 20, 1802), and no.

1722, Sha'ban, 1237 (May 1822). Also see Özbek, "II. Meşrutiyet Istanbul'unda Dilenciler ve Serseriler," and Heyd, *Studies in Ottoman Criminal Law*, 303, 307.

25. McGowan, "The Age of Ayans," 647.

26. Aktepe, "Istanbul'un Nüfus Meselesine Dair Bazı Vesikalar."

27. Fahmy, *All the Pasha's Men*, 11, 311. Muhammad Ali's household and retinue also had a great deal to gain from the agricultural riches of Egypt. For a discussion of the responsibilities and roles of his supporters and his household's members, see Hunter, *Egypt under the Khedives*.

28. For an examination of the disruptions these various economic programs caused in peasants' lives, see, for example, Marsot, *Egypt in the Reign of Muhammad Ali*, 128–29; Tucker, *Women in Nineteenth-Century Egypt*, 27–29; and Cuno, *The Pasha's Peasants*, 153. For a discussion of how state building arises in consequence of war making, see Tilly, *Coercion, Capital, and European States*. Tilly argues that wars necessitate extraction of resources to pay for the military, which in turn leads to repression of the populace. Also necessary for the extractive capacity of the state is an efficient system of courts, treasuries, systems of taxation, regional administrations, and public assemblies.

29. Fahmy, *All the Pasha's Men*.

30. Marsot, *Egypt in the Reign of Muhammad Ali*; Tucker, *Women in Nineteenth-Century Egypt*; Timothy Mitchell, *Colonizing Egypt*; Kuhnke, *Lives at Risk*; and Cuno, *The Pasha's Peasants*; all explore state-societal relations during this era.

31. Bowring, Report on Egypt and Candia, 1839, fol. 339, and Hekekyan Papers, 1843, vol. 2, fols. 148, 175.

32. Gabriel Baer discusses collective punishments of villagers in "The Village Shaykh." For the responsibilities of rural officials in the eighteenth century, see Abd al-Rahim, *Al-Rif al-misri*.

33. Najm, "Tasahhub al-fallahin," 284–86; S 1/13/1/19/12, 14 Muharram 1245 (July 16, 1829); S 1/37/1/523 24 Safar 1247 (July 5, 1831); and Hekekyan Papers, vol. 2, fol. 120.

34. An example of a tadhkira used in the second part of the nineteenth century can be found in Dabtiyyat Misr Mukatabat Arabi, no. 3, dated 29 Sha'ban 1290 (October 22, 1873). For decrees discussing enforcement of the tadhkira, see *Al-Waqa'i' al-Misriyya*, no. 34 2 (Dhu l-Hijja, 1244 [June 5, 1829]: 1, and no. 246 (9 Ramadan, 1246 [February 21, 1831]: 4. For a discussion about the issuance of another sort of identification card, see *Al-Waqa'i' al-Misriyya*, no. 228 (18 Rajab, 1246 [February 21, 1831]): 1. Although women were among the absconders being returned to the countryside, I have not found any reference to women being issued tadhkira.

35. Najm, "Tasahhub al-fallahin."

36. Bayle St. John, *Village Life in Egypt*, 2:59.

37. Toledano, *State and Society*, 182 (discussion of exemptions from conscription in the reigns of Abbas and Ismail). Former soldiers' decision to stay in Cairo after their service is on 198. Bowring notes that employees of manufactories were not conscripted (Bowring, Report on Egypt and Candia, fol. 128).

38. Lane, *Manners and Customs*, 123–24.

39. The most comprehensive study to date of peasant flight from the country-

side is Najm's "Tasahhub al-fallahin." Abd al-Rahman ibn Hasan al-Jabarti, in *Al-Aja'ib al-Athar fi Arajim wa al-Akhbar* (1880; reprint 1966), discusses numerous incidents of unrest in the countryside and city at the end of the eighteenth and beginning of the nineteenth centuries due to taxation and famine and recounts how peasants frequently fled from their villages. For example, accounts of food scarcities and unrest in the rural areas are in 3:272–73; for a discussion of famine and the poor leaving the countryside, see 3:279; the actions of students at al-Azhar who revolt when they do not receive their rations is recounted in 3:298; the suffering of the starving rural and urban populaces (due to crop failures), the depopulation of the countryside, and the necessity of importing wheat from Anatolia is found in 4:220; Bedouin attacks on pilgrim caravans is in 4:242; and further discussions of food prices are in 7:396.

40. Dar al-Kutub al-Qawmiyya (Egyptian National Library), *Al-Waqa'i' al-Misriyya* 34, June 5, 1829, 1.

41. Peters, " 'For His Correction." In addition to Gypsies and peasants, homeless black slaves were singled out as having committed acts of thievery and begging.

42. Bowring, Report on Egypt and Candia, fol. 339. Also see James August St. John, *Egypt and Muhammad Ali*, 2:412; Hekekyan Papers, vol. 2, fols. 148, 175.

43. Diwan al-Khidiwi, box 1, 16 Dhu l-Hijja 1243 (June 29, 1828); S 7/33/1/317, 22 Rabi II 1245 (October 21, 1829). James August St. John, *Egypt and Muhammad Ali*, 2:425–27. Beggars, previously tolerated in Russia's major cities, also found themselves the targets of the police when the government of Peter the Great launched "a full scale assault on begging and vagrancy." These efforts were part of Peter's attempts to modernize Russia and included concerted efforts to distinguish between deserving beggars and impostors. His government also attempted to suppress the charitable actions of private citizens; almsgivers were fined and encouraged to give money to institutions rather than beggars (Lindenmeyr, *Poverty Is Not a Vice*, 30–32).

44. James August St. John, *Egypt and Muhammad Ali*, 2:425–27.

45. Abu-Lughod, *Cairo*, 87–93.

46. Fahmy, "The Era of Muhammad Ali Pasha," 163–64. Fahmy also discusses concerns about sexually transmitted diseases among prostitutes in "Women, Medicine, and Power." Tucker discusses the ban on prostitution initiated in 1834 and notes that despite prohibitions, prostitution continued in cities such as Cairo (*Women in Nineteenth-Century Egypt*, 151–52).

47. Cuno, *The Pasha's Peasants*, 123–24, 153–63.

48. L 2/1/1/ 15/2, 11 Ramadan 1260 (September 24, 1844). Peasants came from various areas of Egypt but also from as far away as Jerusalem. L 2/1/1/ 15/3 4 Shawwal 1260 (October 17, 1844) provides examples of peasants' places of origins, including Jerusalem.

49. L 2/1/16/580/662, 9 Shawwal 1265 (August 28, 1849).

50. For example, see L 2/1/7/169/249, 19 Dhu l-Hijja 1262 (December 8, 1846).

51. See, for example, L 2 /1/16/554/641, 14 Ramadan 1265 (August 3, 1849).

52. Helen Rivlin discusses Muhammad Ali's commissions of inquiry and how he went into the countryside himself to study conditions there (Rivlin, *Agricultural Policy*, 102). Maha Ghalwash examines policies during the reigns of the

Abbas and Said (which included redistributing land to poor peasants) in "Land Acquisition."

53. See, for example, L 2/1/5/204/ 217, 5 Safar 1262 (February 2, 1846).

54. S 1/33/1/10, 5 Safar 1279 (August 2, 1862). Another term for the *orta al-madhnubin* was *firqa islahiyya* (the military reform unit). Further orders calling for the arrest and training of vagabonds are in S 1/19/2/12/8, 12 Jumada II 1280 (November 24, 1863) and S11/8/10/24/10, 17 Jumada I 1283 (September 27, 1866). I discuss actions against rural vagrants of the second half of the nineteenth century in "Prohibitions on Begging." None of the records of arrests for wandering around without work or being homeless mentioned whether the supposedly "idle" were looking for work.

55. Hekekyan Papers, vol. 2, fol. 120; Hamont, *L 'Egypte sous Méhémet Ali*, 1:121–22.

56. Mollat, *The Poor in the Middle Ages*, 270.

57. S 1/72/11/1040, 1053/80 4 Sha'ban 1264 (July 6, 1848).

58. Reimer, "Reorganizing Alexandria," 62.

59. The Ornato's visit is discussed in Hekekyan Papers, 1844, vol. 2, fol. 239. For an overview of the establishment of the Civilian Hospital of Azbakiyya as well as other health care initiatives during this period, see Ibrahim, *Al-Haya al-Ijtima'iya fi Madinat al-Qahira*, 117–23.

60. Issa Bey, *Al-Bimaristan*, 58. See also Mahfouz, *The History of Medical Education*, 12–15, and Amin, "Watha'iq Waqf al-Sultan Qalawun."

61. "Rapport sur le Moristan."

62. Jomard, "Description de la ville du Kaire," 2:322.

63. Bowring, Report on Egypt and Candia, 1839, fol. 352.

64. S 1/79/1/376, 28 Ramadan 1250 (January 28, 1835); S 2/32/1, 7 Muharram 1253 (April 13, 1837); and Shura al-Mu'awana, Register 274/1007/346, 25 Ramadan 1253 (December 23, 1837).

65. Yates, *Modern History*, 1:330, 334, 335.

66. Gallagher, *Medicine and Power*, 20–21. Medieval European hospitals also served various functions. In this regard, see Martha Carlin, "Medieval English Hospitals," and Brodman, *Charity and Welfare*.

67. Yates, *Modern History*, and Lane Poole, *Englishwoman in Egypt*, 1:175

68. For information on Hekekyan's background and training in England, see Mustafa, "The Hekekyan Papers."

69. Hekekyan Papers, 1844, vol. 2, fol. 239.

70. S 3/122/2/68/43, 5 Muharram 1263 (December 24, 1846).

71. For large groups being admitted to Mahall al-Fuqara', see, for example, documents pertaining to the arrest of 40 beggars in L 2/1/1/13/8, 10 Rajab 1260 (July 26, 1844); the arrest of 6 beggars in L 2/1/1/14/20, 10 Rajab 1260 (July 26, 1844); the arrest of 7 beggars in L 2/1/1/17/22 15 Ramadan 1260 (September 28, 1844); and L 2/1/1/17/30, 17 Ramadan 1260 (September 30, 1844).

72. S 1/79/1/376, 28 Ramadan 1250 (January 28, 1835).

73. L 2/1/1/ 15/2, 11 Ramadan 1260 (September 24, 1844).

74. L 2/1/1/23/1, 26 Ramadan 1260 (October 9, 1844).

75. L 2/1/1/23/9, 17 Muharram 1261 (January 26, 1845). I have not found accounts of this threat being carried out.

76. L 2/1/1/180/418, 2 Rabiʿ II 1261 (April 10, 1845).

77. Sabra, *Poverty and Charity*.

78. S 3/122/2/68–69, 5 Muharram 1263 (December 24, 1846) and S 3/122/2/ 115 and 119, 19 Rabiʿ II 1263 (April 6, 1847).

79. I discuss the Qanun al-Muntakhabat's articles on begging in "At the Crossroads."

80. Inalcık, *Economic and Social History*; *The Ottoman Empire*, 47; and "Matbakh."

81. L 2/1/7/142/207, 29 Dhu l-Qaʿda 1262 (November 18, 1846). This is just one example of a foundling. During a period of eight years (between 1846 and 1854), when the most extensive discussion of infant abandonment and admission to the Madrasat al-Wilada is available in the Dabtiyya registers, the numbers generally ranged from one to three foundlings per month (some months there were none).

82. Edward Lane, *Manners and Customs*, 197. The act of leaving a child at a mosque indicated that the child's religion was Islam. Infants were also abandoned at churches. Guerin, *La France catholique*, 50.

83. In "The Charity of the Khedive," I discuss incidents of people seeking medical and other services available to them. The following are examples of registers that contain references to the sick receiving care: L 2/1/1 (1845); L 2/1/13 (1848); L 2/1/42/44 (1853–54); L 2/1/119 and L 2/11/15–16 (1863); L 2/1/124 and L 2/11/18 (1864); L 2/11/40 (1868); and L 2/1/212 (1876).

84. Sami Hamarneh discusses a number of hospitals established in the central Arab lands as well as in Andalusia in "Development of Hospitals in Islam." For further information on hospital construction and medical services in the Mamluk and Ottoman periods, see Sabra, *Poverty and Charity*; Gurkan, *Süleymaniye Daruşşifasi*; Taşkıran, *Hasekinin Kitabi*; and Hoexter, *Endowments, Rulers, and Community*.

85. Foucault, "Governmentality," 100. Also see Foucault's discussion of biopolitics in *The History of Sexuality*, 139–40.

86. Fahmy, *All the Pasha's Men*, 210, and Tagher, *Mémoires de A. B. Clot Bey*.

87. Kuhnke, *Lives at Risk*, 134.

88. For Clot Bey's training in France and the impact many of these ideas had on his own actions in Egypt, see Panzac, "Médecine révolutionnaire."

89. Kuhnke, *Lives at Risk*, 116–19, and Fahmy, *All the Pasha's Men*, 210. Concern about infant mortality grew in part out of fears of depopulation. Madden notes that Muhammad Ali sent European physicians into the countryside to inoculate children against smallpox so as "to prevent the total depopulation of the country." See Madden, *Travels in Turkey, Egypt, and Palestine*, 298. Yet Clot Bey's own policy objectives (and specifically his pronatalist stance) were also realized through the government's involvement in the care of abandoned infants. For his condemnation of abortions, for example, see his *Aperçu*, 2:426–27. Mervat Hatem discusses how the government (and especially Clot Bey) sought to restrict reproductive choices in this era; see "The Professionalization of Health," 70. The Qanun al-Muntakhabat (1844), parts of which were adopted from the French Code pénal, stipulates that the punishment for per-

forming abortions is six months' to two years' imprisonment. The text of Qanun al-Muntakhabat is in Zaghlul's, *Al-Muhama*. Clot Bey was also instrumental in passing laws on abortions and child abandonment in 1857. For these laws, see S 7/33/1/248 17 Sha'ban 1273 (April 12, 1857).

90. L 2/1/15/69/124 26 Rabi' I 1265 (February 19, 1849). While Dabtiyya records recount frequent requests by families and others to have infants wet-nursed and cared for by the state, an account of mortality rates among children in the foundling home is absent. In Europe, maternity wards and foundling homes were sites of infection and disease, and infants who became the charges of wet nurses frequently died.

91. L 2/1/143/15/1105 10 Rabi' II 1270 (January 10, 1854).

92. L 2/1/42/160/1031 30 Rabi' I 1270 (December 31, 1853).

93. L 2/1/12/337/640 16 Rabi' II 1264 (March 22, 1848).

94. L 2/1/10/ 616/1006 26 Sha'ban 1263 (August 9, 1847).

95. L 2/1/6/591/931 4 Ramadan 1262 (August 26, 1846).

96. L 2/1/19/475/1053 27 Jumada I 1266 (April 10, 1850).

97. L 2/1/12/309/606 1 Rabi' II 1264 (March 7, 1848).

98. Examples of orphans are found in L 1/60/9, L 1/60/13, and L 2/11/42/59/130.

99. For hospitals in Europe, see Porter, *Disease, Medicine, and Society*, and Grinshaw and Porter, eds., *The Hospital in History*.

100. L 2/1/43/157/1421, 11 Jumadi I 1270 (February 9, 1854); L 4/1/13/58/ 88, 10 Safar 1272 (October 22, 1855); L 2/1/1/11/4, 3 Ramadan 1260 (September 16, 1844); and Tagher, *Mémoires de A. B. Clot Bey*, 316.

101. While the creation of distinct and specialized facilities were state initiated, at the turn of the century, voluntary charity also witnessed such transformations. These trajectories (wherein charity became more specialized) were similar to developments under way in nineteenth-century France and Germany. See Weindling, "The Modernization of Charity."

102. In *The History of Medical Education in Egypt*, Mahfouz argues that by 1863, the hospital had fallen into ruin (43). Toledano discusses negative portrayals of the Abbas and Said's reigns in *State and Society*, 25–35.

103. Duff Gordon, *Letters from Egypt*, 157, and Mahfouz, *History of Medical Education in Egypt*, 46.

CHAPTER III
AMONG THE POOR OF TAKIYYAT TULUN

1. Mubarak, *Al-Khitat al-Tawfiqiyya*, 4:101. On Tulunid rule, see Kennedy, *Prophet*, 174, 310–11. Regarding the architecture of this mosque, see Corbet, "The Life and Works of Ahmad ibn Tulun."

2. Creswell, *Early Muslim Architecture*, 2:338.

3. Lane Poole, *Cairo*, 22.

4. Corbet, "The Life and Works of Ahmad ibn Tulun," 555.

5. Creswell, *Early Muslim Architecture*, 2:338. Also see Corbet's accusations in "The Life and Works of Ahmad ibn Tulun," 555.

6. Duff Gordon, *Lady Duff Gordon's Letters from Egypt*, 18.

7. Ibid., 18–19.

8. S 1/1/14/34/1 7 Rabiʿ II 1276 (November 3, 1859); S 1/1/15/55/29 27 Jumada I 1277 (December 11, 1860); S 1/7/4/16/14, 20 Rajab 1278 (January 21, 1862); S 1/1/19/77/99, 26 Shaʿban 1278 (February 26, 1862); and Maʿiyya Saniyya Arabi Register 1907/106/25, 23 Shaʿban 1280 (February 2, 1864). A number of these orders pertain to special food or other items to be distributed during or after Ramadan.

9. S 1/1/30/41/2, 13 Jumada II 1282 (November 3, 1865). Baer discusses the Kavala waqf in *A History of Landownership*, 149, 159.

10. S 11/2/5/98, 103,104/323, 17 Jumada I 1290 (June 13, 1873). On a prior occasion, the poor of Tulun were to be transferred to another building, a former broadcloth factory. S 1/1/40/38/102, 3 Jumada II 1286 (September 10, 1869). Another source of funds for Takiyyat Tulun and other mosques and takaya in Egypt during this period was the central treasury (Maliyya) and the Customs Office of Alexandria. S 1/1/39/62/48 19 Shaʿban 1285 (August 18, 1878).

11. McCarthy, "Nineteenth-Century Egyptian Population," 30, 33. McCarthy shows how nineteenth-century European estimates of Egypt's population were frequently incorrect and argues that it is impossible to obtain exact population figures for this period.

12. L 2/11/2/173/869, 25 Rajab 1275 (February 28, 1859), L 1/60/4, and L 1/60/8.

13. L 2/1/12/346/661, 25 Rabiʿ II 1264 (March 31, 1848).

14. L 2/1/41/88/513, 4 Safar 1270 (November 6, 1853).

15. The following documents record the requests made by each of these men (in order of appearance in the text): L 2/1/41/38/427, 23 Muharram 1270 (October 26, 1853); L 2/1/41/153/643, 18 Safar 1270 (November 20, 1853); L 2/1/41/45/809, 5 Rabiʿ I 1270 (December 6, 1853); L 2/1/120/51/2217, 10 Safar 1280 (July 27, 1863); and L 2/1/121/6/2380, 14 Rabiʿ I 1280 (August 29, 1863).

16. L 2/1/124/56/38, 23 Rajab 1280 (January 3, 1864). For more on the precarious position in which "the stranger" found himself, see Rosenthal, "The Stranger in Medieval Islam."

17. L 2/11/2/255/1060, 22 Shaʿban 1275 (March 27, 1859).

18. L 2/1/124/161/490, 25 Shaʿban 1280 (February 4, 1864).

19. L 2/11/53/189/2283, 19 Jumada I 1287 (August 17, 1870).

20. L 2/1/125/149/655, 3 Dhu l-Qaʿda 1280 (April 10, 1864) and L 2/1/125/666/669, Dhu l-Qaʿda 1280 (April 1864).

21. L 2/1/41/144/633, 17 Safar 1270 (November 19, 1853).

22. L 2/1/41/38/429, 23 Muharram 1270 (October 26, 1853).

23. L 2/11/51/ 53/1231, 29 Dhu l-Hijja 1286 (April 1, 1870).

24. L 2/11/15/69/1283, 12 Safar 1280 (July 29, 1863).

25. L 2/1/123/178/318, 5 Rajab 1280 (December 16, 1863).

26. L 2/1/120/29/ 2174, 4 Safar 1280 (July 21, 1863).

27. L 2/1/120/151/2342, 2 Rabiʿ I 1280 (August 17, 1863).

28. L 2/11/16/18/16, 30 Rabiʿ I 1280 (September 15, 1863).

29. L 2/1/41/110/552, 8 Safar 1270 (November 10, 1853).

30. L 2/1/43/196/1499, 20 Jumada I 1270 (February 18, 1854).

31. L 2/11/40/145/2177, 10 Rabiʿ I 1285 (July 1, 1868).

32. L 2/11/18/187/52, 4 Safar 1281 (July 9, 1864).

33. L 2/11/2/129/749 6 Rajab 1275 (February 9, 1859).

34. L 2/11/41/15/2361, 6 Jumada I 1285 (August 25, 1868).

35. L 2/11/42/59/130, 11 Jumada II 1285 (September 29, 1868).

36. Tucker examines how in nineteenth-century Egypt the courts might have considered women who engaged in some trades to be unfit mothers (*Women in Nineteenth-Century Egypt*, 82). For a discussion of child custody cases following divorce or the death of a spouse, see Tucker, *In the House of Law*, 113–47.

37. L 2/1/41/110/552, 8 Safar 1270 (November 10, 1853).

38. L 2/1/41/113,117/561, 10 Safar 1270 (November 12, 1853).

39. L 2/11/39/118/1611, 1 Safar 1285 (May 24, 1868).

40. L 2/11/52/187/1913, 13 Rabi' I 1287 (July 13, 1870).

41. L 2/1/41/82/495, 3 Safar 1270 (November 5, 1853), and L 2/1/41/84/498, 3 Safar 1270 (November 5, 1853).

42. L 2/11/18/114/498, 24 Dhu l-Hijja 1281 (May 31, 1864).

43. Yates, *Modern History*, vol. 1; Edward Lane, *Manners and Customs*, 196. That widows of soldiers, women whose husbands were serving in the army, and the elderly needed assistance from the state illustrates the absence of other means of support for some families. For other possible reasons for the purported "emptiness" of villages, see note 15 in chapter 4.

44. James August St. John, *Egypt and Muhammad Ali*, 2:176. Fahmy discusses women's resorting to prostitution in an effort to provide for their families; see his "Era of Muhammad Ali Pasha," 162–63.

45. S 1/1/9/64/31, 11 Rabi' I 1273 (November 9, 1856). Pensions were distributed through the office of the Ruznamaji (Chief Office of Expenditures). For mention of food rations for the children of disabled soldiers, see Mahfazat al-Ma'iyya al-Saniyya, box 1, document 103/1557, 20 Jumada II 1264 (May 24, 1848) and the Campbell/Bowring correspondence found in Bowring, Report on Egypt and Candia, fol. 28. Information on rations for children of army personnel in the 1850s is in Sami, *Taqwim al-Nil*, vol. 3, pt. 1, 82. Free education was also provided to male children whose fathers were in the army and navy late in the century; see Decree of 10 Muharram 1290 (March 10, 1873) in Sami, *Taqwim al-Nil*, vol. 3, pt. 3, 1051.

46. Edward Lane, *Manners and Customs*, 196, and S 1/46/24/224/30, 8 Jumada I 1280 (October 21, 1863).

47. L 11/8/12/144–148, 16 Rabi' II 1286 (July 26, 1869).

48. L 2/1/54/53/2384, 7 Jumada II 1287 (September 4, 1870).

49. Iliffe paraphrases Jean-Pierre Gutton's definitions of structural and conjunctural poverty in *The African Poor*, 4. For Gutton's discussion, see *La Société et les pauvres*. Also see Mollat, *The Poor in the Middle Ages*, 26–31.

50. My quantification and analysis of the numbers of poor people admitted to state-run shelters (or seeking medical assistance) and my examination of lists of shelter residents were facilitated by two databases. These databases allowed me to search and retrieve data on, for example, the number of admissions in any given month, the ratio of men to women, and the grouping of family units.

51. Cuno, "Joint Family Households," 485–502. Cuno also discusses the composition of rural households in "A Tale of Two Villages."

52. Toledano, *State and Society*, 209.

53. One example of a woman seeking out her husband, whom she accused of having stolen money from her, is found in L 2/11/2/312/1212, 28 Ramadan 1275 (May 1, 1859). This case, which involved the sum of 1,400 piasters, indicates both a woman's ability to travel and the "fiction" that her husband was lacking in resources.

54. Tucker, *Women in Nineteenth-Century Egypt*, 61, 102–03.

55. L 2/1/42/6/732, 26 Safar 1279 (November 28, 1853).

56. L 2/1/43/98/1313, 1 Jumada I 1270 (January 30, 1854).

57. Due to the lack of sufficient fuel, lack of expertise, and the absence of significant investments, industrial endeavors had failed. The Treaty of Balta Liman (1838) abolished agricultural monopolies. Egypt was forced to reduce the size of the army and war industries in compliance with the Treaty of London (1841). Marsot discusses the impact of these treaties on the economic and political transformations effected during Muhammad Ali's rule. Marsot, *Egypt in the Reign of Muhammad Ali*, 238–40. Whether or not Muhammad Ali's industrial efforts would have succeeded had Britain not interceded is the topic of debate: obtaining sufficient fuel for steam-powered machinery had been an ongoing problem, and factory machinery frequently broke down. For further discussion of Egypt's industrialization efforts, see Owen, *The Middle East in the World Economy*, 72.

58. Between 1853 and 1856, the drafting of men for the Crimean War would have also explained heightened attention to rounding up agricultural and military absconders.

59. An example of the roundup and arrest of 272 agricultural absconders, including those who had found work in Cairo, is in L 2/1/19/508, 512, 514, 516/125, 14 Jumada II 1266 (April 27, 1850).

60. See, for example, L 2/1/41/65/196, 30 Muharram 1270 (November 2, 1853); L 2/1/42/82/899, 13 Rabiʿ I 1270 (December 14, 1853); L 2/1/42/73/88, 12 Rabiʿ I 1270; and L 2/1/83/97/1071, 20 Dhu l-Hijja 1274 (August 1, 1858).

61. L 2/1/84/36/1197, 19 Muharram 1275 (August 29, 1858).

62. L 4/1/21/25/40, 4 Rabiʿ I 1277 (September 20, 1860).

63. L 4/1/21/69/52, 15 Rabiʿ II 1277 (October 31, 1860).

64. L 2/1/41/117/568, 10 Safar 1270 (November 12, 1853).

65. L 2/1/41/120/571, 11 Safar 1270 (November 13, 1853).

66. L 2/1/41/82/494, 3 Safar 1270 (November 5, 1853). The head of the Armenian community was informed of the circumstances of Ibrahim al-Fayan's arrest in L 2/1/41/117/562, 10 Safar 1270 (November 12, 1853). The Syrians were reminded to prohibit members of their community from begging (L 2/1/41/117/563, 10 Safar 1270 [November 12, 1853]), as were the Copts (L 2/1/41/117/564, 10 Safar 1270 (November 12, 1853).

67. L 1/60/3.

68. L 2/1/41/117/567, 10 Safar 1270 (November 12, 1853).

69. L 2/1/125/100/467, 18 Shawwal 1280 (March 27, 1864). For accounts of numerous British nationals' (British, Greek, and Maltese citizens) arrest for vagrancy, prostitution, and other crimes in Alexandria during the 1840s, see PRO FO 97/410, Police Registers—Turkey. David Landes discusses poor Europeans' coming to Egypt in the 1860s in *Bankers and Pashas*, 89.

70. See, for example, S 1/1/34, 1 Rajab 1283 (November 9, 1866).

71. S 11/2/5/98, 103, and 104/ 323,17 Jumada I 1290 (June 13, 1873).

72. L 2/1/42 171/1043, 1 Rabiᶜ II 1270 (January 1, 1854), and L 2/1/122/135/ 103, 29 Rabiᶜ II 1280 (October 13, 1863).

73. L 2/1/122/174/132, 12 Jumada I 1280 (October 25, 1863).

74. John Barnes shows how, with the beginning of the Tanzimat (and following the creation of the Ministry of Religious Endowments for the central Ottoman lands), dervish orders faced strict regulation. The state took over their property, and vagrant dervishes and students had to register so the government could maintain control over their movements and actions (Barnes, *An Introduction to Religious Foundations*, 44–45, 100–101).

75. L 2/11/2/249/1051, 19 Shaᶜban 1275 (March 24, 1859), and L 1/60/3. Yusuf and his wife might have been confined to the shelter before September 1859.

76. L 2/11/2/190–91/909, 1 Shaᶜban 1275 (March 5, 1859), and L 1/60/4.

77. Toledano discusses daman (guarantees) and damin (guarantors) in the context of obtaining employment in mid-century Cairo (*State and Society*, 199, 203, and 209). Such sureties were promises and not, to the best of my knowledge, monetary.

78. L 2/11/2/165/840, 19 Rajab 1275 (February 22, 1859).

79. L 2/1/41/140/617, 14 Safar 1270 (November 16, 1853).

80. L 1/60/3 and L 2/11/2/ 274/1108, 3 Ramadan 1275 (April 6, 1859).

81. L 2/11/2/287/1142, 7 Ramadan 1275 (April 10, 1859), and L 1/60/4.

82. L 2/11/2/274/1111, 3 Ramadan 1275 (April 6, 1859), and L 1/60/3.

83. L 2/1/42/173/1048, 2 Rabiᶜ II 1270 (January 2, 1854).

84. L 2/1/43/15/1106, 10 Rabiᶜ II 1270 (January 10, 1854).

85. L 2/11/3/165/1641, 24 Dhu l-Hijja 1275 (July 25, 1859), and L 1/60/9.

86. L 2/11/2/279/1122, 4 Ramadan 1275 (April 7, 1859), and L 1/60/3.

87. L 2/11/2/285/1136, 6 Ramadan 1275 (April 8, 1859), and L 1/60/4.

88. L 2/11/2/300/1180, 17 Ramadan 1275 (April 20, 1859).

89. L 2/11/2/309/1204, 24 Ramadan 1275 (April 27, 1859).

90. L 2/11/3/60/1391, 29 Shawwal 1275 (June 1, 1859).

91. L 2/1/124/7/346, 12 Rajab 1280 (December 23, 1863).

92. L 2/11/1/63/134, 24 Rabiᶜ I 1275 (November 1, 1859).

93. L 2/11/1/15/481, 20 Jumada I 1275 (January 25, 1859).

94. For an example of an individual who had his name taken off the list of deserving persons, see the petition of Abd Allah Hasan, who left Takiyyat Tura for medical treatment. Mahfazat Abdin (boxes of petitions), April 25, 1915. Discussion of the high number of applicants to shelters of Cairo and Alexandria during the British occupation of Egypt is in 2/2/b Majlis al Wuzaraʾ: Ministry of the Interior, Matters of Public Health, Ministry of Health.

95. L 2/11/3/87/1467, 13 Dhu l-Qaᶜda 1275 (July 14, 1859); L 1/60/9; and L 1/60/13.

96. L 2/11/3/44/1343, 13 Shawwal 1275 (May 16, 1859); L 1/60/8; and L 1/60/13.

97. L 2/11/3/73/1421, 5 Rabiᶜ I 1275 (October 13, 1858); L 1/60/13; and L 1/60/18.

98. S 1/46/24/205/15, 24 Rabiʿ II 1280 (October 8, 1863), and S 1/46/24/224/30, 18 Jumada I 1280 (October 13, 1863).

99. Burkhardt, *Arabic Proverbs*, 7.

100. A discussion of the allocation of funds from other religious endowments toward the expenses of Takiyyat Tulun is in S 1/1/30/41/2, 13 Jumada II 1282 (November 3, 1865).

101. Members of the various French missions established schools, orphanages, and medical services in Egypt (as well as in Istanbul) during the 1870s and frequently approached Khedive Ismail to request donations. Their requests and the records of Ismail's contributions are in Asr Ismail, boxes 56/3 and 56/4. Also see M. Octave Sachot, "Rapport addressé à son excellence Monsieur Victor Duruy Ministre de l'Instruction Publique sur l'état des Sciences, des Lettres, et de l'Instruction Publique en Egypt" (1868).

102. Ismail had, in the words of Afaf Lutfi al-Sayyid Marsot, "grandiose" plans for Egypt, many of which seemed within the realm of possibility due to the importance of Egypt and the profitability of cotton grown there during the Civil War in the United States. With the end of the cotton boom, however, and due to Egypt's ever greater debts—thanks to projects initiated during the reign of his predecessor, Said, Egypt during the reign of Ismail witnessed financial collapse and ultimately Ismail's dethronement (Marsot, *A Short History of Modern Egypt*, 67–70).

103. During this era, a concern for appearances as well as charitable impulses clearly lay behind the government's calls for the admittance of beggars to shelters. In this regard, see S 1/1/37/29/27, 5 Shaʿban 1284 (December 2, 1867), and M 7/2/164/238, 17 Jumada II 1296 (June 7, 1879).

104. In *State and Society*, Toledano counters conceptions of "decline."

105. The Ministry of Religious Endowments (Diwan al-Awqaf) was established in 1851 and re-created in 1863. For this office's refusal to care for the poor, see L 19/24/24, November 5, 1879, cited in Cole, *Colonialism and Revolution*, 216. Offices concerned with matters of public health, such as those of the Ministry of Religious Endowments or those pertaining to hospitals, had some of their funds depleted due to expenditures by the family of the viceroy. In a document dated November 30, 1878 (a period when the British and the French were responsible for balancing the Egyptian government's budget), a commission inquiring about expenditures noted that doctors on government payrolls frequently served the viceroy's family, not the public at large. For this document, see 2/2/b Majlis al Wuzara'.

106. This committee, known as the Committee for the Conservation of Monuments of Arab Art, composed of Europeans and Egyptians, was concerned with preserving Islamic works of art and architecture throughout Egypt.

CHAPTER IV
THE SPECTACLE OF THE POOR

1. Baedeker, *Egypt: Handbook for Travelers*, 265.

2. Swinglehurst, *Cook's Tours*, 95.

3. Murray, *A Handbook for Travelers*, 127.

4. Baedeker, *Egypt: Handbook for Travelers*, 16.

5. Hobson, *Helouan*, 5.

6. Hutnyk, *The Rumour of Calcutta*, 86. Timothy Mitchell discusses this en-framing in terms of the introduction of a particular order and structure, show-ing how representations of Egypt (for example, in world exhibitions) set forth for Europeans a particular conception of Egypt (*Colonizing Egypt*). Hutnyk (18–21) presents a discussion of enframing in which he shows how this concept leads to a particular way in which the world comes to be viewed, arguing that the dominant frame through which Calcutta is viewed is economics and poverty.

7. Thompson, *Sir Gardner Wilkinson*, 167–68. Wilkinson's *Handbook for Travelers in Egypt* was published in 1847.

8. Waterfield, *Letters from Egypt*, 111, 120.

9. Timothy Mitchell discusses how portrayals of Egypt's poverty (its over-population and insufficiency of arable land) continue to pervade the develop-ment literature; see in "America's Egypt."

10. Yates, *Modern History*, 1:274.

11. Ibid., 276.

12. Ibid., 330–32.

13. Ibid., 339.

14. Edward Lane, *Manners and Customs*, 196–97 (on depopulation); Bayle St. John, *Village Life in Egypt*, 2:59 (pauper women); James August St. John, *Egypt and Muhammad Ali*, 1:78 (depopulation) and vol. 2:176 (prostitution).

15. R. R. Madden, *Egypt and Muhammad 'Ali*, 42. On disease as the cause of village depopulation, see McCarthy, "Nineteenth-Century Egyptian Popula-tion." Also see Marsot, "The History of Muhammad Ali." In this article Marsot claims that travelers' depictions of rural depopulation served political ends. Confirming Marsot's findings, Janet Ross (Lucie Duff Gordon's daughter) re-marked that in the 1860s village men would disappear whenever a government steamer approached. So it is likely that during that era, the depopulation on which travelers remarked was, in fact, caused by able-bodied men who hid until the outsiders (that is, government officials or foreigners) left (Waterfield, *Letters from Egypt*, 311). Fahmy, making use of Egyptian government correspondence corroborating travelers' accounts, concludes that the villages were frequently deserted due to government conscription drives (*All the Pasha's Men*, 99–107).

16. Bartlett, *The Nile Boat*, 53; von Crowins Smith, *Pilgrimage to Egypt*.

17. See, for example, Waterfield, *Letters from Egypt*, 317–18.

18. These "unsanitary habits" included a failure to keep infants clean. See Whately, *Letters from Egypt to the Plain Folks at Home*, 101, and Edward Lane, *Manners and Customs*, 63. Also see Mary L. Whately's *Child Life in Egypt* (Philadelphia: Union Press, 1866).

19. Marsot's discussion of negative portrayals is in "The History of Muham-mad Ali." On the creation of this binary opposition and its political ramifica-tions, see Said, *Orientalism*.

20. Madden, *Travels in Turkey, Egypt, and Palestine*, 1:309–10, 319. In 1792 William Tuke had pioneered more humane treatment of the insane at an asylum in York, England (under the management of the Society of Friends). His im-provements, which included care without the use of excessive force or restraints,

led to important legislation in England. For efforts to eradicate the use of chains and corporal punishment in nineteenth-century British asylums, see Skull, *Museums of Madness*, 119–20.

21. James August St. John, *Egypt and Muhammad Ali*, 2:310.

22. Moreau, "Recherches sur les aliénés," 110. Yates, *Modern History*, 1: 334–35.

23. Lane Poole, *Englishwoman in Egypt*, 1:167, 175.

24. Janet L. Abu-Lughod warns against using Clot Bey's work as an indicator of the developments under way in Egypt during the nineteenth century, for he is full of praise only for Muhammad Ali. The same can be said of Clot Bey's discussions of the completion of his own projects (*Cairo*, 83, n. 4).

25. Bartlett, *The Nile Boat*, 51.

26. See, for example, von Crowins Smith, *Pilgrimage to Egypt*, 361.

27. Urquhart and Tuke, "Two Visits to the Cairo Asylum." At the time of their visit, the Egyptian government had declared bankruptcy, but Dr. Tuke expressed hope that "[w]ith the expected revival of Egyptian finance, this asylum may participate in the advantage."

28. Ibid., 49.

29. Wilkinson, *Handbook for Travelers in Egypt*, 136. Wilkinson, like Bartlett, noted that "[t]he lunatics have lately been removed to another hospital, under the superintendence of Europeans; and the sad treatement they before experienced no longer continues."

30. Judith Walkowitz documents the Victorians' fascination with slums and disease in *City of Dreadful Delight*, esp. 1–80. She notes how George Sims introduced his exposé on London slum housing as "a book of travel" (27).

31. Von Crowins Smith, *Pilgrimage to Egypt*, 360.

32. European travelers to Egypt noted that the funds of al-Azhar had been drastically diminished; however, this institution continued to serve the poor of Cairo and students and ulema of the university. For information on its use as a distribution point of food during this era, see ch. 2, n. 4. Kenneth M. Cuno discusses how scholars such as Gabriel Baer and Helen Rivlin have relied on the remarks of Abd al-Rahman al-Jabarti, who was opposed to the reforms of Muhammad Ali, for proof that this institution's financial strength was severely undermined ("Ideology and Juridical Discourse," 161 n. 92). A thorough analysis of the financial soundness of religious endowments and their abilities to provide for the needy in the nineteenth century awaits further research.

33. On the period of the Egyptian government's bankruptcy, see Landes, *Bankers and Pashas*; Owen, *The Middle East*; and Cole, *Colonialism and Revolution*.

34. Fahmy, *All the Pasha's Men*.

35. De Chamberet, *Enquête*, 192.

36. Thomas Cook and Son encouraged tourists who took part in the Cook tours to make donations to support the medical facilities they had established in Luxor. Although the Cook hospital was initially located in hotel rooms, in 1891 the Cooks obtained permission from the khedive to build a larger hospital facility, which provided free medical care to the poor in Luxor 2/13/B Majlis al-Wuzara', Nizarat al-Dakhiliyya — al-Mustashfayat; letter from Thomas Cook

and Son to the khedive dated Cairo April 28, 1883; and Piers Brendon, *Thomas Cook*, 229. Brendon, citing the *Excursionist* of March 14, 1891, notes that in the first year it was open, the hospital served six thousand patients. Advertisements of the medical work being done at the Cook hospital, as well as solicitations for donations, are found in numerous editions of *The Lancet*. See November 20, 1897 (1316); July 2, 1898 (59); and October 17, 1903 (1311). In 1921 the Cooks gave the hospital building and medical supplies as a gift to the Egyptian government (*The Lancet*, December 3, 1921, 1197). Cartoons in *Punch* also recognized Britain's imperial responsibility to those in need through portrayals of, for example, Britain coming to the rescue of war and famine victims (*Punch*, May 2, 1900, 311).

37. Pemble, *Mediterranean Passion*, 47, 100.

38. *The Lancet*, July 28, 1894, 206. Pemble, *Mediterranean Passion*, 84. Discussions about the numerous locations in Egypt serving as health and vacation resorts are found in *The Lancet*, September 15, 1888, 548; June 8, 1889, 1167; January 16, 1892, 170; June 23, 1894, 1594; October 27, 1894, 970; July 6, 1895, 62; June 2, 1900, 1617; May 3, 1902, 1288; and December 6, 1902, 1584. Extensive coverage of developments and services provided at Helwan is in *The Lancet*, July 31, 1897, 289, and October 9, 1897, 932–37. A number of books provided detailed information on the health benefits of residing or at least wintering in Egypt. See Sandwith, *Egypt As a Winter Resort*; Bentley and Griffenhoofe, *Wintering in Egypt*; and Hobson, *Helouan*.

39. *The Lancet*, May 30, 1891, 1219.

40. In "The Problem of Hygiene in Egypt" (Chadwick Lecture Series), by Andrew Balfour, *The Lancet*, September 6, 1919, 417–21, esp. 420. Gyan Prakash discusses British depictions of Indians as "diseased" in "Body Politic in Colonial India," 189–222.

41. In "The Problem of Hygiene in Egypt," by Balfour, 417.

42. PRO, FO 633/64, *Progress on the Finances, Administration, and Condition of Egypt and the Progress of Reforms* (1895) 12. The capitulations also served as an obstacle to ensuring the health of the Egyptian populace. Since the Egyptian government could not regulate foreign companies, items such as milk products went unmonitored and the employment of children could not be prohibited (*The Lancet*, April 20, 1907, 1128, and June 20, 1908, 1779). British colonial officials also discussed their inability (due to their capitulations) to monitor child labor in foreign-owned industries. See PRO/FO 371/450, Correspondences from April through July 1908.

43. Tignor discusses the different technical priorities of Lord Cromer (formerly Sir Evelyn Baring) in chapter 7 of *Modernization and British Colonial Rule*.

44. Ibid., 21–22. For a discussion of the influence the Indian colonial experience had on British colonial officials in Egypt, see Owen, "Lord Cromer's Indian Experience."

45. Tignor, *Modernization and British Colonial Rule in Egypt*, 56.

46. Evelyn Baring (Lord Cromer) to Rivers Wilson, October 14, 1883. C.C. PRO, FO 633/5, "The Government of Subject Races," cited in "The Influence of Lord Cromer's Indian Experience," by Owen, 114. Preventing the peasantry

from becoming a dangerous class is in correspondence from Northbrook to Salisbury, April 8, 1875, Salisbury Papers, Special Correspondence, "Baring. T.G.," cited in "Lord Cromer's Indian Experience," by Owen, 114. Owen's discussions of the attempts to ease the financial burdens of the Egyptian peasantry are in "Lord Cromer's Indian Experience," 114–18. Although British statesmen regarded the abolition of corvée as a British initiative, Nathan Brown convincingly argues that it was prompted by the desire on the part of large estate owners to retain peasants' labor on their own estates. (Brown, "Who Abolished Corvée Labour."

47. See Tignor, *Modernization and British Colonial Rule in Egypt*, 317–18, 348–57.

48. For a critique of colonial policy in Egypt, particularly a discussion of the lack of funds for carrying out extensive sanitation work, see the overview of Lord Cromer's annual report for 1905 in *The Lancet*, February 27, 1897. A discussion of improvements made in the Qasr al-Ayni Hospital is in *History of Medical Education*, by Mahfouz, and *The Creation of the Medical Profession*, by Sonbol. For a discussion of the first efforts made to improve facilities at the insane asylum at Abbasiyya, see Sandwith, "The Cairo Lunatic Asylum," and *Reports on the Egyptian Government Hospital for the Insane* (1895–1902).

49. PRO, FO 78/3438, Turkey (Egypt) Domestic Various. James MacKie, a surgeon in the Deaconess Hospital in Alexandria, Egypt, to Lord Granville, October 27, 1882. One health initiative, an endowment for the establishment of ophthalmic hospitals, was identified at a meeting of the British Medical Association (1907) as beneficence "calculated to reconcile the [Egyptian] people to our [British] rule" (*The Lancet*, August 24, 1907, 532).

50. Citing correspondence between Gorst and Cromer (PRO, FO 633/14), Tignor illustrates how the British were cautious about sponsoring education for the Egyptian populace (*Modernization and British Colonial Rule in Egypt*, 320). For further discussion of the influence the Indian colonial experience had on British colonial officials in Egypt, see Owen, "The Influence of Lord Cromer's Indian Experience."

51. *The Lancet*, July 28, 1894, 206.

52. Ibid., October 25, 1902, 1160–61, esp. 1160.

53. Ibid., April 30, 1904, 1241–43, esp. 1243.

54. Balfour's statement is in "The Problem of Hygiene in Egypt," 418. Medical personnel from the outset of the occupation had included male doctors from the Indian Medical service, St. Thomas's Hospital, and Charing Cross Hospital (*The Lancet*, July 28, 1883). Medical personnel learned of openings in the profession through a section in *The Lancet* entitled "The British Medical Man Abroad." See, for example, *The Lancet*, September 2, 1902, 735. Female nurses from St. Bartholomew's and St. Thomas's Hospitals taught at Qasr al-Ayni Hospital, and English matrons supervised the work of privately funded dispensaries (*The Lancet*, July 14, 1888, 91, and July 11, 1914, 117).

55. *The Lancet*, September 23, 1911, 881. Yet it was because of its diseases that Egypt offered "so attractive and untouched a field of scientific investigation" for British medical practitioners (*The Lancet*, October 29, 1910, 1299). Sanitary work, as in the case of efforts to isolate the sick during cholera epi-

demics, was met with resistance by the public; *The Lancet*, inferring that religious customs were one obstacle to medical progress, documented an attack on a cholera ambulance in Alexandria and a fight between a disinfector and an "angry mob," as well as rumors that cholera was a European effort to poison Muslims (June 27, 1896, 1835). David Arnold's article "Perspectives on the Indian Plague" documents indigenous resistance to the plague administrators on the Indian subcontinent (in *Selected Subaltern Studies*, ed. Guha and Spivak, 391–426).

56. *The Lancet*, July 6, 1901, 59.

57. Ibid., April 30, 1904, 1242.

58. Ibid., July 11, 1914, 117.

59. Ibid., September 9, 1893, 643–44. The issue of infant mortality also received attention in parliamentary discussions in Britain. See *The Lancet*, March 4, 1905, 611, and United Kingdom, *Hansard's Parliamentary Debates*, 141: 1098.

60. *The Lancet*, April 30, 1904, 1242; September 15, 1888, 547; May 3, 1902, 1272; January 5, 1895, 58; and April 9, 1904, 1010. The Egyptian populace's increased use of hospital services could be compared with what *The Lancet* authors identified as their aversion to hospitals prior to British rule. The hospitals of that period were described as lacking in cleanliness, decency, and ventilation. Speaking of hospital conditions prior to the British occupation, a writer in *The Lancet* (March 29, 1884, 593) remarked: "Fortunately, perhaps, the natives have a well-founded aversion to entering any hospital, and the buildings themselves are in consequence seldom overcrowded."

61. See *The Lancet*, June 27, 1896, 1835. For numerous descriptions of the training and employment of patients in the Abbasiyya insane asylum, see the various publications of the Egyptian Sanitary Department, *Report on the Egyptian Government Hospital for the Insane* (1895–1902).

62. See Sandwith, "Cairo Lunatic Asylum." Also see *The Lancet*, January 8, 1897, 143. For the separation of the "dangerous" insane from the "quiet" insane, see Egyptian Sanitary Department, *Report on the Egyptian Government Hospital for the Insane for the Year 1901*, 1. The removal of mechanical restraints is described in *The Lancet*, April 24, 1897, 1158–59. Egyptian attendants' mistreatment of the insane is discussed in idem, *Report on the Egyptian Government Hospital1895*, 40. The abuse of the insane by their families is discussed in *The Lancet*, June 4, 1910, 1567. The public's abuse of the insane is described in *The Lancet*, June 14, 1902, 1732, and July 6, 1907, 37. Ministry of the Interior, *Lunacy Division Report for the Year 1917*, 85–86.

63. *The Lancet*, September 14, 1912, 778. Overcrowding was also attributable, noted Warnock in his reports on developments in the principal insane asylum, to a decreased rate of mortality, which diminished by 50 percent (*The Lancet*, June 27, 1896, 1835). For Warnock's account of the reform and changes introduced to the insane asylums while he was the director at Abbasiyya, see Warnock, "Twenty-Eight Years' Lunacy Experience." For a study of insane asylums in Egypt during the British occupation, see Mayers, "A Century of Psychiatry."

64. Issues of racial superiority and the "infantalization" of the Middle East as a whole are put forth in Said, *Orientalism*.

65. British depictions of Egyptians' susceptibility to disease also fell along class lines. Earlier issues of *The Lancet* claimed that the Egyptian upper class did not know the "rudiments" of cleanliness and were prone to disease and sickness (*The Lancet*, October 25, 1902, 1161); later editions, however, identified the Egyptian upper classes as prime catalysts in spreading information and knowledge about health and hygiene. (See, for example, *The Lancet*, April 29, 1911, 1511.) "[T]he poorest Europeans" were particularly prone to diseases such as the plague, for they "lead lives as unhealthy as do the natives" and "work with the natives bare-footed or almost bare-footed" (*The Lancet*, May 3, 1902, 1288). In the case of Sumatra, Ann Stoler discusses how the European colonial elite attempted to keep Europeans who were infirm, old, insane, and impoverished out of sight for fear that their presence would undermine the image of the colonizers as healthy and powerful ("Rethinking Colonial Categories").

66. 2/2/b Majlis al Wuzara': Ministry of the Interior, Matters of Public Health, Ministry of Health.

67. *The Lancet*, January 2, 1892, 64.

68. Ibid., January 5, 1895, 58–59.

69. Ibid., December 13, 1902, 1665. For another description of Takiyyat Tura, see *The British Medical Journal*, September 28, 1889, 738–39.

70. PRO, FO 371/1040, correspondence between Kitchener and Sir Edward Gray, November 21, 1913. Further discussions of the duties of the Ministry of Religious Endowments and its reorganization are in *Problème des waqfs en Egypte*, by Sékaly.

71. Chirol, *Egyptian Problem*, 172. Chirol was a journalist for the *Times*. *The Egyptian Problem* was based on his articles appearing in the *Times* from October 1919 through April 1920. By contrast, de Chamberet described the services provided by the Ministry of Religious Endowments as an important contribution to the care for the poor (*Enquête*, 202–3).

72. For a discussion of Egyptian concern about waqf mismanagement, see Sékaly, *Problème des waqfs en Egypte*, 110–11. John Barnes discusses the abuse of funds in the Central Ottoman lands in *Introduction to Religious Foundations*. For negative portrayals of waqf management throughout Ottoman history, see Singer, "Charity's Legacies."

73. See Sékaly, *Problème des waqfs en Egypte*, and Tignor, *Modernization and British Colonial Rule*, 263, 297, 315.

74. See *Mayzaniyya Iradat wa Masrufat al-Awqaf al-Khayriyya al-Mashmula bi Nizarat al-Hadar al-Fakhima al-Khidiwi fi al-Sana 1906*, 15. For information on the administration of these shelters between 1883 and 1923, see 2/alif Majlis al-Wuzara'.

75. For more information on these takaya, see Diwan al-Awqaf, 1904, no. 883; 1918, no. 24; 2/alif Majlis al-Wuzara', 2/2/b Majlis al-Wuzara'; and de Chamberet, *Enquête*, 198–99.

76. Diwan al-Awqaf, 1908, no. 23/886, p. 19.

77. Diwan al-Awqaf, 1918, no. 24, p. 38; 2/2/b Majlis al-Wuzara'.

78. Cooper, *The Women of Egypt*, 330.

79. Chirol, *Egyptian Problem*, 170–71.

80. Cooper, *Women of Egypt*, 330.

81. PRO, FO 633/79, *Reports by His Majesty's Agent and Consul-General on the Finances, Administration, and Condition of Egypt and the Soudan in 1909*, 34.

82. See 2/alif Majlis al Wuzara': Ministry of the Interior, Matters of Public Health, and 2/2/b Majlis al Wuzara': Ministry of the Interior, Matters of Public Health, Ministry of Health for public health initiatives in the late 1850s. Dr. Naguib Mahfouz notes that the medical school and hospital of Qasr al-Ayni were in miserable condition at the point of Ismail's succession, but nonetheless it is important to note that the poor continued to seek assistance from the state, either for abandoned children or medical treatment, until at least 1870. See my "Charity of the Khedive," and Mahfouz, *History of Medical Education in Egypt*, 43.

83. United Kingdom, *Hansard's Parliamentary Debates*, 139:1213.

84. A discussion of the inadequate facilities can be found in *The British Medical Journal*, September 28, 1889, 738–39; Egyptian Sanitary Department, *Report on the Egyptian Government Hospital for the Insane for the Year 1895*, 48; and *The Lancet*, December 13, 1902, 1664–65. Additional reports are also found in 2/2/B, Majlis al-Wuzara', "Report on the State of Public Health in Egypt," 1918; Ministry of the Interior, *Lunacy Division Report, 1917*, 83–85; 2/13/J Majlis al-Wuzara': Ministry of the Interior, al-isbataliyyat, May 29, 1884 (a discussion of what to do with the quiet insane).

85. 2/2/b Majlis al Wuzara': Ministry of the Interior, Matters of Public Health, Ministry of Health.

CHAPTER V
THE FUTURE OF THE NATION

1. Nazmi, "La Protection de l'enfance," 82. For the most extensive discussion of eugenics, see Dr. Paul-Valentin, "La Protection de l'enfance" (paper presented at the Conference on the Protection of Children), published in *L'Egypte Contemporaine*. In this chapter I use the term "Royal Society" to refer to what was called first the Khedival Society for Political Economy, Statistics, and Legislation and then the Sultanic Society.

2. Speakers in the lecture series included British, French, and American specialists in economics and legal matters.

3. Magda Baraka discusses the composition of the Egyptian upper class, their lifestyles and activities, their visions of modernizing Egypt, and their overall contributions to Egyptian society; see *The Egyptian Upper Class*.

4. "Rijal Misr al-amalin."

5. Donald Reid discusses professional syndicates (such as those of doctors, journalists, and engineers) in "The Rise of Professions," 24–57.

6. Wissa, "Freemasonry in Egypt," 145–46, 154–55.

7. Nadir Özbek examines how philanthropic projects presented a challenge to Abdul Hamid II in "The Politics of Poor Relief."

8. Nadim, *Sulafat al-Nadim fi Muntakhabat*. For the political activities of Abd Allah Nadim, see the foreword written by Abd al-Man'am Ibrahim al-Jami'i in *Majalat al-Ustadh* (Cairo: Matba'a al-Ha'ya al-Misriyya al-Amma li al-Kitab, 1994).

9. "Jama'iyyat al-Urwa al-Wuthqa al-Khayriyya al-Islamiyya," 448.

10. Shalabi, *Harakat al-Islah al-Ijtima'iyya fi Misr*. Shalabi's argument also applies to the activities of the Coptic Benevolent Society and the promotion of education by other ethnic groups. The neglect of education was in part due to Cromer's experiences in India and nationalist agitation among the educated classes. Citing correspondence between Gorst and Cromer (PRO/FO 633/14), Tignor illustrates how the British were cautious about sponsoring education for the Egyptian populace (*Modernization and British Colonial Rule*, 320).

11. *Al-Jam'iyyat al-Khayriyya al-Islamiyya*, 7–9, 19.

12. Heyworth-Dunne, *An Introduction to the History of Education*, 278–85, and Dor, *L'Instruction publique en Egypt*, 269.

13. Guerin, *La France catholique*, 55–58. France's participation in charitable efforts were described as having a moral influence on Egypt. See Anonymous, *La France éducatrice*, 30.

14. Whately established her first school for Muslim girls in 1858. Bliss, *The Encyclopedia of Missions*.

15. In 1921, of 8,892 people who received assistance from the Coptic Benevolent Society, 3,939 were Muslims, 4,937 were Copts, and 16 were foreigners. Abdin Collection, box 207, Al-Jam'iyyat al-Ijtima'iyya Ghayr Muslima, "Taqrir al-Jam'iyya al-Qibtiya al-Khayriyya," May 18, 1922.

16. Kramer, *Jews in Modern Egypt*, 104, 100. Religious and ethnic minorities considered themselves Egyptian and directed many of their activities toward nationalist causes, as Joel Beinin illustrates in *The Dispersion of Egyptian Jewry*. Such was the case, for example, of the satirist and journalist Ya'qub Sannu' and Yusuf Aslan Qattawi, a prominent Jewish businessman who sat on the board of the Bank Misr, and his son René, who encouraged the foundation of the Association for Egyptian Jewish Youth in 1935. This association called on Egyptian Jews to take part in Egypt's national revival (Beinin, *Dispersion*, 82–83, 46).

17. Kitroeff, *Greeks in Egypt*, 145.

18. On rural population pressures during the period following 1880, see Owen, *Cotton and the Egyptian Economy*, 236–45. Selma Botman discusses the increase in Cairo's population in the first half of the twentieth century; see her *Egypt from Independence to Revolution*, 22–23. Jacques Berque discusses the impoverishment of Egyptian peasants and their migration to urban areas during the British occupation; see *Egypt*, 287, 618–19.

19. Greiss, "La Mendicité en Egypte," 209.

20. *Ministry of the Interior Police Regulations*, "Public Security," article 152, and "Prevention of Crime," articles 6 and 37 (Cairo: National Printing Press, 1901).

21. Greiss, "La Mendicité en Egypte," 205–6. Greiss does not discuss the exact areas where begging was prohibited. I assume that the European sections and business districts of Cairo were two key areas where strictures on begging were implemented. Efforts to eliminate begging—even in these areas—was nearly impossible. Letters to the editor of English-language newspapers such as the *Egyptian Gazette* note harassment by street peddlers, and guidebooks mention continued government efforts to curtail begging and urge tourists to give money to established charities instead of beggars.

22. 2/2/b Majlis al Wuzara': Ministry of the Interior, Matters of Public Health, Ministry of Health.

23. "Mawt al-Atfal fi al-Mudun al-Kabira," *Al-Muqtataf* (June 1886):522–34. An article on the care of the poor and children in the United States is in *Al-Muqtataf* 9(1878):238–40, and on wet-nursing in France in *Al-Muqtataf* 4(1882):306. Advice on breast-feeding is in *Al-Muqtataf* (June 1883):52–53. Information on the health of the general British populace is in *Al-Muqtataf* (August1883):54–55.

24. Beth Baron discusses the iconography of Egypt as female in "Nationalist Iconography." Her focus on Safiyya Zaghlul as the mother of Egypt is on pages 123–24.

25. "Rijal Misr al-ʿamalin: muʾassas mashruaʿ malgaʾ al-hurriyya," *Al-Lataʾif al-Musawwara*, April 28, 1919, 2–3.

26. Nazmi Bey, "Tarbiyat al-Atfal" and "La Protection de l'enfance," 82, 89.

27. PRO/FO 633/80, *Reports by His Majesty's Agent and Consul-General on the Finances, Administration, and Condition of Egypt and the Soudan in 1910*, 43, and PRO/FO 633/81, *Reports by His Majesty's Agent and Consul-General on the Finances, Administration, and Condition of Egypt and the Soudan in 1911*, 37.

28. *The Lancet*, April 29, 1911, 1151.

29. Shaʿrawi, *Harem Years*, 94–98.

30. Baron, *Women's Awakening*, 175.

31. For a discussion of the political aspect of women's charitable activities, see Marsot, "The Revolutionary Gentlewoman in Egypt"; Baron, *Women's Awakening*, 175; and Badran, *Feminists, Islam, and the Nation*, 48–52. Seth Koven and Sonya Michel provide an overview of the linkages between charity work, child welfare, and political participation; see "Womanly Duties."

32. Badran, *Feminists, Islam, and the Nation*, 51.

33. Baron, *Women's Awakening*, 174, and *Feminists, Islam, and the Nation*, 51.

34. Malak Hifni Nasif's list of demands are found in the *Egyptian Gazette*, May 2, 1911, and discussed in Badran, *Feminists, Islam, and the Nation*, 69. Juan Cole discusses the class-based orientation of Nasif's views in "Feminism, Class, and Islam," 401.

35. In this regard, see Badran's *Feminists, Islam, and the Nation* for her discussion of the political and charitable activities of the Egyptian Feminist Union. Nadje al-Ali provides an overview of women's continued involvement in charitable work through the reign of Gamal Abdel Nasser; see *Secularism, Gender, and the State*, 51–127.

36. Ideas about crime, criminality, and punishments were transferred from the Indian colonial context. Discussions of the crime prevention and punishment techniques used in South Asia, which were proposed for the Egyptian context, are in PRO/FO 78/3839, Turkey (Egypt) Domestic Various, March 1885.

37. Coles, *Recollections and Reflections*, 100.

38. Memorandum on crime in Egypt, in PRO/FO 633/75, *Reports by His Majesty's Consul-General on the Finances, Administration, and Condition of Egypt and the Soudan in 1905*, 115. The view that prosperity resulted in an increase in crime was echoed in a presentation made to the Khedival Society for Political Economy, Statistics, and Legislation in November 1911. For a text of this presentation, see Maunier, "Des Rapports."

39. Machell argued that for Egyptians, "human life is of little value" (PRO/

FO 633/75, *Reports by his Majesty's Consul-General on the Finances, Administration, and Condition of Egypt and the Soudan in 1905*, 115).

40. Lord Cromer noted that in years when the Nile was low and harvests were subsequently poor, the poverty and distress of the peasantry were increased and therefore crime rates were higher (PRO/FO 633/70, *Reports by His Majesty's Consul-General on the Finances, Administration, and Condition of Egypt and the Soudan in 1900*, 35).

41. PRO/FO 633/76, *Reports by His Majesty's Consul-General on the Finances, Administration, and Condition of Egypt and the Soudan in 1906*, 59–60.

42. Methods of criminal identification are discussed in *The Lancet*, July 20, 1895, 184, and in PRO/FO 633/75, *Reports by His Majesty's Consul-General on the Finances, Administration, and Condition of Egypt and the Soudan in 1903*, 50.

43. For details of the prison director Crookshank's trip to England, where he was studying the use of workshops in prisons so as to establish the same at the Giza prison, see 14/alif, Majlis al-Wuzara', February 4, 1889, and 14/alif, Majlis al-Wuzara', March 11, 1889. PRO/FO 633/53, "Further Correspondence Respecting the Affairs of Egypt, 1885," 88–102. PRO/FO 633/63, *Report on the Finances, Administration, and Condition of Egypt and the Progress of Reforms, 1894*, 16. *The Lancet*, November 19, 1910, 1514. For photographs of some of the industries in these prisons, see Wright, *Twentieth Century Impressions*, 411–14. The labor provided by prisoners was intended to cut down on prison expenditures and provided free labor for the construction of roads and canals, in addition to prisons (PRO/FO 633/53, 88–102). Prisoners' labor was also utilized for industrial projects outside the prison. In this regard, see *Bulletin des lois et décrets*.

44. Coles, *Recollections and Reflections*, 109.

45. *The Lancet*, April 20, 1895, 1006, and March 21, 1896, 817. PRO/FO 633/64, *Progress on the Finances, Administration, and Condition of Egypt and the Progress of Reforms, 1895*, 12. PRO/FO 633/65, *Progress on the Finances, Administration, and Condition of Egypt and the Progress of Reforms, 1896*, 17. Juveniles reformatories were a recent innovation in Britain, Mary Carpenter's reform school having been established only in 1852. See Hopkins, *Childhood Transformed*, 198–99.

46. PRO/FO 633/68, *Report on the Finances, Administration, and Condition of Egypt and the Soudan in 1898*, 28. See Coles, *Recollections and Reflections*, 115, and 14/alif, Majlis al-Wuzara', August 29, 1894, for the necessity of observing the conditions and projects of boys' reformatories in Europe.

47. Coles, *Recollections and Reflections*, 115–18. Coles and other British officials remarked on the success of the juvenile reformatory, noting that the recidivism rate was only 15 percent and that upon their release 60–70 percent of the boys who had received training in the reformatory continued to work in the same handicrafts in which they had been trained (Coles, *Recollections and Reflections*, 119).

48. PRO/FO 633/70, *Reports of His Majesty's Agent and Consul-General on the Finances, Administration, and Condition of Egypt and the Soudan in 1900*, 37; PRO/FO 633/77, *Reports of His Majesty's Agent and Consul-General on the*

Finances, Administration, and Condition of Egypt and the Soudan in 1907, 30; and Truscott, *The Parliamentary Debates,* 999, question concerning law on juvenile vagrants, May 9, 1908. Industrial schools in England were a recent phenomenon. With the Industrial Schools Act of 1857, numerous schools were established for the care of street children (interestingly, young boys were referred to as "street Arabs"), and Hopkins notes that in the 1870s there were fifty philanthropic societies assisting children (Hopkins, *Childhood Transformed,* 200).

49. Ahmed Sami, "Juvenile Vagrants and Delinquents," 251. The statement about arresting juveniles was made in 1919. Also see Greiss, "La Mendicité en Egypte," 207.

50. Nazmi Bey, "La Protection de l'enfance"; Caloyanni, "Opening Address for Conference"; Mahmoud Sami, "First Paper"; and Paul-Valentin, "La Protection de l'enfance."

51. Ahmed Sami, "Juvenile Vagrants and Delinquents."

52. Nazmi Bey, "La Protection de l'enfance," 82

53. Roger Owen discusses the "catching up" feature of modernity and the part played by the elite in bringing their nations up to par with the industrialized West; see his "Modernizing Projects," 246. Although his discussion primarily pertains to the Middle East in the era following colonialism, it is clear that Egypt's elites embarked on such projects as early as the first decades of the twentieth century.

54. Mahmoud Sami, "La Protection de l'enfance," 8. Also see Nachat, "Le Patronage," and Ahmed Sami, "Juvenile Vagrants."

55. Neuberger, *Hooliganism.*

56. Al-Quran 9:60. The two articles were reprinted in *Al-Lata'if al-Musawwara,* May 26, 1919, 10–11.

57. Koven, "Dr. Barnado's 'Artistic Fictions.'"

58. "Khutbat al-Doktor Abd al-Aziz Bey Nazmi," *Al-Lata'if al-Musawwara,* May 26, 1919, 2–3, 6–7.

59. Abdin Collection, box 203, Jami'yyat.

60. "Rijal Misr al-amalin."

61. "Azimat sayeda fi Asyut," *Al-Lata'if al-Musawwara,* January 31, 1921, 1, 2, 4–8.

62. "Intiqad lajnat Malga' al-Hurriyya," *Al-Lata'if al-Musawwara,* February 28, 1921, 2. The association that founded the Malga' Abna al-Shawari'a included American and European members.

63. Sandra Cavallo discusses how competition is a key factor in philanthropy; see "The Motivations of Benefactors," 50–53.

64. *Al-Watan,* January 17, 1910, 1.

65. PRO/FO 371/113, translations of articles pertaining to Christian proselytizing from *Misr al-Fatat,* May 9, 1911; *Al-Alam,* May 10, 1911; *Al-Hurriyya,* April 2, 1911; and *Al-Ahali,* May 10, 1911.

66. *Al-Islah,* December 28, 1903, 1–2; *Al-Liwa,* January 12, 1904, 1–2; *Al-Watan,* August 11, 1905, 1; September 5, 1905, 1; and December 22, 1905, 1.

67. See, for example, PRO/FO 371/450, Correspondences from April 1908 through July 1908.

68. McBarnet, "The New Penal Code." On the actions of White Slavery soci-

eties in Egypt, see Dunne, "Sexuality and the 'Civilizing Process' in Modern Egypt."

69. Bianchi, *Unruly Corporatism*, 70–71.

70. Ibid., 73.

71. Abdin Collection, Malaji (Shelters), box 529, statistics of January 4, 1923.

72. Martinez-Vergne, *Shaping the Discourse on Space*, 91.

73. On the importance of language and the press for confirming a nationally imagined community, see Anderson, *Imagined Communities*, 47.

74. Abbas Hilmi was the last of Egypt's rulers to be identified by the title khedive. His successor Husayn Kamil, who ruled during World War I, was recognized with the title sultan. His own successor, Fuad, was recognized first as sultan and then king.

75. Abdin Collection, box 203, Jam'iyyat.

76. Ibid.

77. For censorship of the press and political dissent during this era, see Marsot, *Egypt's Liberal Experiment*, 76, 142.

78. Botman, *Egypt from Independence to Revolution*, 121. Richard P. Mitchell discusses the range of activities carried out by the Muslim Brotherhood in *Society of the Muslim Brothers*.

79. Beinin and Lockman, *Workers on the Nile*, 67 and 272.

80. "Foreword" (presented by Dr. Ahmed Hussein, Minister of Social Affairs, October 3, 1950), in *Social Welfare in Egypt*.

81. *Social Welfare in Egypt*, 82.

82. Garrison, "Public Assistance in Egypt," 285.

83. Gallagher, *Egypt's Other Wars*, 40–55.

84. Ibid., 71–72.

85. Garrison, "Public Assistance in Egypt," 282.

86. Nadir Özbek discusses the use of newspapers in advertising the actions of Abdul Hamid II in the early twentieth century; see "Imperial Gifts."

87. Marsot, *Egypt's Liberal Experiment*, 197–98.

88. Garrison, "Public Assistance in Egypt," 288.

CHAPTER VI
CONCLUSION

1. Hoexter, "Waqf Studies," 476.

2. We do not have sufficient information on the ability of families to care for their members in prior centuries to be able to compare the nineteenth century with earlier eras. As contributors to *The Locus of Care* (Horden and Smith) argue, in the West there never was a golden age of the family. We should not assume that there ever was a golden age for Egypt's needy either.

3. Contributors to Timothy Mitchell's *Questions of Modernity* remind readers that the modern cannot be universalized. As they make clear, the experience of modernity in the Middle East and South Asia must be understood within the context of the specific histories of each region and should not be read as a replication of the West's trajectory.

BIBLIOGRAPHY

ARCHIVAL SOURCES

Egypt: Egyptian National Archives

REGISTERS

Dabtiyyat Iskandiriyya (Police Records for Alexandria). Designated in notes as
L 4, for example, L 4/1/2/page number/entry number, date (Islamic and common era). Such designations apply to each Egyptian archival record found in
the notes.

Dabtiyyat Misr (Police Records for Cairo). Designated as L 1.

Dabtiyyat Misr: Sadir al-Ardhallat (Cairo Police: Petitions and Responses). Designated as L 2/11.

Diwan al-Awqaf (Ministry of Religious Endowments). Listed by register number.

Diwan al-Isbataliyyat (Ministry of Hospitals). Designated as M.

Diwan al-Jihadiyya (Ministry of the Army). Listed by register number.

Diwan al-Khidiwi (Cabinet Records). Designated as S 2.

Diwan Majlis al-Ahkam (Council of Justice Records). Designated as S 7.

Diwan Majlis al-Khususi (Privy Council). Designated as S 11.

Diwan Muhafazat Misr (Cairo Governorate Records). Designated as L 2.

Al-Maʿiyya al-Saniyya (Cabinet Records). Designated as S 1.

Mayzaniyya Iradat wa Masrufat al-Awqaf al-Khayriyya al-Mashmula bi Nizarat
al-Hadar al-Fakhima al-Khidiwi fi al-Sana 1906 (Budget for Religious Endowments, 1906).

Muhafazat Misr: Istihaqqat (Salaries). Ration amounts for the poor and salaries
of administrators in Takiyyat Tulun. Designated as L 1/60/1–20.

Muhafazat Misr: Sadir al-Ardhallat (Cairo Governorate: Petitions and Responses). Designated as L 1/6.

Ruznama (Financial Records). Listed by register number.

Shura al-Muʿawana (Records of the Vice-Royal Suite or Cabinet). Listed by register number.

MAHAFIZ (BOXES)

Abdin (Abdin Collection).

Dabtiyyat Misr (Police Records).

Asr Ismail (Records from the Ismail Period).

Al-Maʿiyya al-Saniyya (Cabinet Records).

Majlis al-Wuzaraʾ (Council of Ministers).

CARD FILES

Al-Dakhiliyya (The Ministry of the Interior).

United Kingdom: Public Records Office (PRO), Kew Gardens

FO (Foreign Office) 78/3839, Turkey (Egypt) Domestic Various.

FO 78/381, John Bowring, Report on Egypt and Candia.

FO 97/410, Police Registers — Turkey.
FO 371/450, Political Egypt, 1908.
FO 633, Annual Reports on Finances and Administration of Egypt and the Sudan.

Turkey: Başbakanlık Arşivi

Cevdet Zaptiye Series.

NEWSPAPERS AND PERIODICALS

Abu Naddara Zurqa
British Medical Journal, The
Egyptian Gazette
Lancet, The
Al-Lata'if al-Musawwara
Al-Muqtataf
Punch
Al-Waqa'i' al-Misriyya
Al-Watan

UNPUBLISHED WORKS

Ahmad, Nahid Hamdi. "Watha'iq al-Takaya fi Misr fi al-Asr al-Uthmaniyya" (Tekke documents of Egypt in the Ottoman Era) Ph.D. diss., Cairo University, 1984.

Baqué, Valérie. "Approches de la marginalité en Egypt, 1880–1930." Paper presented at CEDEJ Forum on Marginality, Cairo, Egypt, 1992.

Cohen, Mark. "Poverty as Reflected in the Cairo Geniza Documents." Paper presented at the annual meeting of the Middle East Studies Association, San Francisco, November 1997.

Dunne, Bruce. "Sexuality and the 'Civilizing Process' in Modern Egypt." Ph.D. diss., Georgetown University, 1996.

Hekekyan, Joseph. Papers. British Museum Department of Manuscripts. Add. 37448–37471, 24 vols.

Mayers, Marilyn Anne. "A Century of Psychiatry: The Egyptian Mental Hospitals." Ph.D. diss., Princeton University, 1984.

Sachot, M. Octave. "Rapport addressé à son excellence Monsieur Victor Duruy Ministre de l'Instruction Publique sur l'état des sciences, des lettres, et de l'instruction publique en Egypt," 1868.

PUBLISHED WORKS

Abd al-Rahim, Abd al-Rahim Abd al-Rahman, *Al-Rif al-Misri fi al-Qarn al-Thamin Ashar* (The Egyptian countryside in the eighteenth century). Cairo: Matba'at Jami'at Ayn Shams, 1974.

Abu-Lughod, Janet L. *Cairo: One Thousand One Years of the City Victorious.* Princeton: Princeton University Press, 1971.

Afify, Muhammad. *Al-Awqaf wa al-Haya al-Iqtisadiyya fi Misr fi al-Asr al-*

Uthmaniya (Religious endowments and economic life in Egypt in the Ottoman Era). Cairo: Al-Ha'ya al-Misriyya al-Amma li-l-Kitab, 1991.

Ahmed, Leila. *Women and Gender in Islam.* New Haven: Yale University Press, 1992.

Aktepe, M. Munir. "Istanbul'un Nüfus Meselesine Dair Bazı Vesikalar" (Some documents pertaining to the problem of Istanbul's Population). *Tarih Dergisi* 9, September 13, 1958, 1–30.

Ali Bey. *The Travels of Ali Bey in Morocco, Tripoli, Cyprus, Egypt, Arabia, Syria, and Turkey between the Years 1803 and 1807*, 2 vols. Philadelphia: M. Carey, 1816.

Al-Ali, Nadje. *Secularism, Gender, and the State in the Middle East: The Egyptian Women's Movement.* Cambridge: Cambridge University Press, 2000.

Amin, Muhammad. "Watha'iq Waqf al-Sultan Qalawun ala al-Bimaristan al-Mansuri." Cairo University, n.d.

Anderson, Benedict. *Imagined Communities: Reflections on the Origin and Spread of Nationalism.* 1983. Reprint, London: Verso, 1990.

Andrews, Jonathan. "'Hardly a Hospital, but a Charity for Pauper Lunatics'? Therapeutics at Bethlem in the Seventeenth and Eighteenth Centuries." In *Medicine and Charity before the Welfare State*, edited by Jonathan Barry and Colin Jones, 63–81. London: Routledge, 1991.

Anonymous. *La France éducatrice et charitable en Egypte.* Paris: Bureaux de la Revue Politique et Parlementaire, January 1910.

Arnold, David. "Perspectives on the Indian Plague, 1896–1900." In *Selected Subaltern Studies*, edited by Ranajit Guha and Gayatri Chakravorty Spivak, 391–426. Oxford: Oxford University Press, 1988.

Badran, Margot. *Feminists, Islam, and the Nation: Gender and the Making of Modern Egypt.* Princeton: Princeton University Press, 1995.

Baedeker, Karl. *Egypt: Handbook for Travelers.* Leipzig: Karl Baedeker, 1878.

———. *Egypt: Handbook for Travelers.* Leipzig: Karl Baedeker, 1914.

Baer, Gabriel. *A History of Landownership in Modern Egypt.* London: Oxford University Press, 1962.

———. "The Village Shaykh." In *Studies in the Social History of Egypt*, edited by Gabriel Baer, 30–61. Chicago: University of Chicago, 1969.

———. "Women and Waqf: An Analysis of the Istanbul Tahrir of 1546." *Asian and African Studies* 17 (1983): 17 (1983): 9–27.

Baraka, Magda. *The Egyptian Upper Class between Revolutions.* Reading: Ithaca Press, 1998.

Barnes, John. *An Introduction to Religious Foundations in the Ottoman Empire.* Leiden: Brill, 1986.

Baron, Beth. "Nationalist Iconography: Egypt As Woman." In *Rethinking Nationalism in the Arab Middle East*, edited by James Jankowski and Israel Gershoni, 105–24. New York: Columbia University Press, 1997.

———. *The Women's Awakening in Egypt: Culture, Society, and the Press.* New Haven: Yale University Press, 1994.

Barry, Jonathan, and Colin Jones, ed. *Medicine and Charity before the Welfare State.* London: Routledge, 1991.

Bartlett, W. H. *The Nile Boat; or, Glimpses of the Land of Egypt.* London: Arthur Hall, Virtue, 1849.

Behrens-Abouseif, Doris. *Egypt's Adjustment to Ottoman Rule: Institutions, Waqf, and Architecture in Cairo (Sixteenth and Seventeenth Centuries)*. Leiden: E. J. Brill, 1994.

Beinin, Joel. *The Dispersion of Egyptian Jewry*. Berkeley: University of California Press, 1998.

Beinin, Joel, and Zachary Lockman. *Workers on the Nile: Nationalism, Communism, Islam, and the Egyptian Working Class, 1882–1954*. Princeton: Princeton University Press, 1987.

Bellingham, Bruce. "Waifs and Strays: Child Abandonment, Foster Care, and Families in Mid-Nineteenth-Century New York." In *The Uses of Charity: The Poor on Relief in the Nineteenth-Century Metropolis*, edited by Peter Mandler, 123–60. Philadelphia: University of Pennsylvania Press, 1990.

Bentley, Arthur J. M., and Rev. C. G. Griffenhoofe. *Wintering in Egypt*. London: Simpkin, Marshall, Hamilton, Kent, 1894.

Berque, Jacques. *Egypt: Imperialism and Revolution*. London: Faber and Faber, 1972.

Bianchi, Robert. *Unruly Corporatism: Associational Life in Twentieth-Century Egypt*. New York: Oxford University Press, 1989.

Bliss, Rev. Edwin Munsell. *The Encyclopedia of Missions*. Vol. 2. New York: Funk and Wagnalls, 1891.

Bonner, Michael. "Poverty and Charity in the Rise of Islam." In *Poverty and Charity in Middle Eastern Contexts*, edited by Michael Bonner, Mine Ener, Amy Singer. Albany: SUNY Press, 2003.

Bonner, Michael, Mine Ener, and Amy Singer. *Poverty and Charity in Middle Eastern Contexts*. Albany: SUNY Press, 2003.

Bosworth, C. E. *The Mediaeval Islamic Underworld: The Banu Sasan in Arabic Society and Literature*. Leiden: E. J. Brill, 1976.

Botman, Selma. *Egypt from Independence to Revolution*. Syracuse: Syracuse University Press, 1991.

Braude, Benjamin, and Bernard Lewis, eds. *Christians and Jews in the Ottoman Empire: The Functioning of a Plural Society*. New York: Holmes and Meier, 1982.

Brendon, Piers. *Thomas Cook: One Hundred Fifty Years of Popular Tourism*. London: Secker and Warburg, 1991.

Brodman, James William. *Charity and Welfare: Hospitals and the Poor in Medieval Catalonia*. Philadelphia: University of Pennsylvania Press, 1998.

Brown, Nathan. "Who Abolished Corvée Labour in Egypt and Why?" *Past and Present*, 144 (1994): 116–37.

Bulletin des lois et décrets. Cairo: Imprimerie Nationale, 1893.

Burkhardt, John Lewis. *Arabic Proverbs*. 1830. Reprint, London: Curzon Press, 1984.

Bynum, W. F., Roy Porter, and Michael Sheperd, eds. *Anatomy of Madness*, New York: Tavistock Publications, 1985.

Çadırcı, Musa. "Tanzimat Döneminde Çıkarılan Men'i Murur ve Pasaport Nizamnameleri" (Rules and regulations pertaining to restrictions on travel and passports in the Tanzimat Era). *Belgeler* 19, (1993): 169–85.

Caloyanni, Megalos A. "La Protection de l'enfance" (Opening Address for Conference on the Protection of Children). *L'Egypte Contemporaine*, (1915): 1–4.

Carlin, Martha. "Medieval English Hospitals." In *The Hospital in History*, edited by Lindsay Grinshaw and Roy Porter, 1–39. London: Routledge, 1989.

Cavallo, Sandra. "The Motivations of Benefactors: An Overview of Approaches to the Study of Charity." In *Medicine and Charity before the Welfare State*, edited by Jonathan Barry and Colin Jones, 46–62. London: Routledge, 1991.

Çelebi, Evliya. *Narrative of Travels in Europe, Asia, and Africa in the Seventeenth Century*. Translated from the Turkish by the Ritter Joseph von Hammer. 1834. Reprint, New York: Johnson Reprint Corporation, 1968.

Chirol, Sir Valentine. *The Egyptian Problem*. London: Macmillan, 1921.

Çiçek, Rahmi. "Asker Ailelerine Yardımcı Hanımlar Cemiyetinin Faaliyetleriyle Ilgili Bir Belge" (A document pertaining to the activities of a women's organization committed to caring for the families of soldiers). *Tarih ve Toplum* 20, no. 116 (August 1993).

Clot, A. B. *Aperçu général sur l'Egypte*. 2 vols. Paris: Fourtin, Masson, 1840.

Cohen, Mark. "The Foreign Jewish Poor in Medieval Egypt." In *Poverty and Charity in Middle Eastern Contexts*, edited by Michael Bonner, Mine Ener, and Amy Singer. Albany: SUNY Press, 2003.

Cole, Juan. *Colonialism and Revolution in the Middle East*. Princeton: Princeton University Press, 1993.

———. "Feminism, Class, and Islam in Turn-of-the-Century Egypt." *International Journal of Middle East Studies* 13 (1981): 397–407.

Coles, Charles E. *Recollections and Reflections*. London: St. Catherine Press, 1918.

Comité de Conservation des monuments de l'art Arabe, exercise 1882–83. Cairo: Imprimerie Nationale, 1892.

Cooper, Elizabeth. *The Women of Egypt*. New York: Frederick A. Stokes, 1914.

Corbet, Eustace K. "The Life and Works of Ahmad ibn Tulun." *Journal of the Royal Asiatic Society*, (1891): 527–62.

Creswell, K.A.C. *Early Muslim Architecture*. 3 vols. Oxford: Clarendon Press, 1932.

Crowins Smith, Jerome von. *Pilgrimage to Egypt*. Boston: Gould and Lincoln, 1852.

Cuno, Kenneth M. "Ideology and Juridical Discourse in Ottoman Egypt: The Uses of the Concept of *Irsad*." *Islamic Law and Society*, (May 1999): 136–163.

———. "Joint Family Households and Rural Notables in Nineteenth-Century Egypt." *International Journal of Middle East Studies* 27 (1995): 485–502.

———. *The Pasha's Peasants*. Cambridge: Cambridge University Press, 1992.

———. "A Tale of Two Villages: Family, Property, and Economic Activity in Rural Egypt in the 1840s." In *Agriculture in Egypt from Pharaonic to Modern Times*, edited by Alan K. Bowman and Eugene Rogan, 301–29. Proceedings of the British Academy 96. Oxford: Oxford University Press, 1999.

de Chamberet, Raoul. *Enquête sur la condition du fellah égyptien*. Dijon: Imprimerie Darantière, 1909.

DeJong, Frederick. "Tasawwuf" (in Nineteenth and Twentieth-Century Egypt)." In *The Encyclopedia of Islam*. New ed. Vol. 10. Leiden: E. J. Brill, 1999.

Delaney, Carol. *The Seed and the Soil: Gender and Cosmology in Turkish Village Society*. Berkeley: University of California Press, 1991.

Deny, Jean. *Sommaires des archives turques du Caire*, Cairo: Société royale de géographie d'Egypte, 1930.

Dodwell, Henry. *The Founder of Modern Egypt: A Study of Muhammad Ali.* Cambridge: Cambridge University Press, 1931.

Dols, Michael. *Majnun: The Madman in Medieval Islamic Society.* Oxford: Clarendon Press, 1992.

Dor, Edouard. *L'Instruction publique en Egypt.* Paris: A. LaCroix Veboeckhore, 1872.

Duff Gordon, Lucie. *Lady Duff Gordon's Letters from Egypt.* London: R. B. Johnson, 1902.

———. *Letters from Egypt.* 1865. Reprint, London: Virago Press, 1983.

Düzdağ, Mehmet Ertuğrul. *Şeyhülislam Ebüssuud Efendi Fetvaları Işığında 16. Asır Türk Hayatı.* Istanbul: Enderun Kitabevi, 1972.

Edwards, Amelia. *A Thousand Miles up the Nile.* 1877. Reprint, New York: Scribner, Welford, and Armstrong, 1890.

Egyptian Sanitary Department. *Report on the Egyptian Government Hospital for the Insane for the Year 1895.*

———. *Report on the Egyptian Government Hospital for the Insane for the Year 1901.*

Ener, Mine. "At the Crossroads of Empires: Policies toward the Poor in Early to Mid-Nineteenth-Century Egypt." *Social Science History,* 2002.

———. "The Charity of the Khedive." In *Poverty and Charity in Middle Eastern Contexts,* edited by Michael Bonner, Minc Ener, and Amy Singer. Albany: SUNY Press, 2003.

———. "Getting into Takiyat Tulun." In *Outside In: On the Margins of the Modern Middle East,* edited by Eugene Rogan. London: I. B. Tauris, 2002.

———. "Prohibitions on Begging and Loitering in Nineteenth-Century Egypt." *Die Welt des Islams,* 39 (1999) 319–39.

Fahmy, Khaled. *All the Pasha's Men: Mehmed Ali, His Army, and the Making of Modern Egypt.* Cambridge: Cambridge University Press, 1997.

———. "The Era of Muhammad 'Ali Pasha." In *The Cambridge History of Egypt,* edited by M. W. Daly, 2:139–79. Cambridge: Cambridge University Press, 1998.

———. "The Police and the People in Nineteenth-Century Egypt." *Die Welt des Islams* 39 (1999): 340–377.

———. "Women, Medicine, and Power in Nineteenth-Century Egypt." In *Remaking Women: Feminism and Modernity in the Middle East,* edited Lila Abu-Lughod, 35–72. Princeton: Princeton University Press, 1998.

Al-Fangari, Mahmud Shawqa. *Al-Jam'iyyat al-Khayriyya al-Islamiyya.* Cairo: Matba 'a al-Tobjiyya al-Tarikhiyya, 1991.

Fernea, Elizabeth Warnock. "Children in the Muslim Middle East." In *Children in the Muslim Middle East,* edited by Elizabeth Warnock Fernea. Austin: University of Texas Press, 1995.

Forster, Charles Thornton, and F. H. Blackburne Daniell. *The Life and Letters of Ogier Ghiselin de Busbecq.* 2 vols. London: C. Kegan Paul, 1881.

Foucault, Michel. "Governmentality." In *The Foucault Effect: Studies in Governmentality,* edited by Graham Burchell, Colin Gordon, and Peter Miller. London: Harvester/Wheatsheaf, 1991.

———. *The History of Sexuality.* 1976. Reprint, New York: Vintage Books, 1990.

————. *Madness and Civilization*. 1965. Reprint, New York: Vintage, 1988.

Fuchs, Rachel. *Abandoned Children, Foundlings, and Child Welfare in Nineteenth-Century France*. Albany, SUNY Press, 1984.

Gallagher, Nancy. *Egypt's Other Wars: Epidemics and the Politics of Public Health*. Syracuse: Syracuse University Press, 1990.

————. *Medicine and Power in Tunisia, 1780–1900*. Cambridge: Cambridge: University Press, 1983.

Garrison, Jean L. "Public Assistance in Egypt: An Ideological Analysis," *Middle East Journal* 32 (1978): 279–290.

Geremek, Bronislaw. *Poverty: A History*. Oxford: Blackwell Publishers, 1994.

Ghalwash, Maha. "Land Acquisition by the Peasants of Mid-Nineteenth Century Egypt: The *Ramya* System." *Studia Islamica* (1998): 121–39.

Ghazaleh, Pascale. "Masters of the Trade: Crafts and Craftspeople in Cairo, 1750–1850." *Cairo Papers in Social Science* 22, no. 3 (Fall 1999).

Ginio, Eyal. "Living on the Margins of Charity: Coping with Poverty in an Ottoman Provincial City." In *Poverty and Charity in Middle Eastern Contexts*, edited by Michael Bonner, Mint Ener, and Amy Singer. Albany: SUNY Press, 2003.

Goitein, Schlomo D. *A Mediterranean Society*. 4 vols. Berkeley: University of California Press, 1967.

Gordon, Linda. *Pitied but Not Entitled: Single Mothers and the History of Welfare*. Cambridge, Mass.: Harvard University Press, 1994.

Greiss, Kamel. "La Mendicité en Egypte et sa repression." *L'Egypte Contemporaine* 26 (March 1916): 203–227.

Grinshaw, Lindsay, and Roy Porter, eds. *The Hospital in History*. London: Routledge, 1989.

Guirin, Victor. *La France catholique en Egypte*. Tours: Alfred Mame et fils, 1894.

Gürkan, Kazi Ismail. *Süleymaniye Darüşşifası* (The hospital of the Süleymaniye). Istanbul: Özişik Matbaası, 1965.

Guha, Ranajit, and Gayatri Chakravorty Spivak, eds. *Selected Subaltern Studies*. Oxford: Oxford University Press, 1988.

Gutton, Jean-Pierre. *La Société et les pauvres: l'exemple de la généralité de Lyon, 1534–1789*. Paris: Société d'édition, Les Belles Lettres, 1971.

Hamarneh, Sami. "Development of Hospitals in Islam." *Journal of the History of Medicine and the Allied Sciences*, 17 (1962): 366–84.

Hamont, P. N. *L'Egypte sous Méhémet Ali*. 2 vols. Paris: Léautey et Lecointe, 1843.

Hanna, Nelly. "Construction Work in Ottoman Cairo (1517–1798)." *Supplément aux Annales Islamologiques* (1984).

————. *The State and Its Servants: Administration in Egypt from Ottoman Times to the Present*. Cairo: American University of Cairo Press, 1995.

Hatem, Mervat. "The Professionalization of Health and the Control of Women's Bodies as Modern Governmentalities in Nineteenth-Century Egypt." In *Women in the Ottoman Empire: Middle Eastern Women in the Early Modern Era*, edited by Madeline Ziffi, 66–80. Leiden: E. J. Brill, 1997.

Henderson, John, and Richard Wall. "Introduction." in *Poor Women and Children in the European Past*, edited by John Henderson, 1–28. New York: Routledge, 1994.

Heyd, Uriel. *Studies in Ottoman Criminal Law*. Oxford: Clarendon Press, 1973.

Heyworth-Dunne, John. *An Introduction to the History of Education in Modern Egypt*. 1939. Reprint, London: Frank Cass, 1968.

Hillenbrand, R. "Masdjid (In the Central Islamic Lands)" In *The Encyclopaedia of Islam*. Vol. 6. Leiden: E. J. Brill, 1991.

Hobson, H. Overton. *Helouan: An Egyptian Health Resort and How to Reach It*. New York: Longmans, Green, 1906.

Hodgson, Marshall. *The Venture of Islam*. Vol. 2, Chicago: University of Chicago Press, 1974.

Hoexter, Miriam. "Charity, the Poor, and Distribution of Alms in Ottoman Algiers." In *Poverty and Charity in Middle Eastern Contexts*, edited by Michael Bonner, Mine Ever, and Amy Singer. Albany: SUNY Press, 2003.

———. *Endowments, Rulers, and Community: Waqf al-Haramayn in Ottoman Algiers*. Leiden: E. J. Brill, 1998.

———. "Waqf Studies in the Twentieth Century: the State of the Art." *Journal of the Economic and Social History of the Orient*, 41, mo. 4, (1998): 474–495.

Hopkins, Eric. *Childhood Transformed: Working Class Children in Nineteenth-Century England*. Manchester: Manchester University Press, 1994.

Horden, Peregrine, and Richard Smith. "Introduction." In *The Locus of Care: Families, Communities, Institutions, and the Provision of Welfare since Antiquity*, edited by Peregrine Horden and Richard Smith, 1–18. London: Routledge, 1998.

———, ed. *The Locus of Care: Families, Communities, Institutions, and the Provision of Welfare since Antiquity*. London: Routledge, 1998.

Hufton, Olwen. *The Poor of Eighteenth-Century France*. Oxford: Oxford University Press, 1974.

Hunter, F. Robert. *Egypt under the Khedives, 1805–1879: From Household Government to Modern Bureaucracy*. Pittsburgh: University of Pittsburgh Press, 1984.

Hutnyk, John. *The Rumour of Calcutta: Tourism, Charity, and the Poverty of Representation*. London: Zed Books, 1996.

Ibrahim, Samir Amr, *Al-haya al-Ijtima'iya fi madinat al-Qahira Hilal Nasf al-Awal min al-Garn al-Tasa 'ashr*, Cairo: Al-Ha'ya al-Misriyya al-Amma li-l-Kitab, 1992.

Iliffe, John. *The African Poor*. Cambridge: Cambridge University Press, 1987.

Imber, Colin. *Ebu's-su'ud: The Islamic Legal Tradition*. Stanford: Stanford University Press, 1997.

Inalcık, Halil. *An Economic and Social History of the Ottoman Empire, 1300–1914*. Cambridge: Cambridge University Press, 1994.

———. "Istanbul." In *The Encyclopaedia of Islam*. Volume 4. Leiden, E. J. Brill, 1978.

———. "*Matbakh* (in Ottoman Turkey)." In *The Encyclopaedia of Islam*. Vol. 6. Leiden: E. J. Brill, 1991.

———. *The Ottoman Empire: The Classical Age, 1300–1600*. 1973. Reprint, London: Phoenix, 1994.

Issa Bey. *Al-Bimaristan fi al-Tarikh al-Islami* (The hospital in Islamic history). Cairo: Al-Matba'a al-Qawmiyya, 1939.

Al-Jabarti, Abd al-Rahman ibn Hasan. *Al-Aja'ib al-Athar fi Arajim wa al-Akhbar.* Vols. 1–7. 1880. Reprint, Cairo: Lajnat al-Bayan al-Arabi, 1966.

Al-Jami'i, Abd al-Man'am Ibrahim. *Majalat al-Ustadh.* Cairo: Matba'a al-Ha'ya al-Misriyya al-Amma li al-Kitab, 1994.

Al-Jam'iyyat al-Khayriyya al-Islamiyya. Cairo: Matba'a al-Tarikhiyya, 1991.

"Jam'iyyat al-Urwa al-Wuthqa al-Khayriyya al-Islamiyya" (Yearly report). *Majallat al-Malga' al-Abbasiyya,* 447–55. Pt. 8, vol. 12. 1 Shaban 1330.

Jennings, Ronald. "Pious Foundations in the Society and Economy of Ottoman Trabzon, 1565–1640." *JESHO* 33 (1990): 271–336.

Jomard. "Description de la ville du Kaire." In *Description de l'Egypte.* Vol. 2, no. 2. Paris: Imprimerie de C. L. F. Panckoucke, 1820–1830.

Karpat, Kemal. "The Population and the Social and Economic Transformation of Istanbul: The Ottoman Microcosm." In *Ottoman Population, 1830–1914: Demographic and Social Characteristics.* Madison: University of Wisconsin Press, 1985.

Kashef, A.S.M. "Egypt." In *Social Welfare in the Middle East,* edited by John Dixon, 1–31. London: Croom Helm, 1987.

Kennedy, Hugh. *The Prophet and the Age of the Caliphates.* London: Longman, 1986.

Kitroeff, Alexander. *The Greeks in Egypt, 1919–1937: Ethnicity and Class.* London: Ithaca Press, 1989.

Koven, Seth. "Dr. Barnado's 'Artistic Fictions': Photography, Sexuality, and the Ragged Child in Victorian London." *Radical History Review* 69 (1997): 6–45.

Koven, Seth, and Sonya Michel. "Womanly Duties: Maternalist Policies and the Origins of Welfare States in France, Germany, Great Britain, and the United States, 1880–1920." *American Historical Review* 95 (October 1990): 1076–1114.

———, eds. *Mothers of a New World: Maternalist Politics and the Origins of Welfare States.* New York: Routledge, 1993.

Kramer, Güdrün. *The Jews in Modern Egypt, 1914–1952.* Seattle: University of Washington Press, 1983.

Krieken, Robert van. "The Poverty of Social Control: Explaining Power in the Historical Sociology of the Welfare State." *The Sociological Review* 39, no. 1 (February 1991): 1–25.

Kuhnke, Laverne. *Lives at Risk: Public Health in Nineteenth-Century Egypt.* Berkeley: University of California Press, 1990.

Landau, Jacob. *Jews in Nineteenth-Century Egypt.* New York: New York University Press, 1969.

Landes, David. *Bankers and Pashas.* Cambridge, Mass.: Harvard University Press, 1958.

Lane, Edward. *Manners and Customs of the Modern Egyptians.* 1836. Reprint, London: East West Publications, 1989.

Lane Poole, Mrs. [Sophia]. *The Englishwoman in Egypt: Letters from Cairo.* 2 vols. London: C. Cox, 1851.

Lane Poole, Stanley. *Cairo: Sketches of Its History, Monuments, and Social Life.* London: J. S. Virtue, 1892.

Laqueur, Thomas. *Religion and Respectability: Sunday Schools and Working-Class Culture, 1780–1850*. New Haven: Yale University Press, 1976.

Lees, Lynn Hollen. *The Solidarities of Strangers: The English Poor Laws and the People, 1700–1948*. Cambridge: Cambridge University Press, 1998.

———. "The Survival of the Unfit: Welfare Policies and Family Maintenance in Nineteenth-Century London." In *The Uses of Charity: The Poor on Relief in the Nineteenth-Century Metropolis*, edited by Peter Mandler, 68–91. Philadelphia: University of Pennsylvania Press, 1990.

Libal, Kathryn. " 'The Child Question': The Politics of Child Welfare in Early Republican Turkey." In *Poverty and Charity in Middle Eastern Contexts*, edited by Michael Bonner, Mine Ever, and Amy Singer. Albany: SUNY Press, 2003.

Lindenmeyr, Adele. *Poverty Is Not a Vice: Charity, Society, and the State in Imperial Russia*. Princeton: Princeton University Press, 1996.

Lis, Catharina, and Hugo Soly. *Poverty and Capitalism in Pre-Industrial Europe*. Atlantic Highlands: Humanities Press, 1979.

———. " 'Total Institutions' and the Survival Strategies of the Laboring Poor in Antwerp, 1770–1860." In *The Uses of Charity: The Poor on Relief in the Nineteenth-Century Metropolis*, edited by Peter Mandler, 38–67. Philadelphia: University of Pennsylvania Press, 1990.

Madden, Robert Richard. *Egypt and Muhammad 'Ali: Illustrative of the Condition of the Slaves and Subjects and c. and c.* London: Hamilton, Adams, 1841.

———. *Travels in Turkey, Egypt, and Palestine*. 2 vols. London: Henry Colburn, 1829.

Mahfouz, Naguib Bey. *The History of Medical Education in Egypt*. Cairo: Government Press, 1935.

Mandler, Peter. "Poverty and Charity in the Nineteenth-Century Metropolis: An Introduction." In *The Uses of Charity: The Poor on Relief in the Nineteenth-Century Metropolis*, edited by Peter Mandler, 1–38. Philadelphia: University of Pennsylvania Press, 1990.

Marcus, Abraham. *The Middle East on the Eve of Modernity: Aleppo in the Eighteenth Century*. New York: Columbia University Press, 1989.

———. "Poverty and Poor Relief in Eighteenth-Century Aleppo," *Revue du Monde Musulman et de la Méditerranée* 55–56 (1990): 171–79.

Marsot, Afaf Lufti al-Sayyid. *Egypt in the Reign of Muhammad Ali*. Cambridge: Cambridge University Press, 1984.

———. *Egypt's Liberal Experiment*. Berkeley: University of California Press, 1977.

———. "The History of Muhammad Ali: Fact or Fiction." *Journal of the American Research Center in Egypt* (1978): 107–12.

———. "The Revolutionary Gentlewoman in Egypt." In *Women in the Muslim World*, edited by Lois Beck and Nikki Keddie, 261–76. Cambridge, Mass.: Harvard University Press, 1978.

———. *A Short History of Egypt*. Cambridge: Cambridge University Press, 1988.

Martinez-Vergne, Teresita. *Shaping the Discourse on Space: Charity and Its Wards in Nineteenth-Century San Juan, Puerto Rico*. Austin: University of Texas Press, 1999.

Maunier, René. "Des Rapports entre le progrès de la richesse et l'accroissement de la criminalité en Egypte." *L'Egypte Contemporaine* (1912): 27–42.

McBarnet, A. C. "The New Penal Code: Offences against Morality and the Marriage Tie and Children." *L'Egypte Contemporaine* 10:374–87.

McCarthy, Justin. "Nineteenth-Century Egyptian Population." *Middle East Studies* 12, no. 3 (October 1976):1–40.

McChesney, Robert D. *Charity and Philanthropy in Islam: Institutionalizing the Call to Do Good.* Indianapolis: Indiana University Center on Philanthropy, 1995.

McClure, Ruth K. *Coram's Children: The London Foundling Hospital in the Eighteenth Century.* New Haven: Yale University Press, 1981.

McGowan, Bruce. "The Age of Ayans." In *An Economic and Social History of the Ottoman Empire, 1300–1914,* edited by H. Inalcık and D. Quataert, 637–758. Cambridge: Cambridge University Press, 1994.

Ministry of the Interior [Egypt]. *Lunacy Division Report for the Year 1917.*

Ministry of the Interior Police Regulations. Cairo: National Printing Press, 1901.

Minutoli [Baroness]. *Recollections of Egypt.* Philadelphia: Carey, Lea, and Carey Publishers, 1827.

Mitchell, Richard P. *Society of the Muslim Brothers.* London: Oxford University Press, 1969.

Mitchell, Timothy. "America's Egypt: Discourse of the Development Industry." *Middle East Report* (March–April 1991): 18–34.

———. *Colonizing Egypt.* Cambridge: Cambridge University Press, 1988.

———. "The Stage of Modernity." In *Questions of Modernity,* edited by Mitchell. Minneapolis: University of Minnesota Press, 2000.

———, ed. *Questions of Modernity.* Minneapolis: University of Minnesota Press, 2000.

Mollat, Michel. *The Poor in the Middle Ages: An Essay in Social History.* New Haven: Yale University Press, 1986.

Moreau, J. "Recherches sur les aliénés en Orient." *Annales Médico-Psychologiques* 1 (1843): 103–33.

Mubarak, Ali. *Al-Khitat al-Tawfiqiyya.* 20 vols. Cairo: al-Ha'ya al-Misriyya al-ʿAmma li-l-Kitab, 1980.

Murray, John. *A Handbook for Travelers in Egypt.* London: John Murray, 1875.

Mustafa, Ahmed ʿAbdel-Rahim. "The Hekekyan Papers." In *Political and Social Change in Modern Egypt,* edited by P. M. Holt, 68–75. London: Oxford University Press, 1968.

Nachat, Hassan. "Le Patronage des jeunes libres." *L'Egypte Contemporaine* (1914): 209–22.

Nadim, Abd Allah. *Majalat al-Ustadh.* Cairo: Matbaʿa al-Ha'ya al-Misriyya al-Amma li al-Kitab, 1994.

———, comp. *Sulafat al-Nadim fi Muntakhabat.* Cairo: Matbaʿa Hindiyya bi-Misr, 1914.

Najm, Zayn al-Abdin. "Tasahhub al-fallahin fi ʿasr Muhammad Ali: Asbabuhu wa nataʿijhu" (The absconding of peasants in the era of Muhammad Ali: Its reasons and effects). *Al-Majalla al-Tarikhiyya al-Misriyya* 36 (1989): 259–316.

Nazmi Bey, Abd el-Aziz. "La protection de l'enfance au point de vue médical et social." *L'Egypte Contemporaine* (1911): 81–93.

———. "Tarbiyat al-Atfal," *Majalat al-Malaji' al-Abbasiyya* 12, no. 6 (1 Jumada II, 1330 May 18, 1912).

Neuberger, Joan. *Hooliganism: Crime, Culture, and Power in St. Petersburg, 1900–1914*. Berkeley: University of California Press, 1993.

Owen, Roger. *Cotton and the Egyptian Economy*. Oxford: Clarendon Press, 1969.

———. "The Influence of Lord Cromer's Indian Experience on British Policy in Egypt, 1883–1907." *St. Antony's Papers* 17 (1965).

———. *The Middle East in the World Economy, 1800–1914*. 1981. Reprint, London: A. Tauris Press, 1993.

———. "Modernizing Projects in Middle Eastern Perspective." In *Rethinking Modernity and National Identity in Turkey*, edited by Sibel Bozdogan and Resat Kasaba, 245–51. Seattle: University of Washington Press, 1997.

Özbek, Nadir. "Imperial Gifts and Sultanic Legitimation during the Reign of Sultan Abuldhamid II, 1876–1909." In *Poverty and Charity in Middle Eastern Contexts*, edited by Michael Bonner, Mine Ener, and Amy Singer. Albany: SUNY Press, 2003.

———. "II. Meşrutiyet Istanbul'unda Dilenciler ve Serseriler" (Beggars and vagrants of the Second Constitutional Period's Istanbul). *Toplumsal Tarih* 64 (1999): 34–43.

———. "The Politics of Poor Relief in the Late-Ottoman Empire, 1876–1914." *New Perspectives on Turkey*, no. 21 (Fall 1999) 1–34.

Panzac, Daniel. "Médecine révolutionnaire et révolution de la médecine dans l'Egypte de Muhammad Ali, le Dr. Clot Bey." *Révue du Monde Musulman et de la Méditerranée* 52/53 (1989): 95–110.

Paul-Valentin. "La Protection de l'enfance." *L'Egypte Contemporaine* (1915): 21–51.

Peirce, Leslie. *The Imperial Harem: Women and Sovereignty in the Ottoman Empire*. Oxford: Oxford University Press, 1993.

Pemble, John. *The Mediterranean Passion: Victorians and Edwardians in the South*. Oxford: Clarendon Press, 1987.

Peters, Rudolph. "'For His Correction and As a Deterrent Example for Others': Mehmed Ali's First Criminal Legislation (1829–1830)." *Islamic Law and Society* 6 (1999): 164–92.

Petry, Carl. "A Paradox of Patronage during the later Mamluk Period." *The Muslim World* 73, nos. 3–4 (July/October 1983): 182–207.

Porter, Roy. *Disease, Medicine, and Society in England, 1550–1860*. London: Macmillan, 1987.

Prakash, Gyan. "Body Politic in Colonial India." In *Questions of Modernity*, edited by Timothy Mitchell, 189–222. Minneapolis: University of Minnesota Press, 2000.

Raf'i, Abd al-Rahman. *Asr Muhammad Ali*. Cairo: Dar al-Maʿarif, 1989.

"Rapport sur le Moristan ou Hôpital du Kaire, addressé au Général en Chef Bonaparte par le Citoyen Desgenettes." in *La Décade Egyptienne, Journal Littéraire et d'Economie Politique*. Vol. 1. Cairo: Imprimerie Nationale, year VII of the French Republic.

Reid, Donald. "Cultural Imperialism and Nationalism: The Struggle to Define and Control the Heritage of Arab Art in Egypt." *International Journal of Middle East Studies* 24 (1992): 57–76.

———. "The Rise of Professions and Professional Organization in Modern Egypt." *Comparative Studies in Society and History* 16 (January 1974): 24–57.

Reimer, Michael J. "Reorganizing Alexandria: the Origins and History of the Conseil de l'Ornato." *Journal of Urban History* 19, no. 3 (1993).

"Rijal Misr al-amalin: mu'assas mashrua' malga' al-hurriyya." *Al-Lata'if al-Musawwara*, April 28, 1919, 2–3.

Rivlin, Helen. *The Agricultural Policy of Muhammad Ali in Egypt*. Cambridge, Mass.: Harvard University Press, 1961.

Rosenthal, Franz. "The Stranger in Medieval Islam." *Arabica* 44 (1997): 33–75.

Ross, Ellen. "Survival Networks: Women's Neighborhood Sharing in London before World War I." *History Workshop Journal* 15 (1983): 4–27.

Rugh, Andrea. Orphanages in Egypt: Contradiction or Affirmation in a Family-Oriented Society." In *Children in the Muslim Middle East*, edited by Elizabeth Fernea, 124–41. Austin: University of Texas Press, 1995.

Sabra, Adam. *Poverty and Charity in Medieval Islam*. Cambridge: Cambridge University Press, 2001.

Said, Edward. *Orientalism*. New York: Vintage Books, 1978.

St. John, Bayle. *Village Life in Egypt with Sketches of the Said*. 2 vols. Boston: Ticknor, Reed, and Fields, 1853.

St. John, James August. *Egypt and Muhammad Ali; or, Travels in the Valley of the Nile*. 2 vols. London: Longman, Rees, Orme, Brown, Green, and Longman, 1834.

Sami, Ahmed. "Juvenile Vagrants and Delinquents." *L'Egypte Contemporaine* (February 1923): 250–72.

Sami, Amin. *Taqwim al-Nil* (Nile almanac). 3 vols. Cairo: Dar al-Kutub al-Misriyya, 1916–36.

Sami, Mahmoud. "La Protection de l'enfance" (First Paper in the Conference on the Protection of Children). *L'Egypte Contemporaine* (1915): 5–20.

Sanders, Paula. *Ritual, Politics, and the City in Fatimid Cairo*. Albany: SUNY Press, 1994.

Sandwith, F. M. "The Cairo Lunatic Asylum, 1888." *The Journal of Medical Science* 34, no. 148 (January 1889): 473–90.

———. *Egypt As a Winter Resort*. London: Kegan Paul, 1889.

Schimmel, Annemarie. *Mystical Dimensions of Islam*. Chapel Hill: University of North Carolina Press, 1981.

Sékaly, A. *Le Problème des waqfs en Egypte*. Paris: Libririe Orientaliste Paul Geuthner, 1929.

Shalabi, Hilmi Ahmad. *Harakat al-Islah al-Ijtima'iyya fi Misr*. Cairo: al-Ha'ya al-Misriyya al-Amma li-l-Kitab, 1988.

Sha'rawi, Huda. *Harem Years: The Memoirs of an Egyptian Feminist*. Translated by Margot Badran. London: Virago Press, 1986.

Shaw, Stanford. *The Financial and Administrative Organization and Development of Ottoman Egypt, 1517–1798*. Princeton: Princeton University Press, 1962.

Shefer, Miri. "Charity and Hospitality: Hospitals in Three Islamic Capitals in the Early Modern Period." In *Poverty and Charity in Middle Eastern Contexts*, edited by Micheal Bonner, Mine Ener, and Amy Singer. Albany: SUNY Press, 2003.

Singer, Amy. "Charity's Legacies: A Reconsideration of Ottoman Imperial Endowment-Making." In *Poverty and Charity in Middle Eastern Contexts*, edited by Micheal Bonner, Mine Ener, and Amy Singer. Albany: SUNY, 2003.

———. *Constructing Ottoman Beneficence*. Albany: SUNY Press, 2002.

———. "The Ottoman Empire As a Welfare State: The Case for and Against." in *Halil Inalcık Armağani*, edited by Nejat Göyünç, Jean-Louis Bacque-Grammont, and Ozer Ergenç. Istanbul: Eren Yayınevi, forthcoming.

Skocpol, Theda. *Protecting Soldiers and Mothers: The Political Origins of Social Policy in the United States*. Cambridge, Mass.: Harvard University Press, 1992.

Skull, Andrew T. *Museums of Madness*. New York: St. Martin's Press, 1979.

Social Welfare in Egypt. Cairo: Royal Government of Egypt Ministry of Social Affairs, 1950.

Sonbol, Amira al-Azhary. "Adoption in Islamic Society: A Historical Survey." In *Children in the Muslim Middle East*, edited by Elizabeth Warnock Fernea, 45–67. Austin: University of Texas Press, 1995.

———. *The Creation of the Medical Profession in Egypt, 1800–1922*. Syracuse: Syracuse University Press, 1991.

Stillman, Norman. "Charity and Social Services in Medieval Islam." *Societas* (1975): 105–15.

Stoler, Ann. "Rethinking Colonial Categories: European Communities and the Boundaries of Rule." *Comparative Studies in Society and History* 31, no. 1 (1989): 134–61.

Swinglehurst, Edmund. *Cook's Tours: The Story of Popular Travel*. New York: Blandford Press, 1982.

Tabbaa, Yasser. "The Functional Aspects of Medieval Islamic Hospitals," In *Poverty and Charity in Middle Eastern Contexts*, edited by Michael Bonner, Mine Ener, and Amy Singer. Albany: SUNY Press, 2003.

Tagher, Jacques, ed. *Mémoires de A .B. Clot Bey*. Cairo: Institut français d'archéologie orientale, 1949.

Taşkıran, Nimet. *Hasekinin Kitabı* (Book of the Haseki Foundation). Istanbul: Yenilik Basımevi, 1972.

Thompson, Jason. *Sir Gardner Wilkinson and His Circle*. Austin: University of Texas Press, 1992.

Thornton, Thomas. *The Present State of Turkey*. 2 vols. London: Joseph Mawman Publishers, 1809.

Tignor, Robert. *Modernization and British Colonial Rule in Egypt, 1882–1914*, Princeton: Princeton University Press, 1966.

Tilly, Charles. *Coercion, Capital, and European States, AD 990–1990*, Cambridge: Basil Blackwell, 1990.

Toledano, Ehud. "Mehmet Ali Paşa or Muhammad Ali Basha? An Historiographic Appraisal in the Wake of a Recent Book." *Middle East Studies* 21, (October 1985): 141–59.

————. *State and Society in Mid-Nineteenth-Century Egypt.* Cambridge: Cambridge University Press, 1990.

Tourneau, R. "Bayt al-Mal." *Encyclopedia of Islam.* New ed. Vol 1. Leiden: E. J. Brill, 1960.

Truscott, J. A. S. *The Parliamentary Debates.* Vol. 5. London: Wyman and Sons, 1909.

Tucker, Judith. *In the House of Law: Gender and Islamic Law in Ottoman Syria and Palestine.* Berkeley: University of California Press, 1998.

————. *Women in Nineteenth-Century Egypt.* Cambridge: Cambridge University Press, 1985.

United Kingdom. *Hansard Parliamentary Debates,* 4th ser., vol. 139 (1904).

————, vol. 141 (1905).

Urquhart, A. R., M.D., and W. S. Tuke, M.D. "Two Visits to the Cairo Asylum, 1877 and 1878." *The Journal of Mental Science* 25 (1880): 43–53.

Walkowitz, Judith. *City of Dreadful Delight: Narratives of Sexual Danger in Late-Victorian London.* Chicago: University of Chicago Press, 1992.

Walsh, R. *Constantinople during a Period Including the Commencement and Termination of the Greek and Turkish Revolutions.* 2 vols. London: Frederick Westley and A. H. Davis, 1836.

Warnock, John. "Twenty-Eight Years' Lunacy Experience in Egypt (1895–1923)." Parts 1 and 2. *The Journal of Mental Science* 70, no. 289 (April 1924): 233–61; no. 290 (July, 1924): 380–410.

Waterfield, Gordon. *Letters from Egypt (1862–1869) by Lady Duff Gordon.* London: Routledge and Kegan Paul, 1969.

Weindling, Paul. "The Modernization of Charity in Nineteenth-Century France and Germany." In *Medicine and Charity before the Welfare State,* edited by Jonathan Barry and Colin Jones, 190–206. London: Routledge, 1991.

Whately, Mary L. *Child Life in Egypt.* Philadelphia: Union Press, 1866.

————. *Letters from Egypt to the Plain Folks at Home.* London: Seeley, Jackson, and Halliday, 1879.

Wilkinson, G. *Handbook for Travelers in Egypt.* London: John Murray, 1847.

Winter, Michael. *Egyptian Society under Ottoman Rule, 1517–1798.* London: Routledge, 1992.

Wissa, Karim. "Freemasonry in Egypt, 1798–1921: A Study in Cultural and Political Encounters." *British Society for Middle Eastern Studies Bulletin* 16 (1989) 143–61.

Wolper, Ethel Sara. "The Politics of Patronage: Political Change and the Construction of Dervish Lodges in Sivas." *Muqarnas* 12 (1995): 39–47.

Wright, Arnold. *Twentieth Century Impressions of Egypt.* London: Lloyds Greater Britain Publishing, 1909.

Yates, William H. *The Modern History and Condition of Egypt, Its Climate, Diseases, and Capabilities.* 2 vols. London: Smith, Elder, 1843.

Yediyıldız, Bahaeddin. *Institution du Vaqf au XVIIIe siècle en Turquie.* Ankara: Imprimerie de la Société d'Histoire Turquie 1985.

Zaghlul, Ahmad Fathi. *Al-Muhama.* Cairo: Maʿarif Publishers, 1900.

INDEX

Abbas, 47, 63, 74
Abbas Hilmi, 95, 102
Abdul Hamid II, Sultan, 23–24, 76, 168n.7, 173n.86
able-bodied poor, 29–31, 34, 38–40, 46, 65–66, 140
Abu Naddara Zurqa, 79
agricultural absconders, 30, 34–35
Ahmed, Leila, xviii
Aleppo, 7, 15, 27
Alexandria: as destination for peasants fleeing countryside, 13, 33; improving appearance of, 35, 74; location of shelters in, xi, 11, 20, 40, 54; loitering in 13, 64, 74; as site of first Muslim Benevolent Society, 102; as site of juvenile reformatory, 114; as site of Orphanage of St. Vincent de Paul, 103; street-children in, 18
American philanthropists, 120–21
Antwerp, 19
appearances, concern about, 29, 35
Ashura, 27, 151n.11
awqaf. See religious endowments
Al-Azhar: diminishing funds of, 163; distribution of food at, 12, 26, 44, 150–51n.4; as place of sanctuary, 26, 35

Badran, Margot, xviii, 111, 116
Balfour, Andrew, 90–91
Baron, Beth, xviii
Bartlett, W. H., 85–86
bassas (spies) 33
Bayt al-Mal (state treasury), xii, 6, 8, 11, 147
Bowring, John, 34, 38
bureaucratization of poor relief, 11–12, 30, 45, 136, 143
Busbecq, Ogier Ghiselin de, 3, 6

Çelebi, Evliya, 6–7
cerrarlar (troublesome beggars) 28
charitable associations. *See* philanthropic associations
charity's purpose, 4, 27
children, abandoned, xi, xvii, 29, 42–46, 50, 108, 127, 137; abandonment at

churches, 155n.82; ameliorating conditions of, 22; as deserving, 82, 107, 137, 141, 143; dispensaries for, 92; education of, 18; elites' concern for, 100–102, 108, 111, 121; health and hygiene of, 43–44, 91–92, 99–100, 112, 129, 143; living in Mahall al-Fuqara', 39; missionary care for, 103; with mothers, 56–57; and nationalism, 123–24; orphaned, 27, 47, 56, 102–3; programs for, 116; "protection of," 116; as residents of Takiyyat Tulun, 59; seeking charity, 31, 76; street children, 96–97, 115–16; vulnerability of, 2, 20; working in factories, 31, 34.
Chirol, Valentine, 94–97
Civilian Hospital, x, 37–38, 42, 53, 58, 62, 86
civilizing mission, 93
civil society, 23–24, 100–101, 104
cleanliness: European notions of, 89; purported lack of, in Egypt, 88; teaching Egyptians about, 92
Clot, Antoine Barthélémy, xxiii, 40, 43, 50, 84, 86, 87, 155–56n.89, 163n.24
Clot Bey. *See* Clot, Antoine Barthélémy
Code pénal (France), 41
Cohen, Mark, 28
Comité de Conservation des Monuments de l'Art Arabe, 49, 74, 150n.69
conjunctural poverty, 59
conscription: continued after reign of Muhammad Ali, 63; European accounts of, 84–85, 87; impact on families, 50, 56, 58, 61; introduction of, 31–34, 57
Cook, Thomas, 79, 88–89, 163–64n.36
Cooper, Elizabeth, 95–97
Coptic Benevolent Society, projects of, 102, 104, 138, 142, 169nn. 10 and 15; Ministry of Social Affairs supervision over, 130
corvée, 31–32, 57, 85, 87, 164–65n.46
Creswell, K.A.C., 50
crime: cases of 114, 170n.38; criminality of the poor, xvii, xx, 36, 64, 105, 113, 117, 141, 143; fear of, 34; fighting,

crime (*cont.*)
  113; ideas about, 170n.36; new research on, xxi
Cromer, Lord (Evelyn Baring), 90–91, 96–97
Crowins Smith, Jerome von, 85, 87
Cuno, Kenneth, xv, 60

daman (guarantee, bond, surety) 9, 34, 66–69, 160n.77
damin (guarantor) 160n.77
Darülaceze, xx
daya (midwife), 93
Dervish (member of a Sufi order), 33, 66–67, 160n.74
dismissal (from Takiyyat Tulun), 71–72
Dols, Michael, 27
Dual Control, 77
Duff Gordon, Lady (Lucie), 47, 49, 51–53, 62, 69, 72–73, 76, 79, 83–84, 92

Ebu's-su'ud Effendi, Şeyhülislam (chief religious cleric), 28, 151n.15
Egypt's Ottoman identity, xiv, xviii, 148n.52
Elgood, Bonté Sheldon, 93, 107
elites, competition among, 128
England, poor relief in, 15, 16, 19, 20, 21, 41
European charitable programs, Egyptians comparing their own with, 116

Fahmy, Khaled, xv, 18, 88
Fangari, Muhammad Shawqi, 103
Farouk, King, xi, 24, 130–32, 134, 139
Fatimids, 5
flight from Takiyyat Tulun, xxi, 71
France, poor relief in, 15, 20, 40–41
Fuad, King, 128, 130
Fuchs, Rachel, 17

Gallagher, Nancy, 24, 38, 130, 139
Garrison, Jean, 131
gender, as criterion for admittance to Takiyyat Tulun, 55
gharib (stranger), 54
Ginio, Eyal, xix
golden age of the family, 18, 105, 173n.2
Greiss, Kamel, 12, 105–7

Hajj (pilgrimage), poor pilgrims' passage through Egypt and, 43, 50
hakima (female medical specialist), 93
haqq (due or right), 27, 31, 46, 62
health resort, Egypt as, 89, 139
Hekekyan, Joseph, xxiii, 39, 49, 73, 140
Hoexter, Miriam 4
hospitals: European, 45; Islamic 46
Hutnyk, John, 81
hybridity of poor relief, 14
hygiene, discourse about, 90, 105, 108–9, 111–12

iblikhane (women's prison), xx
Id al-Adha, 2, 7
Id al-Fitr, 2
Iftar, 7
infant abandonment. *See* children, abandoned
infant mortality, 92–93, 97, 104, 108–9, 112, 166n.59
insane, the, xi, 37–38, 42–43, 46–47, 84, 86–87, 89, 91, 97, 138
insane asylums, x, 11, 43, 84, 92–93, 97; European attitudes toward, 86–87, 92–93;
irsad, 8
Ismail: charitable contributions of, 74; and military recruitment, 57; in *Punch*, 77; and Takiyyat Tulun's diminishing funds, 51, 73
Istanbul: beggars presence in, 2–3, 12; controlling access to, 30; imaret in, 20; maintenance of order and security in, 139–40; policies toward the poor, xix–xx; provisions for poor of, 6–7, 20; study of the poor in, 15, 139; and Sultan Abdul Hamid II's charitable projects, 23

Jam'iyyat al-Musawah al-Islamiyya (Society of Islamic Benevolence), 128
Jerusalem, 7

kashf, 53, 62
Koven, Seth, 17
Kuhnke, Laverne, xvi, 43

Lane, Edward, 27, 42, 76, 83, 85
Lane Poole, Sophia, 86
Lane Poole, Stanley, 49

Lees, Lynn 16, 73
Lindenmeyr, Adele, 17

Mabarat Muhammad Ali, 96, 111–12, 123
Madden, R. R., 85
Madrasat al-Wilada (midwifery training school and location of orphanage and foundling home) 11, 42–45, 134, 155n.81
Mahall al-Khayriyat, 43–44
Mahfouz, Naguib, 47
Mahir, Ali, 124, 130
Mahmud II, Sultan, challenges of Muhammad Ali to, xiv, 13, 34
Malagi al-Abbasiyya, 118
Malga' al-Abbasiyya, 102
Malga' Abna al-Shawari'a, 118, 120–22
Malga' al-Hurriyya, 118–19, 121–22, 143; care of non-Muslim and Muslim boys, 125–26
Mamluk 5, 7–8, 15, 40
Ma'mur al-Mutasahibin, 30, 151n.22
Mandler, Peter, 17
Marcus, Abraham, xix, 53, 141,
Maristan Qalawun, 20, 49, 52–53, 61, 63, 69, 72, 126, 135–36; European depictions of, 84–87; history of, xi; location of Mahall al-Fuqara', 36–42; as representing modernization of poor relief, 46
Marsot, Afaf Lutfi al-Sayyid, xviii, 13, 85
maternalist policies, 111
maternalist welfare state, 17
maternity schools, 92
mawdi' al-hukm (orphans depository in Mamluk period), 8
Mecca, 7, 48, 73; poor shelters located in, 95
Medina 7; poor shelters located in, 95
Michel, Sonya, 17
Minutoli, Baroness, 76
missionaries, activities, 74, 79, 84; Egyptian concerns about, xviii, 20, 103, 123, 138, 143; examples set by, 96
Mitchell, Timothy, xiv
mixed economy of relief, 9
mosques, as place of rest and refuge, 26
Moureau, J., 86
Muhammad Ali, xiv, xvi–xvii, 39, 50, 107, 140; concern about absconders, 13; criminal legislation and, 41; imita-
tion of Ottoman rulers by, 11, 134; medical advances during era of, 42–43; need for revenues and, 35; negative commentary about, 85–86; policies toward populace and, 46, 63, 137; projects of, 31, 63; public security and, 31; religious endowments of, 51, 73
muhtasib, 28, 40
Muslim Benevolent Society, 97–98, 102–3, 130, 132, 142
Muslim Brotherhood, 24, 129, 134, 139
Muslim Youth Association, 129
mutasahibun, 39. See also agricultural absconders

Nasser, Gamal Abdul, 133
nationalism, 123, 127–28, 144
Nazmi, Abd al-Aziz, 99–100, 105, 109, 117–19, 121, 129

Ornato, Commission of, 37, 39
orta al-madhnubin, 36
Ottoman Empire, xii, 29, 74, 76–77, 135; charitable associations in, 23; controlling migration in, 30; dervishes and, 67; Egypt's importance to, 14; hospitals in, 38, 45, 57, 134; provisions for the poor, 7–8, 41, 134–35, 143; scholarship on history of, xvii; soup kitchens (imaret) in, 7, 38, 41, 134; sultan as source of benevolence in, 8, 41, 131, 134
Owen, Roger, xv

pensions, 57
philanthropic associations, 10, 18, 22, 24, 73, 75, 79, 113, 119, 124–25, 132; elites participation in xi, 98–101, 126; European influence on Egyptian, 101; multidenominational aspect of, 128; purposes of, 138, 142; religious rhetoric of, xviii; rise of 101, 123, 135; and Sultan Abdul Hamid II, 24; those of Western Europe, Russia, and North America, 19; women's involvement in, 111–12,
pious endowments. See religious endowments
politicization of Egypt's poverty, 135
politics of benevolence, 24
politics of Egypt's poverty, 81–82
poor, as subject of analysis in Europe, xviii

poor prisoners' health, 43
press, the: to advertise efforts of philan-
    thropists, 126–27; for drawing atten-
    tion to the poor, 116, 119; as site of
    criticism, 119
private organizations. See philanthropic
    associations
prostitutes, 35, 47 153n.46, 158n.44,
    159n.69
public health, xvi, 13–14, 22, 30, 35, 39,
    42–43, 45–46, 66, 84, 90–94, 97, 103;
    Department of Public Health, 94, 97
public order, 30–31, 36, 64, 67
public security, 13, 29
Punch, 76, 79, 89

Qalawun complex, 26; school for orphans
    at, 26
Qanun al-Filaha, 32–33,
Qanun al-Muntakhabat, 41
Qasr al-Ayni hospital, 47, 52, 74, 165nn.
    48 and 54; 168n.82
Qishla al-Sadaqa, xi, 20, 40, 54

"ragged child," 117
Ramadan tables, 2
reformatory for juveniles, 114–15, 117,
    119, 171nn. 45, 46, and 47; as punish-
    ment for street boys, 115
religious and ethnic minorities, care for
    poor among, 28, 64–65, 103–4,
    125–26
religious endowments, 3–10, 42, 104,
    131, 134–35, 147n.15; Europeans' neg-
    ative views of, 87–88; Ministry of Reli-
    gious Endowments (Awqaf), 74, 95, 97,
    109, 112, 161n.105, 167n.71; mis-
    management of, 93–94, 167n.72, re-
    search on, xix
residence, as criterion for assistance, 28;
    distinctions of in Europe, 29, 36–37
Revolution of 1919, 126, 129
Royal Society, 99–100, 105–6, 109, 113,
    115–16, 142, 148–49n.54
Russia, 15, 19, 116
Ruznamaji (Chief Office of Expenditures)
    158n.45

Said, 47, 74
Saint John, Bayle, 85
Saint John, James August, 35, 57, 85–86

sanitation, 35, 91; British involvement in,
    103
Sannu' Yaqub, 79
screening of residents at Takiyyat Tulun,
    21, 54, 71–72
Senior, Nassau, 49
Shalabi, Hilmi Ahmad, 103
Sha'rawi, Huda, 111
Shefer, Miri, 45
Shepheard's Hotel, 76
shrines, as places to obtain food, 27, 61
Social Affairs, Ministry of, 24, 124, 130–
    31, 134, 139
social control, xvii, 15–18, 66, 137
Société pour la protection d'enfance
    (SIPE), 110, 112, 119, 129
soup kitchens, xix, 10, 134
"strangers," attitudes toward, 28, 54
streetchildren 115, 117–20, 124–25,
    142
structural poverty, 59
sturdy poor. See able-bodied poor
Sufis, 6
Sufi lodges (tekke) ix, xvi, xix, xxii, 5–8,
    61, 141

tadhkira (tezkere), 9, 30, 33–35, 54,
    152n.34; Istanbul's use of, 33
Takiyyat Abdin, 75, 95, 98, 126
Takiyyat Qabbari, xi, 13, 20, 40, 94–95,
    98, 138
Takiyyat Tulun, births at, 57–58; rations
    for poor at, 51
Takiyyat Tura, 71, 75, 94–95, 98, 126,
    138
Tawfiq, xvi, 74, 79–80
taxation, 31–32, 63, 85
taxonomies of locale, space, productivity,
    29
tekke. See Sufi lodges
Thornton, Thomas, 1, 3, 9,
Tignor, Robert, 90
Toledano, Ehud, xvi, xix, 61, 74
tropes of Egypt's poverty, 14, 79, 81, 88
Tucker, Judith, xv–xvi, 61, 146n.4
Tuke, William Samuel, 86
Tunis, 15

unsanitary places in Egypt, discourses of,
    90–91
Urabi, Ahmad, 77, 80, 88

vagabondage xx, 36,
vagrants, 65
vocational training, 101, 105, 126, 171–
    72n.48

Wafd, 131
Walsh, Reverend, 76
Al-Waqa'i' al-Misriyya, 33

waqf. See religious endowments
welfare state, rise of, 17
Whately, Mary, 103
Workhaus, 21, 150n.68

Yates, William, 38, 84, 86

Zakat (alms tax), 1